The Rights Track

The Rights Track

Sound Evidence on Human Rights and Modern Slavery

Todd Landman and Christine Garrington

ANTHEM PRESS

Anthem Press
An imprint of Wimbledon Publishing Company
www.anthempress.com

This edition first published in UK and USA 2022
by ANTHEM PRESS
75–76 Blackfriars Road, London SE1 8HA, UK
or PO Box 9779, London SW19 7ZG, UK
and
244 Madison Ave #116, New York, NY 10016, USA

British Library Cataloguing-in-Publication Data
A catalogue record for this book is available from the British Library.

Library of Congress Control Number: 2022932239

ISBN-13: 978-1-83998-385-6 (Hbk)
ISBN-10: 1-83998-385-X (Hbk)
ISBN-13: 978-1-83998-388-7 (Pbk)
ISBN-10: 1-83998-388-4 (Pbk)

This title is also available as an e-book.

CONTENTS

List of Figures   vi
List of Tables   vii
Acknowledgements   viii

Part I: Background and Context

1. Human Rights in the Twenty-First Century   5

2. Podcasting for Human Rights   25

Part II: Human Rights Themes

3. Mobilising for Human Rights   47

4. Human Rights Evidence   65

5. Freedom of Speech, Religion, Belief and Thought   87

6. Minorities, Migrants and Refugees   107

7. Human Rights and COVID-19   129

Part III: Modern Slavery

8. Slavery Past and Present   157

9. Perpetrators and Survivors   179

10. Business, Economics and Modern Slavery   191

11. Fighting Slavery on the Ground   209

Part IV: The Future of Human Rights

12. Communicating Human Rights   229

Appendix 1: Complete list of Rights Track *podcasts by series, episodes,*
guest (s), title, and duration, 2015-2021   239
Index   243

LIST OF FIGURES

2.1.	The Rights Track visual identity	35
4.1.	Known and unknown human rights violations	68
4.2.	Human rights evidence, inference and error (ε)	70
5.1.	Number of journalists confirmed killed, 1992–2021	95
7.1.	COVID-19 stringency index, January–December 2020 (the United States and United Kingdom)	147
8.1.	States party participation in core international instruments on slavery	161
8.2.	Proportion of states with domestic legislative provisions by region	172
9.1.	Socially embedded slavery: micro, macro and international factors	183
10.1.	Cobalt mining region in the DRC	202

LIST OF TABLES

1.1.   State ratification of core human rights instruments, 2000, 2021   8

2.1.   US podcast listeners, 2013–21   29

3.1.   Selected list of major international human rights organisations   53

5.1.   International human rights law and freedom of expression   90

5.2.   International human rights law and freedom of religion,
       belief and thought   92

ACKNOWLEDGEMENTS

We dedicate this book to the memory of Professor Will Moore, a dedicated human rights scholar and committed advocate for the advancement of human rights.

~

We greatly appreciate the support and dedication of so many different people and organisations that have made this book possible. We met while working at the University of Essex where we created the idea of the Rights Track. Christine had been working with academics at the university to communicate their research and findings as part of her communications role. With her background in broadcast journalism, she was an early advocate of the potential of podcasts in this area. Todd came to the University of Essex in 1993 from the United States as a senior research officer on a project to measure and analyse the relationship between citizenship rights and social movements, and since then has worked on the systematic analysis of human rights, taking him to over fifty countries and engaging with a wide range of stakeholders. He moved to the University of Nottingham in 2015 and has since been instrumental in the founding and development of the Rights Lab Research Beacon of Excellence, which carries out research to help end modern slavery.

The Rights Track had its initial funding in 2015 from the Nuffield Foundation, and then received subsequent funding from the UK Economic and Social Research Council (ESRC) through several Impact Accelerator Awards (2016, 2020–21), the Rights Lab (2017–20) and for its seventh series, the Data Driven Discovery Initiative (3Di) at the University of Nottingham. Over the six years of the Rights Track, we have learned so much from inspiring people who have worked hard to make the world a better place. We are grateful to all the podcast guests featured in this book who gave freely of their time and shared their expertise and knowledge in ways that have allowed us to reach a global audience. The podcast has its own dedicated website (www.rightstrack.org) and is discoverable on Spotify, Amazon Music, iTunes, YouTube and via many other podcast apps and directories. The Rights Track would not have been possible without the financial and in-kind support from so many people around the world who have engaged with us.

The total array of people and organisations who have worked with us is too numerous to mention here. We would like to offer special thanks to the University of Essex, the University of Nottingham, the Rights Lab, the Nuffield Foundation and the ESRC for their financial and institutional support. We would like to thank, in particular, Zoe Trodd, Krissie Brighty-Glover, Phil Brighty, Paul Groves, Helen Taylor and Helen White. Todd wishes to thank Laura Landman, Drew Landman, Kate Landman, Hank Landman, Kelli Landman, Sophia Landman and Briony Landman for all their love and support over the years. Christine would like to thank Jack and Jean Garrington, Alice Brighty-Glover and Catherine McDonald for all their love and support. She would also like to thank Todd for a very special podcasting partnership of which she is immensely proud. Todd and Christine are also very grateful to the anonymous reviewers at Anthem Press for their valuable feedback on the content of the book.

We do hope that you find this book provides sound evidence on the human rights challenges facing us today and that in some way it helps get your thinking about human rights on the right track.

Todd Landman, Nottingham
Christine Garrington, Manningtree
December 2021

Part I

BACKGROUND AND CONTEXT

The *Rights Track* is an unusual and in many ways a unique book. Its genesis lies in over thirty years of human rights research carried out by our host and co-author, Todd Landman, who has engaged in the systematic comparative analysis of human rights problems around the world. His work has also involved travel to over fifty countries and the development of a vast network of human rights students, scholars and practitioners engaged in the struggle for human rights. From the Great Hural of Mongolia to the home of the former Chilean president, his travels exposed him to the panoply of human rights challenges across many different country contexts, institutional arrangements and populations. It turns out that after all these years, his research, travels and expanding network proved to be valuable sources of information in need of a new kind of dissemination. His collaboration with co-author Christine Garrington with her BBC broadcast background and her expertise in producing research podcasts provided the perfect opportunity to create the Rights Track.

The book is thus underpinned by six series of a podcast, created and published between 2015 and 2021, which have sought to bring a new mode of communicating research and practical work on the advance of human rights through dialogue and conversation that is accessible to a wide range of people. Our ambition – to provide sound evidence on the human rights challenges facing us today and get our thinking about human rights on the right track. After six years of discussing human rights with scholars, practitioners and advocates, we realised that we had very rich and very real content in our podcast that demonstrates the struggle for human rights through a very different lens. Across our many conversations, we learned of the incredible dedication, diligence and commitment to human rights across the world, precisely during a time when the world needs human rights the most. Our recordings began a year before the election of Donald Trump in the United States, carried on during the UK's referendum to leave the European Union, included the most intense period of the COVID-19 pandemic and ended during the first year of the new Biden administration. In addition to these major events, we witnessed so many global developments through the eyes and words of our guests, and recorded more than twenty-six hours of conversations with 71 people. Along the way, we learned of the value of our conversational approach and gained tremendous insights into the continued struggle for human rights.

We thus decided to come full circle from the written word, to the spoken word and back again to the written word. What we present here is a fascinating set of conversations and insights across a wide range of human rights topics. Our guests provide clear and compelling stories about the human rights work in which they are engaged, while also reaching beyond their immediate work to reflect on what they have learned about the struggle for human rights and how they view the current and future state of human rights in the world. This conversational and dialogic approach to talking about human rights revealed a number of surprises for us. First, the state of human rights is much better than one would assume by only focusing on popular news media and the immediacy of new forms of information available through social media platforms and the proliferation of alternative news media and commentary. Second, beyond the separate conversations between our host and the many different guests that make up the Rights Track, we discovered that in many ways, our guests were also *talking to each other* across our different episodes. The additional insights about human rights that emerged from making visible the many shared and common themes across our guests demonstrate a surprising degree of consistency in the human rights community. This consistency is grounded in a shared commitment to our common humanity and the need for all our efforts to uphold and value human dignity. Third, our podcast seems to have gathered a momentum of its own. Each episode and series of the podcast prompted fresh ideas for new topics and themes to explore and throughout the six series, we increasingly experienced previously unknown experts and advocates contacting us asking to be a guest. The Rights Track reached new audiences, explored new themes and grew in popularity. For these and other reasons, we feel that now is the time to bring these conversations out in book form.

Part I sets the scene for the rest of the book. Chapter 1 'Human Rights in the Twenty-First Century' provides an overview of the state of human rights in the post-911 era. It sets out a brief theoretical and conceptual framework, grounded in the international law of human rights in order to orient the reader to how we talk about human rights. It challenges a number of popular misconceptions about human rights and complements the discussion with tables and figures on the growth and proliferation of human rights laws, trends in human rights protection and the growing challenge to human rights with the rise of populism. Chapter 2 'Podcasting for Human Rights' explains the advantages of communicating human rights research and advocacy through the medium of podcasting, the popularity and trends in podcasting and how a focus on the dialogical and conversational features of podcasts provides new insights into how to understand human rights challenges. It outlines the basis for the Rights Track, the ways in which it was organised and how the host sought to elicit the strongest contributions from the guests, primarily through a structured and improvisational approach to interviewing and making connections between the theory and practice of human rights.

Chapter 1

HUMAN RIGHTS IN THE TWENTY-FIRST CENTURY

Abstract

This chapter situates our six years of human rights podcasting in the larger context of the first two decades of the twenty-first century. This period was bracketed by the terrorist attacks in the United States on 11 September 2001 and the insurrection on the Capitol in Washington DC on 6 January 2021. The years between these two events included the 'War on Terror' and the step away from hard fought human rights commitments, two major wars in Afghanistan and Iraq, the rise and fall of Islamic State (IS), the emergence of modern slavery as a global challenge that captured the world's attention, a wave of natural and human disasters, a global pandemic, and continued contestation over identity, difference and justice. We argue that podcasts capture the power of voice across a wide range of human rights scholars, practitioners, and activists, and that the content and insights contained in this book are needed now more than ever to keep us on the right track.

The Power of Voice

The main questions for this book are: How can we raise and broaden human rights awareness and how can the advance of human rights be achieved? Answers to these questions are crucial at a time when significant arguments have been waged against the purpose and utility of human rights, and the world has experienced, and continues to experience, a once in a hundred-year disruption from the COVID-19 global pandemic. We elected to address these questions through the *power of voice*. We had conversations with 71 scholars and practitioners working across a wide range of human rights issues. We recorded over twenty-six hours of podcasts and released 58 original episodes and 2 omnibus episodes. Our guest list includes academic 'scholar-activists' and specialists from law, political science, geography, business, economics, American studies, development studies, sociology, history, psychology, public health and intelligence to understand the ways in which their research and practical experience provide a greater understanding of the many human rights challenges facing us today. These guests were joined by non-academic specialists who work on statistics and data science; supply chains and production; journalism and free speech; justice and accountability; faith and religion; refugees, minorities and migrants; victims and survivors; modern slavery; forced labour; forced marriage; prisoners; and children. Across our different episodes, we used the Rights Track to provide a different kind of space than is typical for these specialists, who in turn provided voice to the 'voiceless', those groups of marginalised and obscured groups of people around the world who have experienced a disproportionate abuse of their human rights.

In talking about human rights over six years and six series, the Rights Track developed a unique means of capturing the voices of the people working every day to make the world a better place across a complex array of human rights. Our dissemination platforms, social media campaigns and general outreach approach have yielded over thirty thousand downloads, the incorporation of our content into educational curricula, training materials and the popular media. Through face-to-face and online conversations, we captured many different perspectives on the struggle for human rights from many different and diverse people. Hearing about their work in their own voices gave us a newfound appreciation for their authenticity and their unstinting commitment to the advance of human rights. We also built a large and complex 'conversational network' between and among our guests as well as our listeners that collectively offers a careful assessment of the current state of human rights, based on systematic evidence, and a call to action to address the many remaining and ongoing challenges.

Our dialogic and conversational approach allowed us to hear from our guests in their own words about how they are carrying out their work on human rights, probing their motivations, interrogating their methods and understanding how they use their work to advance human rights at the many different levels that comprise the system of global governance. In order to situate these conversations in its broader context, this chapter assesses the state of human rights over the first two decades of the twenty-first century. As the world struggles to emerge from the COVID-19 pandemic, which we show has exacerbated pre-pandemic inequalities and disproportionalities, we argue that human rights are now more important than ever. Across our chapters run important and enduring themes, such as mobilisation for human rights, measurement and analysis of human rights, minorities and discrimination, freedom and coercion and the need to transcend nationalist and exclusionary discourses, particularly at a time when global cooperation and solidarity for all peoples are sorely needed. The international framework for human rights continues to provide important signposts on how states should use their resources to provide and realise protections for individuals and groups, how these obligations extend to non-state actors and how the work of the people with whom we spoke continues to bring sound evidence to bear on the problems of human rights and modern slavery.

A Precarious Triumph

At the end of the twentieth century, there were many human rights triumphs heralding a bright future for the twenty-first century. The world had survived two world wars during its first half, and from these horrific events that caused so much loss of life, the international community came together in 1948 and articulated a commitment to a set of human rights and human values that would grow in importance and effect over the rest of the century. Long a part of philosophical debate and grasped by revolutionaries and visionaries in the United States and France in the eighteenth century, human rights found formal and legal expression through the 1948 Universal Declaration of Human Rights, followed by a proliferation of international human rights law, which codified an increasing number of different rights. The Universal Declaration was soon followed by the 1966 International Covenant on Civil and Political Rights and the 1966 International Covenant on Economic, Social and Cultural Rights. Together, this new International Bill of Rights set the direction for the next several decades on how states and individuals would relate to one another and provided a moral compass on the fundamental rights that inhere in all of us as humans. These developments have been an astonishing global achievement in setting out a set of protections and aspirations with universal applicability for all humans.

In addition to the International Bill of Rights, the international community continued to promulgate new international legal instruments delineating new and more specific sets of rights, while states themselves increasingly signalled their commitment to these rights through the act of signature and ratification of international treaties. By 2000, state ratification of these different international human rights instruments included between 95 and 190 countries. These instruments articulated over sixty human rights through express legal protection across many dimensions and facets of human life and by 2021, state commitment to these rights had increased further both in the number and proportion of states that had ratified these instruments (see Table 1.1). These human rights include individual rights that protect people from unnecessary interference from the state; individual rights that allow people to express themselves through voice and collective action; individual rights to health, education and welfare; and group rights to particular kinds of identity

Table 1.1 State ratification of core human rights instruments, 2000, 2021.

Name of Instrument	Date When Opened for Signature	States Parties 2000 N (%)	States Parties 2021 N (%)
International Covenant on Civil and Political Rights (ICCPR)	1966	146 (75.6)	173 (87.8)
International Covenant on Economic, Social, and Cultural Rights (ICESCR)	1966	142 (73.6)	171 (86.8)
International Convention on the Elimination of all Forms of Racial Discrimination (CERD)	1966	156 (80.8)	182 (92.3)
Convention on the Elimination of All Forms of Discrimination Against Women (CEDAW)	1979	164 (85.0)	189 (95.9)
Convention Against Torture and Other Cruel, Inhuman, or Degrading Treatment or Punishment (CAT)	1984	122 (63.2)	171 (86.8)
Convention on the Rights of the Child (CRC)	1989	190 (98.4)	196 (99.5)

Source: Landman, T. (2005) *Protecting Human Rights: A Comparative Study.* Washington, DC: Georgetown University Press, p. 61; Office of the High Commissioner for Human Rights (2021) Status of Ratification Interactive Dashboard, available at: https://indicators.ohchr.org/.

and culture.[1] States, for their part, have obligations to respect, protect and fulfil these rights within their maximum available resources.[2]

Alongside these formal legal instruments, there has also been the development of international, regional and domestic institutions charged with the responsibility to promote and protect these rights. At the international level, the United Nations established treaty bodies to monitor the progress of state commitments, the Office of the High Commissioner for Human Rights, and Special Rapporteurs with the responsibility to act on behalf of certain categories of human rights. International non-governmental organisations (NGOs) mobilised their members and supporters to advocate for human rights and to hold state and non-state actors accountable for the violation of human rights. The UN Global Compact and the UN Guiding Principles on Business and Human Rights articulated the human rights obligations of private sector and

---

1   T. Landman, *Studying Human Rights* (London and Oxford: Routledge, 2006), 16. See also T. Landman, *Human Rights and Democracy: The Precarious Triumph of Ideals* (London: Bloomsbury, 2013).
2   T. Landman and E. Carvalho, *Measuring Human Rights* (London and Oxford: Routledge, 2009), 25–26. See also G. Alfredsson and A. Eide, *The Universal Declaration of Human Rights: A Common Standard of Achievement* (The Hague, Boston and London: Martinus Nijhoff Publishers, 1990).

corporate organisations. Regional organisations such as the Council of Europe (COE), the Organisation for Security and Cooperation in Europe (OSCE), the European Union (EU), the Organisation of American States (OAS) and the African Union (AU) established their own founding human rights documents and institutions. At the domestic level, national constitutions embraced and codified rights, while many states formed dedicated national institutions for human rights.

By the end of the twentieth century, enough states ratified the Rome Statute to establish the International Criminal Court (ICC), which internationalised criminal liability and provided the court with 'universal jurisdiction' over crimes against humanity and gross violations of human rights, a long-standing goal of many human rights organisations that dates back to the 1920s. In 1998, the UK passed the Human Rights Act, which brought the values, aspirations and protections of the 1951 European Convention for Human Rights into domestic law. In that same year, the UK detained former Chilean dictator Augusto Pinochet at the request of Spanish authorities for alleged crimes committed against Spanish citizens during the long period of authoritarian rule between 1973 and 1989. The Law Lords upheld his detention and although he returned to Chile on grounds of ill health, the case firmly established the principle of universal jurisdiction, which forever changed the landscape for the advance of human rights.

The Pinochet case came close on the heels of other significant developments. Throughout the 1970s and 1980s, more and more countries embraced democratic forms of governance, from Southern Europe, to Latin America, to parts of Eastern Europe, Asia and Africa. The end of the Cold War brought the collapse of the Soviet Union and the reunification of Germany. The International Criminal Tribunal for the former Yugoslavia (1993–2017) sought justice for the victims and survivors of the conflict in the Balkans. The International Criminal Tribunal for Rwanda, established in 1995, was the first international tribunal to deliver verdicts in relation to genocide. Truth Commissions in South America, Central America, the Caribbean, South Africa, Sierra Leone and East Timor provided the opportunity for victims and perpetrators to take part in the public acknowledgement of past wrongs, and in part pursue different forms of reconciliation and restorative justice.[3]

These and other developments led to the observation that the world at the end of the twentieth century was experiencing the 'precarious triumph of human rights'.[4] Fascism and Communism had been defeated, the inter-

---

3 P. Hayner, *Unspeakable Truths: Transitional Justice and the Challenge of Truth Commissions*, 2nd ed. (London and Oxford: Routledge, 2011).

4 David Rieff, "The Precarious Triumph of Human Rights," *New York Times Magazine*, August 8, 1999, 36–41. See also T. Landman, *Democracy and Human Rights: The Precarious Triumph of Ideals*

national law of human rights had expanded in 'breadth and depth'[5] with more human rights codified in law and more states confirming their formal commitment to these rights, and justice and accountability for past wrongs were beginning to be achieved. This triumph, however, was indeed precarious, since international human rights law is difficult to enforce and implement. New groups challenge the status quo, and states who bear the primary responsibility for the promotion and protection of human rights can just as easily rescind them during times of crisis. The much proclaimed 'end of ideology'[6] and 'end of history',[7] it would appear from subsequent developments, were indeed drastically and mistakenly premature.

A Tale of Two Decades

Against this idea of the precarious triumph of human rights, the first 20 years of the twenty-first century have presented many different challenges for the advance of human rights in the world. Most notably, this period began with the terrorist attacks on 11 September 2001 on the World Trade Centre in New York, the Pentagon in Washington, DC, and Shanksville, Pennsylvania. The period ended with a violent attack on the US Capitol in an effort to stop the certification of Electoral College votes in the House of Representatives and the Senate on 6 January 2021. This was the first such violent attack and occupation of the Capitol since the War of 1812, and it led to the second impeachment of President Donald Trump and an investigation of the event itself by the House of Representatives. The 9/11 attacks were externally motivated, coordinated and implemented, while the attack on the Capitol was a wholly domestic affair, reflecting increased polarisation of American politics and widespread discontent across certain parts of the electorate mobilised by a renewed appeal to populism, nationalism and isolationism. In between these two events, the world witnessed a number of significant events that undermined the global commitment to human rights that had progressed over the course of the twentieth century. The 9/11 attacks ushered in the 'War on Terror' with the invasion of Afghanistan in 2001 and the Second Gulf War in Iraq in 2003, where human rights rhetorically and practically took a back seat to security interests and counter-terror efforts. Across Democratic and

---

(London: Bloomsbury, 2013).

5   T. Landman, *Protecting Human Rights: A Comparative Study* (Washington, DC: Georgetown University Press, 2005), 1.

6   D. Bell, *The End of Ideology: On the Exhaustion of Political Ideas in the 1950s* (New York: Free Press, 1960).

7   F. Fukuyama, *The End of History and the Last Man* (Harmondsworth: Penguin, 1992).

Republican administrations, the United States engaged in 'extraordinary rendition'[8] of terror suspects, detained 'enemy combatants' at Guantanamo Bay, increased its use of drone warfare and the targeted assassination of suspected terrorists[9] and engaged in the systematic use of torture and 'enhanced interrogation techniques'.[10] Only in the summer of 2021 did the United States withdraw all of its troops from Afghanistan, while it still has forces present in Iraq. The withdrawal of the United States and other countries saw the rapid advance and political takeover of Afghanistan by the Taliban, and renewed concern over the protection of human rights, particularly those of women under the newly formed Islamic Emirate of Afghanistan.[11]

One year before the 9/11 attacks, under the leadership of Prime Minister Tony Blair and New Labour, the UK consolidated and made permanent its anti-terror legislation.[12] The UK was an active and committed ally in the invasions of Afghanistan and Iraq (along with other NATO members), where it lobbied alongside the United States for UN Security Council authorisation for military action.[13] One dominant perspective at this time argued that democracies and 'open societies' experience more terrorist attacks[14] and thus need to curb freedoms and roll back human rights protections to provide much needed security against future terrorist attacks.[15] The United States passed the Patriot Act[16] and formed the new Department of Homeland

---

8   R. Cordell, "Measuring Extraordinary Rendition and International Cooperation," *International Area Studies Review* 20, no. 2 (2017): 179–197.

9   M. Zenko, "Obama's Final Drone Strike Data, Council on Foreign Relations," January 20, 2017. https://www.cfr.org/blog/obamas-final-drone-strike-data.

10   Senate Select Committee on Intelligence, *The Official Senate Report on CIA Torture Committee Study of the Central Intelligence Agency's Detention and Interrogation Program* (New York: Simon and Schuster, 2015).

11   See T. Landman et al., *Afghanistan: Prospects and Challenges* (University of Nottingham, 2021). https://www.nottingham.ac.uk/research/beacons-of-excellence/rights-lab/resources/reports -and-briefings/2021/november/afghanistan-prospects-and-challenges.pdf.

12   T. Landman, "The United Kingdom: Terror and Counter-Terror Continuity," in *National Insecurity and Human Rights: Democracies Debate Counterterrorism*, ed. A. Brysk and G. Shafir (Berkeley: University of California Press, 2007), 75–91.

13   A. Mumford, *Counterinsurgency Wars and the Anglo-American Alliance* (Washington, DC: Georgetown University Press, 2017), 161–195.

14   T. Plümper and E. Neumayer, "The Friend of my Enemy Is My Enemy: International Alliances and International Terrorism," *European Journal of Political Research* 49, no. 1 (2010): 75–96.

15   W. Enders and T. Sandler, *The Political Economy of Terrorism* (Cambridge: Cambridge University Press, 2006).

16   United States of America: Uniting and Strengthening America by Providing Appropriate Tools Required to Intercept and Obstruct Terrorism Act of 2001 (USA Patriot Act) [United States of America], October 26, 2001. https://www.refworld.org/docid/3dea43144.html.

Security in an effort to have a more coordinated and multi-agency approach to counter terrorism within its own borders, while it used its hard and soft power policies,[17] instruments and tools to pursue terrorists around the world. The Bali attack of 12 October 2002, the Madrid train bombing of 11 March 2004, the London attacks of 7 July 2005 and the Mumbai attack of 26–29 November 2008 all helped fuel a sense of insecurity and supported the rise of public opinion for curbing liberties in the name of fighting terrorism.[18]

Halfway through these two decades, the world witnessed the 'Arab Spring' across the Middle East and North Africa (MENA), with popular uprisings in Tunisia, Libya, Egypt, Yemen, Syria and Bahrain that led to the toppling of their leaders and the promise of new and freer political futures.[19] These futures, however, were not to be realised, as the political turmoil unleashed by the uprisings was met with fierce opposition, authoritarian governments, the descent into civil war, prolonged political instability, foreign interventions and the rise of the Islamic State (aka ISIL, ISIS, IS and *Daesh*), with its origins in Al-Qaeda. Both Al-Qaeda and IS carried out renewed terrorist attacks across the world.[20] The Human Rights Data Analysis Group (HRDAG) estimated that 191,369 people died in the Syrian conflict between March 2011 and June 2013,[21] with many more deaths and millions of displaced people and refugees since then with no resolution to the conflict in sight. Even in Tunisia, where the popular uprising saw the installation of constitutional democratic government,[22] President Kais Saied on 25 July 2021 invoked emergency powers, fired the prime minister, suspended parliament for 30 days and declared that he would govern alongside a new prime minister.[23]

---

17 J. Nye, *Soft Power: The Means to Success in World Politics* (New York: Public Affairs, 2004).

18 T. Parker, *Avoiding the Terrorist Trap: Why Respect for Human Rights Is the Key to Defeating Terrorism* (London: World Scientific, 2019).

19 M. Lynch, *The Arab Uprising: The Unfinished Revolutions of the New Middle East* (New York: Public Affairs, 2013).

20 M.L. Haas, *The Arab Spring: The Hope and Reality of the Uprisings* (London and Oxford: Routledge, 2019).

21 M. Price, A. Gohdes, and P. Ball, "Updated Statistical Analysis of Documentation of Killings in the Syrian Arab Republic," Report Commissioned by the UN Office of the High Commissioner for Human Rights, San Francisco: Human Rights Data Analysis Group, 2014. https://hrdag.org/wp-content/uploads/2014/08/HRDAG-SY-UpdatedReportAug2014.pdf.

22 A. Breuer, T. Landman, and D. Farquhar, "Social Media and Protest Mobilization: Evidence from the Tunisian Revolution," *Democratization* (2014): 1–29.

23 W. Todman, "A Coup in Tunisia?" Centre for Strategic and International Studies, July 27, 2021. https://www.csis.org/analysis/coup-tunisia.

Armed conflict between 2000 and 2020 saw a mix of trends, with fluctuations in the number of 'minor conflicts' (i.e. those with 25 or more battle deaths) and wars (> 1,000 battle deaths). In 2002, there were between twenty-five thousand and thirty thousand battle deaths, with a peak in 2014 of close to hundred thousand deaths and forty-five thousand in 2020. Between 2000 and 2011, there was a decline in the number of minor conflicts and wars, while between 2012 and 2020, trends in both types of conflict increased dramatically with eight wars and over fifty minor conflicts. The wars include those in Afghanistan, Syria, Somalia, Yemen, Nigeria, Ethiopia (Tigray), Eritrea and Nagorno-Karabakh in Azerbaijan. The increase in minor conflicts has been largely driven by IS with additional non-IS conflicts across many regions.[24] Conflicts such as these have profound effects on the protection of human rights, including gross violations such as extrajudicial killing, arbitrary detention, torture, child soldiers, rape and sexual assault, and enslavement.[25] Conflict also leads to massive internal displacement of people and a flow of refugees and asylum seekers out of regions mired in conflict of the kind witnessed across Europe.

The democratic transitions and achievements that characterised the last 20 years of the twentieth century began to falter, ushering in a new period of democratic 'backsliding' across 16 'new' and 'old' democracies around the world ranging from Bolivia to Zambia.[26] The 'opening' in China from the late 1970s saw a return to a harder authoritarian state under President Xi Jinping,[27] while the transformations in Myanmar saw the fall from grace of Aung San Suu Kyi over the displacement of the Rohingya people and the re-emergence of military rule. The new century also saw the rise of populism and nationalism with the UK voting to leave the European Union on 23 June 2016, followed by the elections of populist leaders, such as Donald Trump in the United States (8 November 2016), Jair Bolsonaro in Brazil (28

---

24   H. Strand and H. Hegre, *Trends in Armed Conflict, 1946–2020*, Peace Research Institute Oslo (PRIO) Policy Brief, 2020. https://www.prio.org/Publications/Publication/?x=12756.

25   On Islamic State and modern slavery, see N. Al-Dayel, A. Mumford, and K. Bales, "Not Yet Dead: The Establishment and Regulation of Slavery by Islamic State," *Studies in Conflict and Terrorism*, 2020. https://www.tandfonline.com/doi/full/10.1080/1057610X.2020.1711590.

26   The 16 countries include Bolivia, Brazil, the Dominican Republic, Ecuador, Greece, Hungary, Macedonia, Nicaragua, Poland, Russia, Serbia, Turkey, Ukraine, United States, Venezuela and Zambia. See S. Haggard and R. Kaufman, *Backsliding: Democratic Regress in the Contemporary World* (Cambridge: Cambridge University Press, 2021), 13. See also International Institute for Democracy and Electoral Assistance, *The Global State of Democracy: Building Resilience in a Pandemic Era* (Stockholm: International IDEA, 2021), 78pp. https://www.idea.int/gsod/sites/default/files/2021-11/the-global-state-of-democracy-2021_1.pdf.

27   S. Morgan, *The Chinese Economy* (Newcastle: Agenda Publishing, 2021).

October 2018), Viktor Orbán in Hungary (8 April 2018) and Boris Johnson in the UK (24 July 2019). These political developments have led to a further questioning of long-held human rights achievements and commitments, and the destabilisation of post–World War II alliances and partnerships that have underpinned them. The advent of the Internet, social media and the spread of misinformation have created a 'post truth era' in which opinion matters more than fact. The hyper-connectivity, mobility and increased communication across countries have at the same time created more cosmopolitanism and universal appreciation of our globalised world and more inward-looking politicians seeking to make gains through appeals to fear of 'the other' and a nostalgic return to politics of the past. The defeat of Donald Trump in the 2020 elections has seen the Biden administration partially shift the balance back to an embrace of human rights, multilateralism and global partnerships, while Orbán and Johnson are being increasingly alienated by the European Union, and Bolsonaro is struggling with his own brand of populism in Brazil, including a pre-emptive attack on electoral integrity.

Within the human rights community, a division over the importance and sustainability of human rights for the future has also appeared. On the one hand, Douzinas's *End of Human Rights*[28] turned fresh and critical eyes to the theory and philosophy used to justify the value of human rights. Hopgood's *Endtimes of Human Rights*[29] issued a critique of the elitist and 'sacral' language of 'Human Rights' within the United Nations as being increasingly out of touch with local and grassroots understanding and use of 'human rights'.[30] On the other hand, Landman's *Protecting Human Rights*,[31] Simmons's *Mobilizing for Human Rights*,[32] Sikkink's *Justice Cascade*[33] and *Evidence for Hope*[34]

---

28 C. Douzinas, *The End of Human Rights: Critical Thought at the Turn of the Century* (London: Hart Publishing, 2000).

29 S. Hopgood, *The Endtimes of Human Rights* (Ithaca: Cornell University Press, 2013). See also D. Lettinga and L. van Troost, eds., *Debating the Endtimes of Human Rights: Activism and Institutions in a Neo-Westphalian World* (The Hague: Amnesty International, 2014).

30 Hopgood intentionally labels the international use of human rights with capital letters and grassroots use of the term with lowercase letters to illustrate his point about the 'sacral' language of rights and its gap with everyday uses of the term on the ground.

31 T. Landman, *Protecting Human Rights: A Comparative Study* (Washington, DC: Georgetown University Press, 2005).

32 B. Simmons, *Mobilizing for Human Rights: International Law in Domestic Politics* (Cambridge: Cambridge University Press, 2009).

33 K. Sikkink, *The Justice Cascade: How Human Rights Prosecutions Are Changing World Politics* (New York: W.W. Norton, 2011).

34 K. Sikkink, *Evidence for Hope: Making Human Rights in the 21st Century* (Princeton: Princeton University Press, 2017).

and Comstock's *Committed to Rights*[35] demonstrate that the proliferation of international human rights law and institutions has had a positive impact on the exercise and enjoyment of human rights. Smith-Cannoy's *Insincere Commitments*[36] shows us that the gap between the formal commitment to international human rights law and the lived reality of rights on the ground can act as a significant lever for positive social change. Her work echoes earlier analyses in Risse, Ropp and Sikkink's *Power of Human Rights*[37] that shows how concerted efforts from 'transnational advocacy networks' (TANs) working with powerful states and the United Nations can bring human rights change across many countries in the world.

Modern Slavery

During the latter two decades of the twentieth century and with increasing acceleration in the early twenty-first century, the issue of modern slavery came to the fore in international and domestic policy circles. Slavery has existed for nearly four thousand years as a common practice across many different societies and systems of government.[38] In addition to the commonality of slavery among ancient civilisations, transatlantic and imperial forms of slavery are the most commonly known, which were formally abolished in England in 1833, the United States in 1865 and Brazil in 1888.[39] Less than forty years after the Brazilian abolition of slavery, the world saw the first purportedly human rights treaty prohibiting slavery (and the slave trade) emerge with the 1926 Slavery Convention. Article 1(1) of the convention defines slavery as 'the status or condition of a person over whom any or all of the powers attaching to the right of ownership are exercised'. This convention, characterised as the 'first true international human rights treaty',[40] gives primacy to the ideas of *ownership* and *property*. Further developments in international

---

35   A. Comstock, *Committed to Rights: UN Human Rights Treaties and Legal Paths for Commitment and Compliance* (Cambridge: Cambridge University Press, 2021).

36   H. Smith-Cannoy, *Insincere Commitments: Human Rights Treaties, Abusive States, and Citizen Activism* (Washington, DC: Georgetown University Press, 2012).

37   T. Risse, S.C. Ropp, and K. Sikkink, eds., *The Power of Human Rights: International Norms and Domestic Change* (Cambridge: Cambridge University Press, 1999).

38   See F. Braudel, *Civilization and Capitalism* (New York: Harper and Row, 1981–1984); S.E. Finer, *The History of Government, Vol. I: Ancient Monarchies and Empires* (Oxford: Oxford University Press, 1997).

39   R. E. Conrad, *Children of God's Fire Children of God's Fire: A Documentary History of Black Slavery in Brazil* (Princeton: Princeton University Press, 1983), xxviii, 515; P. Winn, *Americas: The Changing Face of Latin America and the Caribbean* (Berkeley: University of California Press, 2006).

40   P. Sieghart, *The International Law of Human Rights* (Oxford: Oxford University Press, 1983), 13.

human rights law and international humanitarian law have articulated more fully the definition of slavery.[41] Provisions on slavery and other related forms of exploitation are also set out in other international instruments and norms.[42] In addition, the various regional human rights instruments for Europe, the Americas, Africa and the Arab region all have provisions addressing the problem of slavery, servitude, forced labour and/or trafficking in women, as well as dignity, respect and free choice of work.

The 'social construction'[43] of *modern* slavery is born of mobilisation from human rights and anti-slavery NGOs alongside a growing recognition among states that the unacceptable conditions of work, human trafficking and other forms of exploitation had not abated in the twentieth century. Rather, the practice changed from one based on the strict understanding of property to one of the 'denial of agency', through force, threat and coercion.[44] Scholars and practitioners working on modern slavery have developed the Bellagio-Harvard Guidelines on the Legal Parameters of Slavery (2012), which focus on the right to ownership, the powers attached to the right of ownership and the notion of possession. In focusing on these elements as foundational to slavery, the guidelines emphasise the notion of control and lack of agency for victims of slavery, where different forms of coercion maintain power over individuals.[45] The key phrase from the guidelines with respect to ownership asserts that it constitutes 'control over a person in such a way as to significantly

---

41 These include the 1956 Supplementary Convention on the Abolition of Slavery, the Slave Trade, and Institutions and Practices Similar to Slavery (Article 7a); the 1998 Rome Statute (Article 7.2.c); the International Tribunal for the Former Yugoslavia (Article 5c); the 2000 United Nations Palermo Protocol on Trafficking in Persons; and the 2005 Council of Europe Convention on Action against Trafficking in Human Beings.

42 Article 8 of the 1966 International Covenant on Civil and Political Rights and Article 7 of the 1998 Rome Statute of the International Criminal Court (ICC) have provisions. Slavery is part of the 1945 Charter of the International Military Tribunal (Art 6 (c)) and in the Statute of the International Criminal Tribunal for the Former Yugoslavia (Article 5 (c)), where enslavement in qualifying circumstances is defined as a crime against humanity. The International Labour Organisation (ILO) has provisions in its 1930 Forced Labour Convention (No. 29), 1957 Forced Labour Convention (No. 105), 1999 Worst Forms of Child Labour Convention (No. 182) and 2014 Forced Labour Protocol addressing forced or compulsory labour, and slavery and related exploitation of children.

43 J. Donnelly, "The Social Construction of International Human Rights," in *Human Rights in Global Politics*, ed. T. Dunne and N. Wheeler (Cambridge: Cambridge University Press, 1999), 71–102.

44 T. Landman, "Out of the Shadows: Transdisciplinary Research on Modern Slavery," *Peace Human Rights Governance* (2018)): 1–15.

45 J. Cockayne, N. Grono, and K. Panaccione, "Slavery and the Limits of International Criminal Justice," *Journal of International Criminal Justice* 14, no. 2 (2016): 253–267; A. Choi–Fitzpatrick, *What*

deprive that person of his or her individual liberty, with the intent of exploitation through the use, management, profit, transfer or disposal of that person'. This notion of ownership is then linked to possession.

The United Nations has embraced this agenda, which has been articulated through the promulgation of Sustainable Development Goal (SDG) 8.7, which demands that states 'take immediate and effective measures to eradicate forced labour, end modern slavery and human trafficking and secure the prohibition and elimination of the worst forms of child labour, including recruitment and use of child soldiers, and by 2025 end child labour in all its forms'. The *Global Slavery Index (GSI)* produced initially by Walk Free, an anti-slavery NGO, estimated that in 2013 there were 29 million people in modern slavery, followed by its estimate of 36 million in 2014 and 45.8 million in 2016.[46] The ILO and Walk Free estimated the number of people in modern slavery in 2017 to be 40.3 million. While prevalence rates are difficult to estimate and vary across countries in the world, no country is free of the problem, and efforts to combat slavery focus on its 'root causes', its criminal elements, liberation for those that are enslaved and provision of support and care for victims and survivors of modern slavery.

Natural and Human Disasters

Beyond these trends in human rights law, policy and practice, the world over the past two decades has seen increasing concerns over climate change and global warming, and has experienced a number of natural and human made disasters, each of which has had profound implications for human rights. These human rights effects are not only the deaths that resulted from these events, but also the displacement of peoples and public health emergencies, where marginalised and vulnerable groups bore the brunt of the devastation disproportionately. The 'Boxing Day' tsunami of 2004 in the Indian Ocean began with a large earthquake in Indonesia, while the resulting tsunami killed over 230,000 people. The areas most directly affected include the Aceh region in Indonesia, parts of Sri Lanka, Thailand, India, the Maldives, Myanmar and Somalia, among other areas.[47] The 2011 Tōhoku earthquake and tsunami in Japan led directly to the Fukushima nuclear power plant dis-

---

Slaveholders Think: How Contemporary Perpetrators Rationalize What They Do (New York: Columbia University Press, 2017).

46   Walk Free, *Global Slavery Index*, 2016. Walk Free, *Global Slavery Index*, 2018. https://www .globalslaveryindex.org/.

47   *Nature Geoscience*, "Editorial: Tsunamis Revisited," *Nature Geoscience* 12 (2019): 149. https:// www.nature.com/articles/s41561-019-0328-4.pdf.

aster, where the combination of a natural event and a human made facility brought untold destruction and death. More than 18,000 people died and a further 154,000 people evacuated, with core meltdowns at the facility, hydrogen explosions and the release of widespread radioactive contamination.

The United States, known for its seasonal challenges with large and destructive hurricanes, experienced widespread devastation and displacement from hurricanes Katrina (2005) in New Orleans, Sandy (2012) in the New York and the Northeast, and Maria in Puerto Rico (2017), formally a commonwealth and protectorate of the United States. Katrina displaced over 200,000 people from the Gulf Coast to Texas, Georgia, Florida and Washington DC, while 1,800 people died.[48] The hurricane exacerbated the pre-Katrina lack of adequate housing with a disproportionate impact on poor Black communities. Sandy was one of the most devastating hurricanes in US history, raising significant questions over infrastructure and resilience, while its devastation affected countries in the Caribbean, its path caused havoc up the East Coast of the United States and at its peak covered a quarter of the Continental United States.[49] Maria led to 180,000 people leaving Puerto Rico, while the country experienced a prolonged period of power outages, economic devastation and significant hardship for its poorest communities. These more notable natural disasters are part of a much longer history typical of weather systems that move every summer from their origins in the Caribbean to Florida and up the East Coast of the United States.

In addition to tsunamis, hurricanes and other natural disasters, parts of the world have seen accelerated and more intense wildfires, primarily in Australia and the United States. Between July 2019 and March 2020, the wildfire season in Australia scorched 46 million acres, affected over three billion animals[50] and displaced 65,000 people.[51] In the United States, fires have raged each summer through the west and northwest, affecting the states of California, Nevada and Washington. Natural, intentional and unintentional ignition of these fires has led to wide areas of these states to be under

48   Amnesty International, "10 Years after Katrina, Many New Orleans Residents Permanently Displaced," 2015. https://www.amnestyusa.org/10-years-after-katrina-many-new-orleans-residents-permanently-displaced/.
49   S. Gibbons, "Hurricane Sandy, Explained," *National Geographic*, February 2019. https://www.nationalgeographic.com/environment/article/hurricane-sandy.
50   World Wildlife Fund, *Australia's 2019–2020 Bushfires: The Wildlife Toll*, 2020. https://www.wwf.org.au/news/news/2020/3-billion-animals-impacted-by-australia-bushfire-crisis.
51   Internal Displacement Monitoring Centre, *The 2019–2020 Australian Bushfires: From Temporary Evacuation to Longer-Term Displacement*, 2020. https://www.internal-displacement.org/sites/default/files/publications/documents/Australian%20bushfires_Final.pdf.

prolonged states of emergency, as the fires rip through forests and burn down entire towns, the most notable of which was Paradise, a community of 27,000 people where nearly 95 per cent of the homes, business and schools were destroyed in November 2018.[52] Climate scientists see a strong correlation between patterns of climate change, global warming and the rise in the frequency and intensity of these fires, which bring untold devastation to the human and non-human population.[53]

A Global Pandemic

In December 2019, the world started receiving reports that a dangerous virus had appeared in Wuhan, China, which in January 2020 the Chinese publicly shared the genetic sequence as COVID-19. Cases of the virus had spread within China and then moved first to Thailand and beyond as evidence mounted that the virus was indeed capable of human-to-human transmission. By the end of January, the World Health Organisation (WHO) reported that there were 7,818 confirmed cases. The virus spread quickly thereafter with early waves appearing in Iran, followed by an increasing number of cases in Europe (e.g. Spain and Italy), the United Kingdom and the United States. By March 2020, many countries were introducing various forms of national lockdowns, economic restrictions, domestic and international travel restrictions and a series of public health mitigations to help reduce community transmission,[54] while scientists around the world set to work on developing vaccines.

The first global pandemic since the 1918 Spanish flu, COVID-19 and its effects dominated the world throughout 2020 and 2021 with several waves affecting countries around the world, while the Omicron variant emerged late in 2021 as a new 'variant of concern', leading to renewed restrictions and speculation about vaccine effectiveness. The initial wave of the virus

---

52   A. Gee and D. Anguiano, "Last Day in Paradise: The Untold Story of How a Fire Swallowed a Town," *The Guardian*, December 20, 2018. https://www.theguardian.com/environment/2018/dec/20/last-day-in-paradise-california-deadliest-fire-untold-story-survivors.

53   S.W. Running, "Is Global Warming Causing More, Larger Wildfires?" *Science Express*, July 6, 2006. 10.1126/science.1130370; Q. Sun, C. Miao, M. Hamel, A.G.L. Borthwick, Q. Duan, D. Ji, and H. Li, "Global Heat Stress on Health, Wildfires, and Agricultural Crops Under Different Levels of Climate Warming," *Environment International*, 128 (July 2019): 125–136. https://www.sciencedirect.com/science/article/pii/S0160412018328654.

54   The Blavatnik School of Government at the University of Oxford has been tracking government response to COVID-19, see https://www.bsg.ox.ac.uk/research/research-projects/covid-19-government-response-tracker.

spread to Latin America, severely affecting Ecuador, Peru, Mexico, Brazil, Colombia and Argentina. The delayed and contested response to the virus in the United States in the spring of 2020 led to severe transmission and over 600,000 deaths, with President Trump himself getting the virus sometime between late September and October 2020[55] during the campaign for the November presidential elections. In spring 2020, UK prime minister Boris Johnson contracted COVID-19 and was moved to intensive care to receive treatment followed by a full recovery. Early 2021 saw the UK enter a new period of lockdown, which was not fully eased until July, where the country still saw daily case rates exceeding 30,000, even with close to 70 per cent of the population fully vaccinated. In India, COVID-19 was slow to start, but by May 2021, the peak of its second wave reached 400,000 cases a day with over 4,000 deaths a day. Johns Hopkins University has confirmed over 214 million cases worldwide, over 4.4 million deaths and over 5 billion vaccine doses administered at the time of writing.[56] In late 2021, the Omicron variant emerged with grave new concerns over its transmissibility and ushered in the reintroduction of travel restrictions, mask mandates and a drive to roll out booster vaccines.

The pandemic itself and the variation in government response to the pandemic have had profound effects on human rights. It has been popular to declare that 'the virus does not discriminate', but the evidence is clear that poor and marginalised communities and people of colour suffered disproportionately from the virus. The world experienced economic downturns, disruption and contraction; mass unemployment (particularly low wage and low skilled jobs); and devastating pressure on public health services. Various government restrictions disrupted education at all levels, cancelled social and public events and pushed billions of people back into their homes, with extreme effects on the elderly and vulnerable. Elections and many elements of the electoral cycle were disrupted or compromised,[57] while new forms of remote working using technology and new platforms emerged, changing our understanding of employment, commuting and interacting with our co-workers and colleagues. Public discourse around the virus and govern-

---

55 Mark Meadows, former Trump chief of staff claims that the president contracted COVID-19 on 26 September, a claim which remains contested. See M. Meadows, *The Chief's Chief* (All Seasons Press, 2021). Meadows reports that Trump tested positive for COVID-19 on 26 September and not in October as was widely reported.

56 Johns Hopkins University Coronavirus Resource Centre, available here: https://coronavirus.jhu.edu/map.html.

57 T. Landman and L. Di Gennaro Splendore, "Pandemic Democracy: Elections and COVID," *Journal of Risk Research* 23, no. 7–8 (2020): 1060–1066. doi: 10.1080/13669877.2020.1765003.

ment response sowed division across many societies, particularly democracies, where mass publics used to a wide range of freedoms lashed out at their newfound confinement and government messaging about social distancing, mask wearing and vaccine take-up. Scientists and health officials scrambled not only to develop effective vaccines, but also struggled to provide a clear articulation of the risks and uncertainties associated with epidemiology and virology in ways that gave comfort to the public. The virus became politicised in ways that increased transmission, hospitalisations and deaths.

Black and Racial Justice Mobilisation

In the midst of the pandemic in the United States on 25 May 2020, Minneapolis Police Officer Derek Chauvin held to the ground and killed George Floyd, a 46-year-old Black man suspected of using a counterfeit $20 bill to buy goods from a convenience store. This killing was not an outlier, but rather consistent with police violence towards Black Americans well documented by qualitative and quantitative evidence, and which came several years after the police killing of Michael Brown in Ferguson, Missouri, in August 2014.[58] It also came three years after the 'Unite the Right' white supremacist rally in Charlottesville, Virginia, in August 2017 organised to protest the removal of confederate statues, which descended into violence and left one counter-protestor Heather Heyer dead and over thirty others wounded.[59] In the George Floyd case, police officer Derek Chauvin was tried and convicted in 2021 for murder and sentenced to twenty-two and a half years in prison. The compelling evidence that Chauvin held George Floyd's neck under his knee for almost nine minutes was incontrovertible for the jury, and given its aggravated nature, the judge in the case was empowered to issue a longer sentence, which many saw as a sign of justice after a year of racial tension and contestation.

The polarisation of American politics around questions of race and justice has been an enduring feature of the political landscape since the founding and through antebellum slavery, the Civil War, Reconstruction and the Civil Rights Movement, but this succession of salient events fuelled a series of popular mobilisations throughout the rest of 2020 led primarily by the Black Lives Matter organisation. Black Lives Matter was founded in 2013 following

---

58 T. Landman, "There is No Escaping the Data: African Americans Face Injustice at Every Turn," *The Conversation*, November 26, 2014. https://theconversation.com/theres-no-escaping-the-data-african-americans-face-injustice-at-every-turn-34771.
59 T. Landman, "Charlottesville, Donald Trump, and the Dark Side of Populism," *The Conversation*, August 14, 2017. https://theconversation.com/charlottesville-donald-trump-and-the-dark-side-of-american-populism-82459.

the killing of another Black man Trayvon Martin and the exoneration of his killer George Zimmerman in Florida and has become a group that seeks to make visible the injustices that African Americans face throughout many different dimensions of American life.[60] These protests in the midst of the pandemic spread across large parts of the United States, as well as across to the UK and Europe, where fundamental questions of race, rights and justice were raised along with strong calls for more concerted efforts to address long-standing issues of systemic racism. The 1966 International Convention on the Elimination of All Forms of Racial Discrimination (see Table 1.1) clearly sets out what constitutes 'racial discrimination':

> Any distinction, exclusion, restriction or preference based on race, colour, descent, or national or ethnic origin which has the purpose or effect of nullifying or impairing the recognition, enjoyment or exercise, on an equal footing, of human rights and fundamental freedoms in the political, economic, social, cultural or any other field of public life.[61]

As part of the United Nations institutional structures, the UN Working Group of Experts on People of African Descent published its findings in 2016 from its country visit to the United States. The report's conclusions found significant concerns with respect to racial discrimination in the criminal justice system and 'barriers to civil and political participation'. It found 'disparities in access to education, health, housing and employment'. It found 'multiple forms of discrimination'.[62] These types of reports and other evidence raise broader questions around the tension between 'legal equality' and 'social equal-ity' of people around the world,[63] both in terms of the calls from the Black Lives Matter movement and other movements for racial equality. There are ongoing debates on the degree to which racism in all its manifestations is a

---

60 See https://blacklivesmatter.com/about/.
61 UN General Assembly, International Convention on the Elimination of All Forms of Racial Discrimination, December 21, 1965, United Nations, Treaty Series, vol. 660, p. 195, Article 1.1. https://www.refworld.org/docid/3ae6b3940.html.
62 UN General Assembly Report of the Working Group of Experts on People of African Descent on its mission to the United States of America, August 18, 2016. https://undocs.org/en/A/HRC/33/61/Add.2.
63 For a careful analysis of law and black lives matter, see M.O. Olatokun, "Does the Law Think that Black Lives Matter? A Reflection upon the Role of the Public Sector Equality Duty in Promoting Racial Equality Before the Law," *The Theory and Practice of Legislation* 9, no. 1 (2021): 83–95.

function of individual views and actions or is owing to broader societal and institutional structures.

Structure of the Book

With this broader context about human rights developments in mind as background, we have structured the book across a number of common themes and topics that emerged from our many conversations over six years of the Rights Track. To begin, Chapter 2 explains why we chose podcasting as our medium of communication and provides an overview of how podcasting, in the words of Steve Jobs, has created a new 'generation of radio listeners'. We recount our early discussions to create the resource and how it developed over the period from 2015 to 2021. The chapters in Part II of the book share what we have learned across a set of human rights themes: mobilising for human rights (Chapter 3); human rights evidence (Chapter 4); freedom of speech, religion, belief and thought (Chapter 5); minorities, migrants and refugees (Chapter 6); and human rights and COVID-19 (Chapter 7). Part III tackles the global challenge of modern slavery with separate chapters on slavery past and present (Chapter 8), perpetrators and survivors (Chapter 9), business, economics and modern slavery (Chapter 10) and fighting slavery on the ground (Chapter 11). Part IV brings together the many important lessons we have learned from the Rights Track about the effective ways to communicate human rights and how we have come full circle to bring this mode of communication to you in book form. Across the four parts of the book, we reveal many common themes and challenges in the struggle for human rights in general and the struggle to end modern slavery in particular. Consistent with the language of the United Nations, all of our guests have demonstrated the 'mutually reinforcing and interdependent' nature of human rights, as well as the significant intersectionality that affects the degree to which individuals enjoy and exercise their human rights. Our dialogic and conversational approach sees us talking *to* our guests and *with* our guests; while without knowing it in advance, we learned that our guests have also *been talking to each other.* We hope that you enjoy joining in with our conversations and that what you read here puts you on the right track in thinking about human rights.

Chapter 2

PODCASTING FOR HUMAN RIGHTS

Abstract

This chapter considers podcasts as a space and medium for important and impactful conversations that in and of themselves can have a role in promoting and advancing human rights. It lays out the thinking behind the Rights Track podcast, from its inception and planning to its production processes and editorial values, as well as its development over six series. This account is set against the backdrop of a rise in the popularity of podcasts, especially in the United States and the United Kingdom, against a political background that has been less favourable to human rights, and in the context of a growing understanding of the need for human rights scholars to engage actively, communicate accessibly and be creative in their approach to impact.

~

'Podcasting is the next generation of radio listeners.'

– Steve Jobs, Apple

'Podcasts are transforming the way people listen to audio content.'

– Ian Macrae, Ofcom

'The Rights Track podcast gets the hard facts about the human rights challenges facing us today and gets our thinking about human rights on the right track.'
– Todd Landman and Christine Garrington, The Rights Track

The Rise of the Podcast

In early 2006, Apple creator Steve Jobs demonstrated the Mac's built-in audio editing software GarageBand to show how to make a podcast and said that podcasting was the next generation of radio listeners. He was right in many ways. A year later, according to Edison Research,[1] 22 per cent of Americans aged 12 and over said they were familiar with the term 'podcasting'. In 2021, that figure had risen to 78 per cent – an estimated 222 million Americans. Of course, familiarity does not necessarily translate into listeners, although there is compelling evidence of increases here too with well over half of Americans (57 per cent) saying in 2021 that they had 'ever listened to a podcast' and monthly podcast listening figures rising from 37 per cent in 2020 to 41 per cent in 2021. Quite how podcasting became 'a thing' is not entirely clear, but it is worth noting that, while many people think of it as a relatively new phenomenon, there are some key milestones dating back as far as the beginning of the World Wide Web in the mid-1990s.

Writing for *The Guardian* in 2004,[2] journalist Ben Hammersley reports that all the ingredients are in place for a new boom in 'amateur radio'. The ingredients he refers to are the availability and popularity of mp3 players such as Apple's iPod, cheaply and even freely available audio editing software and the now established idea of using the Internet as a platform for blogging. At this point, however, there was still some uncertainty about what this new form of media would be called. Was it simply 'online radio'? Was it 'audioblogging'? Or was it 'podcasting'? Hammersley is often credited with being the first to write seriously about podcasting, but the technological roots of its development began much earlier.

In 2000, the first system that enabled the selection, automatic downloading and storage of serial episodic audio content on PCs and portable devices was launched by early mp3 manufacturer i2GO. Another key player in this arena was software developer Dave Winer, who is credited with authoring the RSS format, a web feed allowing users to receive timely updates from their favourite websites. He and fellow Internet entrepreneur Adam Curry are often credited with 'inventing' the podcast, but that is something that remains contested today. By the end of 2005, 'podcast' was declared the word of the year by the New Oxford American Dictionary.[3] The definition back then still alluded to it as an extension of traditional radio: 'a digital recording of a radio broadcast or similar program, made available on the Internet for downloading to a personal audio player'. Jump forward 15 years and the definition now relates more directly to the system developed by i2GO:

---

1 Edison Research. https://www.edisonresearch.com/podcast-research/.
2 Audible revolution, *The Guardian*, Ben Hammersley. https://www.theguardian.com/media/2004/feb/12/broadcasting.digitalmedia.
3 MacDailyNews.   https://macdailynews.com/2005/12/06/new_oxford_american_dictionary_announces_word_of_the_year_podcast/.

A digital audio file of speech, music, broadcast material, etc., made available on the internet for downloading to a computer or portable media player; a series of such files, new instalments of which can be received by subscribers automatically.[4]

Thus by 2006, the technical capabilities for podcasting were well and truly in place, but who would use it and why? The possibilities for both professional and amateur content creators looked promising, but would the idea fly? In Hammersley's *Guardian* piece, podcasting pioneer Christopher Lydon, a *New York Times* and National Public Radio journalist, says that 'everything is inexpensive. The tools are available. Everyone is saying that anyone can be a publisher, anyone can be a broadcaster. [...] Let's see if that works'. Hammersley talks about Lydon's podcasts as 'combining the intimacy of voice, the interactivity of a weblog and the convenience and portability of an mp3 download'. He says this provides the best of both worlds, not just for the listener who can consume the content of their choosing any time anywhere, but also for journalists like Lydon, who tells Hammersley that with no publisher to appease and no editor to report to, he feels 'unleashed' to work directly with his audience. Our experience with the Rights Track confirms this view, where we responded to listener requests and direct approaches from potential guests throughout the six series. Through our approach, we remained timely and relevant with our content, responding to global developments in human rights, emerging human rights stories and of course, the COVID-19 pandemic.

One or two famous faces can probably take credit for boosting the profile and success of podcasts in the early stages. US president George W. Bush had his weekly address delivered as a podcast in 2005, while comedian Ricky Gervais set a Guinness World Record[5] for the most downloaded podcast at 261,670 per episode in 2007. After his terrestrial radio show was cancelled, broadcaster Marc Maron launched his WTF podcast,[6] going on to secure guests such as President Barack Obama, Jodie Foster and John Cusack to feature in a podcast which has gone on to produce more than 1,000 episodes. Celebrity podcasts today are commonplace. Barack Obama and Bruce Springsteen are among the latest somewhat unlikely podcasting duo to debut their show *Renegades: Born in the USA* on Spotify.[7] Academics have also adopted

---

4 Oxford English Dictionary. https://www.oed.com/viewdictionaryentry/Entry/273003.
5 Ricky Gervais Guinness World Record. http://news.bbc.co.uk/1/hi/entertainment/5107424.stm.
6 Marc Maron WTF Podcast. http://www.wtfpod.com/podcast.
7 Renegades: Born in the USA. https://open.spotify.com/show/42xagXCUDsFO6a0lcHoTlv.

the podcast format, including the popular podcast from Harvard historian Jill Lepore entitled 'The Last Archive'.[8]

In 2013, Apple announced it had 1 billion podcast subscribers and a year later the phenomenally successful *Serial* podcast[9] was launched by *This American Life*, achieving 68 million downloads by the end of Season One. Leading up to this point, some surveys had shown a drop or at least a levelling-off of podcast listeners, but following the debut of *Serial*, which popularised the true crime podcast genre, audience numbers started to rise once again. Between 2015 and 2021, it is fair to say that podcasting has had a meteoric rise, both in terms of content production and healthy listenership. In 2019, the popular music platform Spotify acquired the podcast networks Gimlet media and Anchor FM establishing itself as a major player in podcasting.[10] In 2021, *Podcast Insights* reported 2,000,000 podcasts and more than forty-eight million podcast episodes (see Table 2.1).[11]

Some key insights from Edison Research's *Infinite Dial 2021* survey include:

- US weekly podcast listeners consume an average of eight podcasts per week
- A rise in women and ethnic minority listeners
- A 7 per cent increase in listeners aged 12–34 and 4 percentage increase in the 55+ age group

Similar trends have been seen in the UK with Ofcom[12] reporting in 2019 that 7.1 million people were listening to podcasts every week with that figure having doubled in the previous five years and half of those people only starting to listen to podcasts two years previously. Those people were consuming an average of seven podcasts per week.

In 2021, as we write this book, podcasting is an established and influential medium. From major broadcasting companies to first-time podcasters, there is an incredible array of content on offer. Back in 2004, Christopher Lydon described podcasts as 'an experiment'. It was an experiment that clearly worked, where the world of ideas has seen a proliferation in the format across

---

8 See Click here to enter text..
9 Serial. https://serialpodcast.org.
10 SpotifyInvestors.https://investors.spotify.com/financials/press-release-details/2019/Spotify-Announces-Strategic-Acquisitions-to-Accelerate-Growth-in-Podcasting/default.aspx.
11 PODCASTINSIGHTS. https://www.podcastinsights.com/podcast-statistics/.
12 Media Nations 2019, Ofcom. https://www.ofcom.org.uk/research-and-data/tv-radio-and-on-demand/media-nations-reports/media-nations-2019.

Table 2.1 US podcast listeners, 2013–21.

Year	% Listeners
2013	7
2014	8
2015	10
2016	13
2017	15
2018	17
2019	22
2020	24
2021	28

Total US Population 12+.

Source: *The Infinite Dial 2021* Edison Research https://www.edisonresearch.com/the-infinite-dial-2021-2/.

a wide range of topics. Our challenge with the Rights Track was to use podcasts to communicate research and advocacy on human rights.

Podcasting about Research

Responding to these trends in podcasting and predating our creation of the Rights Track, former BBC radio journalist and co-author Christine Garrington established herself as a freelance producer of podcasts about social science research. After a 12-year career in journalism (mostly for BBC Radio) she already had many of the editorial and technical skills and know-how to produce quality audio content, although she acknowledges herself that it took some time to get to grips with the fact that podcasting was more than recorded audio made available on a website. It required planning, thematic organisation, branding and establishing a suitable online platform for hosting podcasts.

She had the idea for her first podcast in 2010 while working at the Institute for Social and Economic Research (ISER) at the University of Essex. It was here she came to understand the research process: from the original idea to grant writing, funding, to carrying out the research, to publishing in journals, and communicating and disseminating findings, the latter part being something she had been employed to lead on at the institute, which was funded by the UK's ESRC.[13] This work coincided with a growing focus across the

---

13 See https://esrc.ukri.org/. Landman is a member of the Council for the ESRC, working closely with colleagues on strategic delivery plans, reviewing budget allocations and advising on research funding calls.

Higher Education sector and among the funders of research on its broader impacts for the economy and society. The authors of a 2012 Russell Group[14] paper on 'The social impact of research conducted in Russell Group universities'[15] point to a report showing a combined wealth of £2 billion created by just a small number of breakthroughs across the Russell Group universities. The report adds that research does not just benefit the economy: 'World-class research, in its many guises, can transform our lives and reach areas we may never have thought of' and that it can benefit the 'nation's health, quality of life, culture and environment'.

There had previously been considerable focus on the need to communicate and promote research through non-academic channels, such as the media or accessibly written newsletters and videos. However, there was a growing understanding that for impact to be achieved, what was needed was not simply the outward communication of research. Impact was about the exchange of knowledge, engagement with businesses, policy makers and other organisations who could benefit from the expertise and evidence that those working in universities could provide. To secure funding for research, academics would need to demonstrate a clear understanding of who might benefit from their research, how and when it might have impact and how that impact would be achieved and evidenced. Although Christine was realistic about the potential of any single podcast to 'have societal or economic impact', she could certainly see its potential as a medium for the exchange of ideas, for engagement not just with other academics, but with a wider range of individuals and organisations who might benefit from research across a range of different areas.

Against this backdrop, and given free rein to innovate, she proposed the idea of a podcast as a vehicle for researchers to talk about their work in a way that would make it both relevant and accessible to non-academics and potential beneficiaries of the research. The result was a series of radio-style interviews conducted and recorded by Christine with researchers on topics as diverse as childcare policy, family breakdown, poverty triggers, the cost of long-term sickness and much more. The podcast was billed as an opportunity to hear researchers talking accessibly about the background to and policy/societal context of their research; explain where they got their information from; what they found; and what it meant for policy, practice and people.

---

14 The Russell Group is a collection of large, research-intensive universities in the UK, see https://russellgroup.ac.uk/about/our-universities/.

15 The social impact of research conducted in Russell Group universities, Russell Group Papers Issue 3, 2012. https://russellgroup.ac.uk/media/5235/socialimpactofresearch.pdf.

Working with ISER's web editor to make the podcast available on the institute's website and also create the essential RSS feed so that it would be available on iTunes and later in other podcast directories, Christine quickly came to understand that a podcast was a great way to talk about, communicate and engage with non-academic audiences. It was possible, she saw, to talk not just about the research itself, but about the key issues behind it and to use a podcast as a way of showcasing the credibility and expertise behind the research and, perhaps most importantly, its real-world relevance and applicability to people's everyday lives. This was research that might otherwise not appear anywhere other than a journal article read largely by academic peers. It was, she could see, a great tool in the wider array of activities to share and promote the work of the institute.

Anecdotally, the podcasts proved popular, and Christine saw an opportunity to offer podcasting about research as a freelance service to universities, research centres and individual academics. She foresaw that some might be interested in presenting their own podcast, but with support that would ensure a professional approach and make it less burdensome for already busy academics. Not long after, she proposed a separate podcast for the UK Household Longitudinal Study,[16] a survey of 40,000 households in the UK, a multimillion-pound research project housed at the institute. The study, known as *Understanding Society*, she argued, merited a podcast of its own to showcase its possibilities, the important policy-relevant work being done using it and the fascinating and important findings that were emerging from it. That podcast launched in 2013, covering important subjects such as managing financial well-being in later life; the links between ethnicity, neighbourhoods and life satisfaction; sexual orientation and poverty; the financial value of a university degree; living with sight loss; and how well people sleep.

By this point Christine had conceived the idea of a business that would work with research centres and individual academics interested in using podcasting as a means of communicating research in an accessible and relevant way to non-academic audiences, but it would take a little longer than she hoped to get this off the ground. At this point, the popularity of podcasts seemed to take a dip or, at the very least, level off for a few years. Even the big players like the BBC were slow to see the potential of podcasts and it would be some years still before they would launch their own podcasting app in the form of the now eponymous *BBC Sounds*. In similar fashion, *The Conversation UK*, an online media outlet with the tagline, 'academic rigour, journalistic

---

16 Understanding Society. www.understandingsociety.org.

flair' with millions of readers and downloads, launched its own successful podcast series.[17]

Podcasting about Human Rights

The idea for a podcast about human rights research emanated from a conversation between Christine and co-author Todd Landman in 2014. With a background in radio journalism and a number of years working in a research-intensive environment, Christine was comfortable reading, understanding and communicating the often complex research and findings presented in academic journals, developing a regular format for the podcasts, interviewing researchers and supporting them through the production process to help them make the most of the opportunity. While happy to be the face or the voice of these podcasts, she understood that there were opportunities here for academics to present their own podcast. She was cognizant of the fact that while many academics might like the idea and see the potential benefits of producing a podcast about their research, they would find the editorial and production processes involved in setting up, launching and maintaining a quality podcast challenging, and that this might be a barrier to them getting one off the ground. She needed to find an academic with whom she could collaborate on a podcast. She then met Todd, an experienced and charismatic human rights academic, a seasoned presenter who had worked extensively with more traditional media organisations, and a professional magician, whose style of performance combines academic themes and content with the methods of the modern conjurer and mystery entertainer.[18]

Todd could immediately see the potential of a podcast not just to share his work, but to share ideas and have important and interesting conversations about human rights, but it was agreed that a pilot series in which Christine would interview him about his human rights work would be a good starting point. Using discretionary funds to pay for Christine's podcast production expertise and support, we selected six pieces of Todd's recent research and recorded six episodes for a pilot series, which, at that point, was simply uploaded to Todd's personal website. The experience was a positive one and a good starting point, but both could see that with Todd as the host of his own podcast, where he could use his expertise and knowledge of the field, together with his excellent communication and presentation skills, there was

---

17   See https://theconversation.com/uk/podcasts. As a member of the editorial board for *The Conversation*, Landman advised the team on how to create and deliver an effective podcast.
18   See www.todd-landman.com.

an opportunity to have even more impactful conversations about human rights. With him in the chair and Christine in the role of producer, there was potential to achieve much more, and so the idea for the Rights Track came about.

Web Expertise – The Missing Link

Despite her radio editing and production credentials, the process of producing a pilot series with Todd, without the support of a web and Internet professional, made Christine realise that there was a gap in her knowledge and skills around the hosting and publishing of podcasts beyond the uploading of them to a website. At ISER, she had had support from website manager Paul Groves who had provided considerable advice, support and expertise around the hosting of the podcast; the creation of an RSS feed; and the process of submitting it to iTunes to make it available on Apple's platform. The technology was fast moving and if Christine's research podcasting ambitions, which included the Rights Track, were to become a reality, she would need to build in that resource. Further discussion about how best to take the idea forward led Todd to apply successfully to the Nuffield Foundation[19] for funding to set up and launch Series 1 of the podcast – 12 episodes featuring conversations between him and leading analysts at the forefront of the latest critical thinking on human rights. Presenter – Todd Landman, Producer – Christine Garrington, Web support – Paul Groves. A look back at notes from our first editorial meeting states: 'We play to our strengths as a team'.

Getting Started

Podcasting about human rights with leading analysts was a great starting point, but now there was work to be done to shape the editorial focus not just of the podcast, but also of Series 1 and each episode within it. The name for the podcast had been discussed and agreed before the funding bid was submitted. The team felt the Rights Track played nicely on the idea of human rights while 'track' had a dual meaning of 'audio track' and as a 'pathway' or 'route', something we would later exploit in the podcast's visual identity (as well as the cover image of this book). The name was just the beginning. Considerable thought went into what we were looking to achieve in this podcast, beyond providing an interesting and accessible space for important conversations about human rights. The following simple but carefully chosen

---

19 https://www.nuffieldfoundation.org/.

sentence which appears in the podcast's description helped to clarify our thinking and set out a stall which would keep the podcast on the right track six years, six series and some sixty episodes later.

> The Rights Track Podcast gets the hard facts about the human rights challenges facing us today and aims to get our thinking about human rights on the right track.

It is a sentence we revisited every time we planned a new series and indeed every time we discussed an episode. What was the challenge? e.g. ending modern slavery by 2030. What were the hard facts? e.g. research revealing the real numbers behind the phenomenon. How would the podcast help get our listeners' thinking on the right track? e.g. through sharing, explaining and discussing the real-world implications and impact of those findings.

Once that was clear in our minds, there was podcast artwork to design, an accompanying website to set up, an episode template to produce, topics and guests to identify and invite, recording sessions to be organised and the necessary technology to be acquired. This latter requirement was especially so as Todd announced he was about to take up a new role as pro-vice-chancellor of the Faculty of Social Sciences at the University of Nottingham, some three hours from Christine's base in Essex. The recording of episodes would need to be done remotely, and there would be few opportunities for face-to-face editorial or production meetings and recordings (perhaps an omen for the COVID-19 world that had yet to come).

Already au fait with recording interviews over Skype, Christine foresaw no problems making this work; however, she was concerned to ensure that the podcast's presenter be equipped with a broadcast quality microphone and that his contribution would be recorded locally and mixed at a later point with the Internet-quality recording of the Rights Track guests. The solution was relatively straightforward as Todd owned a broadcast standard digital recorder and could share his local recording via Dropbox (in 2015 a relatively new platform), but one deemed useful for sharing fairly large audio files within the team and also for comment and sign-off from guests. It could also be a central repository for other background documents related to the podcast and individual episode text, show notes, etc. Other platforms deemed suitable for remote working at that point included a Private Facebook group for sharing ideas and discussion about the podcast and Trello board for project management.

Another glance at the project kick-off notes from 2015 shows some clear ideas for the visual identity of the podcast – 'a clean, clear website with strong visual identity', 'bold, moving forward, NOT woeful, pathfinding'. Paul turned his attention to a logo and podcast artwork, while Christine put

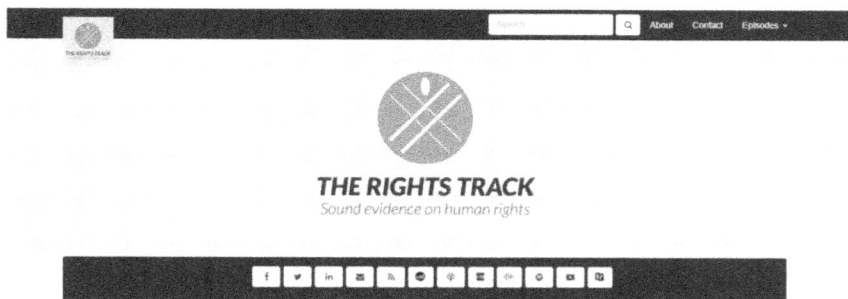

Figure 2.1 The Rights Track visual identity. *Source:* www.rightstrack.org.

forward ideas for a strap line and website text that would reflect the team's thinking about the podcast. For the strap line, the team settled on 'Sound evidence on human rights'.

The team had committed to a podcast episode per month, which was sensible, and it was agreed that the workflow would be fluid – episodes would be recorded and published as we went along rather than having them all recorded and edited pre-publication. Episode length was set at 20–25 minutes, allowing conversations to breathe but not to drift. Christine understood from reading as widely as possible around what was working in podcasting that many people were listening on their commute to work and that the average commute was around this duration, making each episode the perfect length for a listen on the bus, train or underground (i.e. subway).

As far as who Todd would talk to, the ability to link up with and record interviews over the Internet quite literally meant the world was our oyster. There was no shortage of ideas for content, topics or guests, and the challenge was to select the best from a very long list and 'to stay true to our vision for The Rights Track'. Other decisions were made around Todd's style of hosting. He would be 'a neutral adjudicator', 'scrutinising, not hostile' and each episode would be 'informal – conversations not interviews', something the team understood instinctively would be right for the podcast format and something which has been talked about at length in broader discussions around the success of podcasts and how they have found their place in the media landscape.

A list of potential guests and topics was drawn up for Series 1. These would tackle some big ideas and ask and try to get answers to some challenging questions such as: 'Are we better at human rights than we used to be?', 'Do NGOs matter?', 'How do we count victims of torture?', 'How can statistics advance human rights?', 'Does America need a Truth Commission?' With Todd's connections around the globe, it was not difficult to identify, invite and secure excellent guests, each of whom was provided with a clear briefing on the format and style of our podcast and what was expected of them. Although we provided guests with a clear steer on the content we wanted to cover with them, Todd was adamant he did not want to be constrained by providing a set list of questions in advance. The podcasts would be free-flowing conversations. He would have an idea in his mind of how he would get from the beginning to the end of a conversation, but where he would be free to respond naturally and spontaneously to his guests allowing conversations to evolve naturally during the recording and, in some cases, to surprise him and the podcast's listeners. This dialogic approach to the podcast gave the guests the opportunity to present ideas, clarify points and expand on themes as they developed across the course of each episode. Todd focused on the main expertise of each guest and engaged in a probing conversation that yielded fresh content delivered in a relatable fashion, accessible to a wide range of listeners.

Just as journalist Christopher Lydon felt 'unleashed' by his podcast, so Todd felt free to bring his personality as well as his expertise and understanding to bear in the podcast. In an article for *The Guardian* newspaper[20] shortly after launching the Rights Track, Todd would write that podcasting was perfect for academics looking to engage with others, not just around a specific piece of research but around the ideas and concepts behind it in a way that would help all those with an interest to continue upholding and advancing human rights.

> For me, the podcast is like a fireside chat – it allows listeners to hear experts discuss their work in their own voices, and allows the experts to express themselves more freely than in the usual academic forms of dissemination. [...] I hope more academics will recognise podcasting as a way of reaching out, sharing, communicating, and discussing their research and what it means for the real world.

With all the background work done, a clean, clear website in place, a podcast template with theme music and standard introduction scripted, it was time to press the record button and make the Rights Track vision a reality.

Series 1 – International Human Rights Day

To ensure a good start and to make sure the processes put in place worked, the team decided to pre-record two episodes in the autumn of 2015 in

---

20 *Why podcasting Is Perfect for People with Big Ideas*, The Guardian HE Network. https://www.theguardian.com/higher-education-network/2016/jan/13/podcasting-is-perfect-for-big-ideas.

preparation for a launch of the Rights Track on International Human Rights Day on 10 December. This would provide the opportunity on social media – Twitter in particular – to tap into the day's conversations about human rights and draw further attention to the podcast. Paul would undertake the necessary work to make it available and therefore discoverable on iTunes. Six series later, we take it for granted that our podcast is available in all podcast directories and apps, on Spotify, Amazon Music and YouTube, but, at the end of 2015, nothing could beat our delight at seeing the Rights Track on the iTunes platform.

As we entered 2016, we could see that our hard work was paying off. Editorial and production processes had all worked well. The podcast's first three guests Chris Fariss, Amanda Murdie and Will Moore (to whom this book is dedicated) were excellent and gave the team confidence that, at least in part, they were already starting to achieve what they had set out to do. To find out more about what we learned from those guests and for Todd's interpretation of this new kind of content, you will need to read on into the main chapters of the book, but with each conversation came further inspiration and ideas for more conversations. Feedback from our guests who were given the opportunity to listen through to an episode before publication was so positive that we felt sure we were onto a winner. Each episode and the ensuing comments from guests and listeners gave us further food for thought, ideas about who to speak with next in that series and indeed ideas for future series.

Christine and Todd did not allow themselves to feel constrained by the original list of guests as Todd would come away from an episode and say, 'That was great – now we need to talk to x about y' and our process for inviting, securing, recording and publishing a new episode would swing back into action. We began to realise that even though each episode was a self-contained piece of content, there was an ever-moving golden thread connecting episodes going forward and looking backward and that these connections were also taking on a life of their own beyond the podcast, with guests reporting contacting and collaborating with one another as a result of appearing on the Rights Track. This golden thread will also become apparent as you read the chapters here.

Thinking everything through so clearly from the outset meant editing episodes was relatively painless (no wading through endless unstructured material to find the best 20–25 minutes). Our process was quite the reverse. This meant editing could focus quite simply on making guests and the host sound as good as possible, with edits largely dealing with any retakes or smoothing out any pauses, hesitations or retakes of questions. Draft episodes were shared with the guests for sign off, but no substantive content was deleted or changed, preserving the authenticity of each guest and delivering high-quality conversations on a wide range of human rights topics.

As Series 1 was drawing to a close, Todd and Christine were already fired up and keen to keep the podcast going. The first series had focused on academic experts, their research and what our conversations could tell us about the major human rights challenges of the day. Series 2 would feature experts of a different kind: practitioners working in the field to tackle human rights abuses. Funding was secured this time from the UK's ESRC and the Rights Track turned its attention to those involved in the struggle for human rights to learn more about their work and the ways in which academic research was helping them. Todd would speak with a leading businessman on gay rights; a photographer who used his pictures to expose environmental issues; a trade unionist about rights to a basic income; representatives from Amnesty International, Human Rights Watch; and the UK representative of United Nations High Commissioner for Refugees (UNHCR). The Rights Track was securing influential and important guests to talk about the pressing human rights issues of our times.

Modern Slavery

Series 2 had barely got underway when the production team found themselves talking about taking a deep dive into a specific human rights topic for Series 3. Todd was working closely with a new research programme at the University of Nottingham called the Rights Lab[21] that was committed, in line with UN SDG 8.7,[22] to ending modern slavery by 2030. The possibilities for more inspiring conversations such as that with Kevin Bales in Series 1 around counting victims of modern slavery, combined with emerging findings from the Rights Lab seemed a clear and perfect fit for our vision of the Rights Track as a podcast that engaged actively, expertly and accessibly in work that could advance our human rights. And so, another successful partnership emerged. Todd and Christine worked closely with the Rights Lab's Director Zoe Trodd to develop Series 3 of the podcast, giving careful thought to the best aspects of the research to focus on, considering who would make good guests – here was an opportunity for the Rights Track to collaborate and co-produce content in a really impactful way. November 2017 saw the series launch with Todd and Zoe discussing the Rights Lab's 'Blueprint for Freedom' and its cross-disciplinary approach to ending modern slavery. The series would go on to talk about why communities are key to ending slavery, how evidence from

---

21 See https://www.nottingham.ac.uk/research/beacons-of-excellence/rights-lab/index.aspx.
22 Sustainable Development Goals, United Nations. https://www.unodc.org/southeastasiaand-pacific/en/sustainable-development-goals.html.

the research was helping businesses tackle slavery in their supply chains, the need to listen to and incorporate the survivors of slavery into solutions to the problem, the use of satellites and GPS technology in rooting out slavery from the sky and fascinating research looking at the perpetrators of slavery.

There were some technical changes in the background of the podcast too – podcasting advances meant that there were now specialist podcast hosting platforms, the equivalent of blogging platforms such as WordPress and Medium, where podcast creators could host their podcasts, and which would automate the delivery of the Rights Track to the many podcast apps now available. The platform[23] also provided a frontend website doing away with the need for a standalone website and download statistics that would help us evaluate how our podcast was performing. The transition was made smoothly, ensuring the Rights Track was making the most not only of its important conversations and high-quality content but also of a renewed interest in podcasting (among content creators and listeners).

At the end of Series 3, it was agreed that there was simply too much ground to cover in a single series on modern slavery and so it was decided that a follow-up series staying with this topic could work well. This time Todd would speak with other individuals and organisations interested in tackling modern slavery, as well as discussing emerging findings with researchers at the Rights Lab. Todd would travel to the United States to speak with two eminent historians who would tell us about what lessons from the past are useable in today's struggle against slavery. He would also meet with a Church of England bishop working on the Clewer Initiative[24] to help raise awareness of modern slavery, a House of Lords peer involved in the development and passage of the 2015 UK Modern Slavery Act,[25] connect with NGO workers in India working with the poor and marginalised to empower them with the knowledge and understanding to tackle slavery in their communities and homes, and speak with a representative of the United Nations on its Delta 8.7 knowledge platform of resources[26] on what works in tackling modern slavery.

It was this last conversation with James Cockayne at the United Nations that inspired the idea for Series 5 of the Rights Track. It was time to look at the relationship between the United Nations' goal to end modern slavery (SDG 8.7) and many of the other UN SDGs to see what could be learned. The podcast would ask if developing stronger institutions could lead to slavery-free

23 Libsyn. https://libsyn.com.
24 The Clewer Initiative. https://www.thecleweriinitiative.org.
25 See https://www.legislation.gov.uk/ukpga/2015/30/contents/enacted to enter text.
26 Delta 8.7. https://delta87.org.

supply chains or if making businesses better was the route to a world free of slavery by 2030 and ultimately how achieving these goals together might lead to the single aim of a better and more sustainable future for us all. Conversations with authors, researchers, those working in business and campaigners from around the globe would enable the podcast to take what it had learned about modern slavery and look at it in a wider context.

Special Episodes

Series 5 saw Christine and Todd reflecting on the fantastic body of resources they had created with the Rights Track and the idea of a book that might help them reflect on what they had learned from those conversations was beginning to emerge. These discussions also prompted the idea of two special episodes of the podcast where key audio snippets from the podcast to date would be presented in a mini-documentary scripted format that enabled Todd to talk about what the podcast was finding as a whole. One of these special episodes would look at what the first two series of the Rights Track had shown about advancing human rights and the second would explore what had been learned from Series 3 to 5 about how the world could free itself of modern slavery.

Christine and Todd thought these special episodes might neatly wrap up the podcast, which had already run for much longer than they anticipated in those early discussions in 2014. At this point, there had been excellent feedback from listeners and guests; great support from funders; an active Twitter following; media coverage, endorsements and accolades; and more than 20,000 downloads. We felt that we and our listeners had learned so much from the podcast that there was a need to take stock of the conversations, the exchanges and the learning. From the need for NGOs to be savvy about the framing of human rights in a crowded space to the key role of empirical evidence; the thorny issues of freedom of speech, belief and thought; the realities of life for the 'marginalised other' and modern slaves to what more can be done to communicate those realities effectively, the Rights Track had covered a lot of ground. We wanted to write a book about all this, something Anthem Press also believed to be a worthwhile endeavour. At that point, we wondered though if our work on the podcast was done, but as it transpired, that was far from the case. Enter COVID-19.

Human Rights in a Pandemic

As 2020 unfolded, it became clear that if we did not produce a sixth series, the Rights Track would be missing an important and unprecedented opportunity to use the now established podcast to discuss the impacts of the COVID-19 pandemic on the human rights of people all around the world. After success-fully applying for funding from the ESRC's Impact Acceleration Account, Todd and Christine were able to devote eight further episodes of the Rights Track to understanding the complex relationship between COVID-19 and human rights. The series would include conversations with a best-selling author about how the pandemic was affecting women and the citizens of her birthplace of Iran, with an attorney and champion of Black Americans and people of African descent about the unequal effects of the pandemic on the lives and rights of people of colour, with a civil rights campaigner about the impact of COVID-19 on prisons and prisoners and with a leading anti-terrorism expert and former MI5 agent on why human rights are key to not only defeating terrorism, but also useful for understanding and shaping government responses to the pandemic. Across this diverse set of topics, our listeners learned how the pandemic exacerbated pre-pandemic inequalities and had a disproportionate impact on marginalised groups around the world.

The Future

As we write this book, Series 7 of the Rights Track about human rights in a digital world is already in production and ready to launch on International Human Rights Day 2021. After over eighteen months of remote recording, it was gratifying and humbling to come together face-to-face to record the first episode of this series, an experience enjoyed by presenter, producer and guest. Of course, the podcast alone cannot change the world, but we do believe that it plays a role in enriching and informing it. In that respect, it has had and continues to make a small but impactful contribution to the advance of human rights. In producing the podcast and in writing this book reflecting on it, we hope we have gone some way in creating sound evidence on human rights and that we have done so by getting the hard facts about the human rights challenges facing us today.

Part II

HUMAN RIGHTS THEMES

Having set the scene through a discussion of the concept of human rights, major trends in the law and practice of human rights and the value of podcasts for disseminating sound evidence on human rights, Part II comprises a set of chapters on dominant human rights themes that emerged from the Rights Track. These themes emerged organically from our own planning of different series and across our many episodes and include mobilisation; evidence; freedom of speech; freedom of religion, belief and thought; and the rights of minorities, migrants and refugees in the modern world. In the middle of Series 5, the world was struck with a global pandemic and so we dedicated all of Series 6 to the human rights implications of COVID-19.

Chapter 3 'Mobilising for Human Rights' considers how non-governmental organisations frame and mobilise the struggle for human rights, drawing on the insights and thoughts from Meghna Abraham from Amnesty International, Iain Levine from Human Rights Watch and Dixon Osburn from the Centre for Justice and Accountability (CJA), three world-leading human rights NGOs based in London, New York and San Francisco. The rich content from our conversations is situated in a larger consideration of social movements, civil society and so-called transnational advocacy networks, which is informed by our conversation with Amanda Murdie from the University of Georgia and Shareen Hertel from the University of Connecticut. The chapter argues that human rights advocacy is a crowded and highly competitive space, which requires savvy and effective framing of issues to capture the public imagination, alongside frontline interventions designed to improve the protection of human rights.

Chapter 4 delves into the world of empirical evidence and how it is generated in making the case for human rights. Its point of departure is what the Rights Track guest Will Moore calls the 'fundamental problem of unobservability' or the hidden nature of human rights abuses. The chapter's content derives from episodes discussing how to measure torture, how to count human rights violations, the trends in public opinion and attitudes about human rights, the socio-economic dimensions of human rights and how new forms of data and data analytics can be used to map and explain the nature and extent of human rights problems around the world. The content draws on conversations with Patrick Ball from the HRDAG; James Ron from the Humphrey School of Public Affairs at the University of Minnesota; Sakiko Fukuda-Parr from the New School and former director of the United Nations Human Development Report; Chris Fariss from the University of Michigan; Kevin Bales, Doreen Boyd and Sir Bernard Silverman from the University of Nottingham; and Meg Satterthwaite from New York University.

Chapter 5 takes on the thorny issues surrounding the rights to free speech and freedom of religion, belief and thought, with further references to the human rights values of voice and accountability. Set in the ongoing debates surrounding fake news, media biases and the challenges to upholding free speech in universities, other large organisations and society, it teases out the many distinctions and parameters that separate free speech from hate speech, and the challenges that arise from freedom of religion, belief and thought. The content of the chapter draws on our conversations with Elisabeth Witchel from the Committee to Protect Journalists (CPJ); Heidi Beirich from the Southern Poverty Law Centre; Akbar Ahmed, former high commissioner to the UK from Pakistan and professor of Islamic studies at the American University; and the Rt. Rev. Alastair Redfern, bishop of Derby and former member of the House of Lords.

Chapter 6 discusses a range of different human rights for those considered as 'the marginalised other', a term that emerges from our conversation with Bill Simmons from the University of Arizona. We explore these issues through our conversations with Claire Thomas from Minority Rights Group International (MRG) and Gonzalo Vargas Llosa, the United Nations High Commissioner for Refugees representative to the UK. We then turn to the issue of Black Americans through our conversations with Karen Salt and Christopher Phelps from the University of Nottingham, women's rights with Monica Casper from the University of Arizona and LGBTQ+ rights with Richard Beaven, corporate leader and former trustee of Stonewall.

Chapter 7 focuses on human rights and COVID-19. We discovered from our conversations during 2021 that COVID-19 exacerbated existing inequalities within countries and between countries, where marginalised groups were particularly vulnerable to the pandemic as a public health risk, as well as across many dimensions of economy, society and polity. The pace and spread of the pandemic affected communities of people differently and disproportionately. The chapter begins by situating COVID-19 in a larger discussion of ecology, a healthy planet and its relationship with healthy people, drawing on our conversation with award-winning nature photographer Garth Lenz.

We then turn to the impact of COVID-19 on human rights in general with Alison Brysk (University of California Santa Barbara). We go on to consider the impact on different groups of people. We discuss African Americans with Dominique Day (member of the UN Working Group of Experts on People of African Descent), prisoners in the United States with David Fathi (American Civil Liberties Union (ACLU)), refugees in Malaysia with Mahi Ramakrishnan (Beyond Borders Malaysia) and children with Aoife Nolan (University of Nottingham Human Rights Law Centre). We discuss human rights, terrorism and COVID-19 with Thomas Parker (journalist, consultant, educator and counterterrorism expert) to understand how responses to existential crises born of natural causes (the pandemic) and human causes (terrorism) can benefit from human rights-based approaches. We conclude the chapter with our conversation with David Owen (University of Southampton) and Arlene Tickner (Universidad del Rosario in Colombia) on COVID-19, democracy and migration.

Chapter 3

MOBILISING FOR HUMAN RIGHTS

Abstract

This chapter considers how NGOs frame and mobilise the struggle for human rights, drawing on the insights and thoughts from Meghna Abraham from Amnesty International, Iain Levine from Human Rights Watch and Dixon Osburn from the CJA, three world-leading human rights NGOs based in London, New York and San Francisco. The rich content from our conversations is situated in a larger consideration of social movements, civil society and so-called TANs, which is informed by our conversation with Amanda Murdie from the University of Georgia and Shareen Hertel from the University of Connecticut. The chapter argues that human rights advocacy is a crowded and highly competitive space, which requires savvy and effective framing of issues to capture the public imagination, alongside frontline interventions designed to improve the protection of human rights.

~

'There is no alternative to doubling down on the facts.'
— Iain Levine, Human Rights Watch

'Law takes a long time.'
— Dixon Osburn, Centre for Justice and Accountability

'There is hope in the darkness.'
— Shareen Hertel, University of Connecticut

Introduction and Background

Human rights do not exist in a vacuum, nor are they firmly grounded in a single and coherent philosophical position. Rather, they are born of an historical evolution of thinking about the fundamental protections that need to be in place to ensure individual agency, freedom, flourishing and dignity. Philosophical writings on human rights have variously appealed to God, nature and reason as key sources for their origins and articulation.[1] Centuries of writing on human rights that extend from ancient philosophy through to the period of accelerated globalisation in the latter half of the twentieth century[2] have gradually developed a consensus around the need for and the nature and extent of human rights as they apply to people around the world, by virtue of them being human. Rights have been at the heart of national founding moments, as in the cases of the US Declaration of Independence and US Constitution, while the first international and formal articulation of human rights did not appear until the promulgation of the 1926 Slavery Convention.[3] This important milestone for human rights addressing a barbaric practice that had existed for thousands of years was soon followed by the 1948 Universal Declaration of Human Rights, and the subsequent proliferation of international and legally binding instruments for the promotion and protection of human rights. State ratification of these instruments since 1966 has varied greatly across the 193 UN Member States,[4] while the UN system and regional inter-governmental bodies such as the Organisation of American States, the COE and the African Union have developed similar institutions for the promotion and protection of human rights.

This evolution in human rights should not be seen as a natural progression of human thought and political philosophy, but rather as the cumulative outcome of centuries of social struggle from below from marginalised sections of the human population and their representatives, and the articulation, codification and 'legalisation'[5] from above through the concerted efforts of individual states and inter-governmental organisations. This incremental growth in the idea of human rights, the different categories and dimensions of human rights (see below) and the international law of human rights seen in this way

---

1 T. Landman, "The Political Science of Human Rights," *British Journal of Political Science* 35, no. 3 (2005): 549–572; S. Mendus, "Human Rights in Political Theory," *Political Studies* 43 (1995): 10–24; J. Finnis, *Natural Law and Natural Rights* (Oxford: Oxford University Press, 1980); J. Waldron, *Theories of Rights* (Oxford: Oxford University Press, 1984); A, Ingram, *A Political Theory of Rights* (Oxford: Oxford University Press, 1994); P. Jones, *Rights* (London: Macmillan, 1994).
2 M. Ishay, *The History of Human Rights: From Ancient Times to the Globalization Era* (University of California Press, 2004).
3 P. Sieghart, *The International Law of Human Rights* (Oxford: Oxford University Press, 1983).
4 T. Landman, *Protecting Human Rights: A Comparative Analysis* (Washington, DC: Georgetown University Press, 2005); T. Landman, *Human Rights and Democracy: The Precarious Triumph of Ideals* (London: Bloomsbury, 2013).
5 S. Meckled-Garcia, ed., *The Legalization of Human Rights: Multidisciplinary Perspectives on Human Rights and Human Rights Law* (London and Oxford: Routledge, 2006).

are the product of a process of 'social construction'[6] and iterative consensus building across a number of different fora. Such a process of consensus building means that the advance in the de jure protection of human rights has exceeded their de facto realisation, while the contestation over human rights has been led through popular mobilisation and social struggle, increasingly organised and led by social movement organisations and NGOs.[7]

In the policy space between state and interstate actors, human rights NGOs have worked on domestic human rights issues and have developed so-called TANs.[8] These networks provide expert advice, represent a human rights 'epistemic community'[9] and act to advocate on behalf of rights holders to bring about greater awareness of human rights problems and bring about human rights changes. It is often the case that domestic mobilisation can face significant blockages and difficulties in achieving change at the domestic level, while mobilisation at the transnational level uses inter-governmental systems and powerful states to leverage the international community to put pressure on states to address their human rights problems. This 'boomerang' effect means that blockages at the domestic level can in many cases be overcome, and that long-term positive change is possible.[10]

In the highly competitive 'market of ideas', human rights organisations find themselves in a crowded policy space, often contending to make their work visible across networks of domestic actors and form alliances with

6 J. Donnelly, "The Social Construction of International Human Rights," in *Human Rights in Global Politics*, ed. T. Dunne and N. Wheeler (Cambridge: Cambridge University Press, 1999), 71–102.

7 J. Foweraker and T. Landman, *Citizenship Rights and Social Movements: A Comparative and Statistical Analysis* (Oxford: Oxford University Press, 1997); T. Risse, S.C. Ropp, and K. Sikkink, eds., *The Power of Human Rights: International Norms and Domestic Change* (Cambridge: Cambridge University Press, 1999); T. Risse, S.C. Ropp, and K. Sikkink, eds., *The Persistent Power of Human Rights* (Cambridge: Cambridge University Press, 2013); T. Landman, *Human Rights and Democracy: The Precarious Triumph of Ideals* (London: Bloomsbury, 2013), 83–96; K. Sikkink, *The Justice Cascade: How Human Rights Prosecutions Are Changing World Politics* (New York: Norton, 2011).

8 M. Keck and K. Sikkink, *Activists beyond Borders: Advocacy Networks in International Politics* (Ithaca, NY: Cornell University Press, 1998).

9 E. Adler, "The Emergence of Cooperation: National Epistemic Communities and the International Evolution of the Idea of Nuclear Arms Control," *International Organization* 46, no. 1 (1992): 101–145; P. M. Haas, "Epistemic Communities and International Policy Coordination," *International Organization* 46, no. 1 (1992): 1–35.

10 T. Risse, S.C. Ropp, and Sikkink, K., eds., *The Power of Human Rights: International Norms and Domestic Change* (Cambridge: Cambridge University Press, 1999); T. Risse, S.C. Ropp, and K. Sikkink, eds., *The Persistent Power of Human Rights* (Cambridge: Cambridge University Press, 2013).

their transnational partners.[11] There is a competition among organisations for salience, sustainability and relevance, in terms of real concrete impact.[12] Successful mobilisation and impact of groups within this context have often been seen as a function of their ability to mobilise resources (e.g. people, finances and evidence), capture the public imagination through discursive framing and demand making, and sustaining collective action for human rights over long periods of time.[13] Positive outcomes and impact in this world of mobilisation are not inevitable, where movements and organisations celebrate small victories; experience partial reversal and setbacks; and are met with stonewalling, repression and state and non-state violence born of a rejection of their cause.[14] The variable success in human rights change can be affected by the political contexts in which organisations operate, the nature and strength of domestic political institutions, the role of the military and ideological control of government and the resonance of the claims and demands that they are making for particular human rights issues.[15]

Demand making, mobilisation, incremental change, setbacks and partial reversals run through the history of the struggle for human rights. In the West, the struggle for human rights saw mobilisations for civil rights in the eighteenth century, political rights in the nineteenth century, and social and economic rights in the twentieth century. Such struggles were grounded in the notion of citizenship rights, but with the advent of the UN system after World War II, the struggle for human rights became universal and international. The 1948 Universal Declaration of Human Rights applies to all humans regardless of their citizenship status or membership of political communities, a conceptual and legal pivot that nevertheless requires state capacity and institutions for their full realisation and implementation. The gradual and piecemeal recognition and protection of human rights in the latter half of the twentieth century in many ways culminated in the establishment of the ICC in The Hague, which can adjudicate cases of crimes against humanity,

11   C. Bob, *The Marketing of Rebellion: Insurgents, Media, and International Activism* (Cambridge: Cambridge University Press, 2005).
12   A. Cooley and J. Ron, "The NGO Scramble: Organizational Insecurity and the Political Economy of Transnational Action," *International Security* 27, no. 1 (2002): 5–39.
13   T. Landman, *Human Rights and Democracy: The Precarious Triumph of Ideals* (London: Bloomsbury, 2013), 83–96.
14   A. Murdie and C.S. Stapley, "Why Target the 'Good Guys'? The Determinants of Terrorism Against NGOs," *International Interactions* 40, no. 1 ((2014): 79–102.
15   S.C. Poe and C.N. Tate, "Repression of Human Rights to Personal Integrity in the 1980s: A Global Analysis," *American Political Science Review* 88, no. 4 (1994): 853–872; S.C. Poe, C.N. Tate, and L.C. Keith, "Repression of the Human Right to Personal Integrity Revisited A Global Cross-national Study Covering the Years 1976–1993," *International Studies Quarterly* 43 (1999): 291–313.

regardless of where they may have been committed.[16] This idea of 'universal jurisdiction', for which many human rights organisations have advocated since the League of Nations in the 1920s, was given moral and legal reinforcement in the extradition case against General Augusto Pinochet, who at the behest of Spanish legal authorities was placed under house arrest in the UK between October 1998 and March 2000.[17] The case filed against Pinochet was for the violation of human rights that had taken place during his dictatorship (1973–89). In the event, the House of Lords ruled that it was legal to detain Pinochet, but agreed on health grounds that he could return to Chile, where he escaped justice and then died in December 2006. Human rights change in Chile was a function of domestic human rights documentation, social mobilisation, international condemnation and competing factions within the regime itself.[18]

The Contemporary Terrain of Human Rights

While human rights organisations such as Anti-Slavery International (ASI) have existed since the 1830s (see Part III), the 1970s saw an increasing number of human rights organisations that have grown in size and impact as they work on human rights on the ground, at the transnational level and within the halls of the United Nations and other inter-governmental organisations. Systematic comparative analysis across all countries in the world in the last three decades of the twentieth century shows that state membership in inter-governmental organisations, such as the United Nations, is significantly related to the ratification of human rights treaties, while the presence of NGOs is significantly related to better human rights protection.[19] In the first two decades of the twenty-first century, despite (or even because of) the rise in populism seen in the United States (Donald Trump), Brazil (Jair Bolsonaro) and Hungary (Viktor Obán), there has been continued mobilisation from human rights organisations. They are well funded, have large memberships,

---

16   Rome Statute of the International Criminal Court, A/CONF.183/9. https://www.icc-cpi .int/resource-library/documents/rs-eng.pdf.
17   D. Connett, J. Hooper, and P. Beaumont, "Pinochet Arrested in London," *The Guardian*, October 18, 1998. https://www.theguardian.com/world/1998/oct/18/pinochet.chile; F. Webber, "The
   Pinochet Case: The Struggle for the Realization of Human Rights," *Journal of Law and Society* 26, no. 4 (1999): 523–537.
18   D. Hawkins, *International Human Rights and Authoritarian Rule in Chile* (Lincoln, NE: University of Nebraska Press, 2002).
19   T. Landman, *Protecting Human Rights: A Comparative Study* (Washington, DC: Georgetown University Press, 2005), 59–158.

continue to monitor human rights, design human rights interventions and advance human rights protection both in principle and in practice. These organisations comprise single-issue groups, or groups with a broad portfolio of human rights issues that include civil, political, economic, social and cultural rights across all their dimensions (see Table 3.1).

People and Practice

To understand the nature and extent of human rights organisations, the ways in which they frame the struggle for human rights and how they have had an impact on human rights law and practice, our podcast featured a number of people from leading human rights organisations, as well as academics who study the effectiveness of these organisations. Meghna Abraham is head of Economic, Social and Cultural Rights at Amnesty International. Iain Levine is the programme director of Human Rights Watch, a human rights organisation based in New York with different country and regional offices that monitor human rights developments. Dixon Osburn from the CJA discussed his 17-year struggle for gay rights reform in the United States, his work on the case against former Pinochet officer, Pedro Pablo Barrientos, the Khmer Rouge in Cambodia and the use of forensic evidence in the case on genocide in Guatemala during the 1980s. Amanda Murdie from the University of Georgia and Shareen Hertel from the University of Connecticut discussed the ways in which human rights TANs bring about positive yet incremental changes in human rights around the world.

Amnesty International[20]

Amnesty International is one of the most well-known and world-leading human rights organisations. Established in the 1970s, primarily to mobilise letter-writing campaigns on behalf of political prisoners and prisoners of conscience held around the world, it expanded its mandate in 2001 to include a wide range of human rights issues.[21] In addition to its work on civil and political rights, such as torture, arbitrary detention and freedom of speech and expression, it now also carries out work on economic, social and cultural rights. This additional set of rights includes rights to health, education,

---

20   This section of the chapter is based on the Rights Track podcast "Advancing Human Rights the Amnesty Way,"
       published on March 20, 2017. http://rightstrack.org/advancing-human-rights-the-amnesty-way.
21   S. Hopgood, *Keepers of the Flame: Understanding Amnesty International* (Ithaca: Cornell University Press, 2006).

Table 3.1 Selected list of major international human rights organisations.

Name	Date Founded	Human Rights Issues
Amnesty International	1961	Human rights defenders, children's rights, women's rights, refugees and migrants, LGBT rights, free speech, death penalty, forced marriage and FGM
Anti-Slavery International	1839	Slavery, servitude, modern slavery, forced marriage, forced labour, human trafficking
Article 19	1987	Freedom of speech, freedom of expression, freedom of information
Centre for Economic and Social Rights	1993	Economic and social rights, poverty, sustainable development, inequality
Global Rights	1978	Women's rights, access to justice, natural resource governance, disability rights
Human Rights Campaign	1980	LGBT rights, HIV and AIDS, same-sex marriage, hate crimes, discrimination
Human Rights Data Analysis Group	1991	Statistics and human rights, killings, police violence, Truth Commissions, conflict, data modelling
Human Rights Watch	1978	Civil and political rights, gender discrimination, children's rights, refugees, minorities, free speech, right to health, torture, women's rights
HURIDOCS	1982	Human rights and information management, information technology, human rights documentation
International Centre for Transitional Justice	2001	Transitional justice, post-conflict reconciliation, Truth Commissions, mass human rights violations
International Federation of Human Rights Leagues	1922	Human rights defenders, women's rights, migrants' rights, judicial mechanisms, globalisation and human rights
International Service for Human Rights	1984	Women human rights defenders, LGBT rights defenders, business and human rights, democratic freedoms
Minority Rights Group International	1969	Ethnic, linguistic, minority rights, land rights, indigenous rights, modern slavery, disability rights
Physicians for Human Rights	1986	Health, asylum and persecution, killings and mass atrocities, sexual violence, torture, COVID-19, doctors who harm
Transparency International	1993	Corruption, anti-corruption and human rights
World Organization Against Torture	1985	Arbitrary detention, torture, extrajudicial killings, forced disappearances, violence

Source: Compiled by the authors. See also Landman, T. (2006) *Studying Human Rights*. London and Oxford: Routledge, p. 21.

water, food, language and ancestral land among other rights. In addition to expanding the categories of human rights that are the focus of its attention, Amnesty International has embraced what is known as the 'state obligation' approach to 'respect, protect, and fulfil' human rights.[22] In this approach, the international law of human rights places obligations on states to not violate human rights (respect), to regulate and control third party organisations from violating human rights (protect) and to use the maximum available resources to engage in the 'progressive realisation' of human rights (fulfil).

This intersection between different categories and dimensions of human rights provides a rubric, or matrix, of issues in need of analysis, intervention and advocacy from groups such as Amnesty International. Meghna Abraham explained to us that in the area of economic, social and cultural rights, her work has involved collecting evidence and data from a variety of sources on the violations of these rights. She uses the example of forced evictions to illustrate how the violation of the right to housing is akin to the right not to be tortured. There are 'identifiable victims and perpetrators'. There is the 'use of force or coercion'. There is a role for accountability. State and non-state actors are often involved in forcing people from their homes, razing their homes to the ground for large infrastructure projects or moving minority groups and other marginalised groups for ideological and political reasons.[23] Such actions across these groups are not hidden from sight, but advocacy around violations does require considerable work in documenting events. Such documentation involves using satellite images before and after the destruction of property, examining government records, interviewing displaced people and then making representations across a wide range of stakeholders to bring redress to the victims and to hold states accountable for their actions, whether they are directly responsible for them, or failed to prevent third parties from committing them.

Meghna uses a second example from a major report *The Great Palm Oil Scandal* she authored on this industry in Indonesia.[24] She explains that palm oil is a 'key ingredient' for 50 per cent of products found in many supermarkets around the world, such as packaged bread, breakfast cereals, margarine, chocolate, ice cream, biscuits and snack food, as well as detergents, shampoos, creams, soaps, lipsticks and biofuels for cars and power plants. The extraction and production processes have been identified to have problems of forced labour and unsafe

---

22   T. Landman and E. Carvalho, *Measuring Human Rights* (London and Oxford: Routledge, 2009).
23   Illustrative examples include the forced eviction of residents in Bucharest during the Ceauçescu dictatorship in order to build the grand avenue to his 'House of the People', and the forced displacement of the Roma people in post-Communist Bulgaria.
24   Amnesty International, *The Great Palm Oil Scandal* (London: Amnesty International, 2016). https://www.amnesty.org/en/documents/asa21/5184/2016/en/.

working conditions. Her work with Amnesty on this issue focused on one major company, Wilmar International, its subsidiaries and its buyers in order to disentangle the roots of the problem, which she argues reside in gender inequality, the structure of wages and the absence of proper protective equipment for workers, leaving them vulnerable to the harms caused by the use of pesticides.

For the report, Amnesty carried out two field missions to Indonesia, worked with local partner NGOs, conducted 120 in-depth interviews, analysed medical reports, examined protective equipment and assessed the regulatory frameworks and enforcement of labour laws. She gathered multiple forms of data and evidence, used to triangulate and corroborate accounts of labour abuse, gender inequality in the use of casual worker contracts and absence of protection. In addition to the publication of the report, Amnesty sought to foment real change in corporate practice and behaviour. It focused its attention on changing the terms and conditions for workers, and sought greater protection of worker rights. It communicated with consumers to raise awareness about the ubiquity of palm oil in products in an effort to put pressure on companies and identify real concrete changes that could be implemented. Companies in the industry, for their part, did not reject the findings of the report, made public commitments to investigate the issues and to report on the measures that they have taken. For its part, Amnesty followed a project cycle that is now quite typical for human rights NGOs: prepare a concrete case study, challenge the key stakeholders, monitor progress and seek to close the gap between principle and practice. Such an approach, Meghna explains, moves far beyond the 'name and shame' approach adopted by many NGOs[25] and allows for human rights NGOs to be agents of change, holding states and companies accountable for practices that violate basic core economic and social rights commitments. In the end, according to Meghna, Amnesty was able to use the evidence it gathered to say outright that 'you can fix these problems and end these abuses'.

Human Rights Watch[26]

Based in New York City, Human Rights Watch investigates and reports on human rights abuses taking place worldwide. Since its establishment over forty years ago, it has now grown to include 450 staff working in 65 locations

---

25 E. Hafner-Burton, "Sticks and Stones: Naming and Shaming the Human Rights Enforcement Problem," *International Organization* 62, no. 4 (2008): 689–716.
26 This section of the chapter is based on the Rights Track podcast "Evidence for Change: The Work of Human Rights Watch," published on April 27, 2017. http://rightstrack.org/evidence-for-change-the-work- of-human-rights-watch-0.

and covering human rights issues in over ninety countries. It has regional offices in Africa, the Americas, Europe and Central Asia, the MENA and the United States. Iain Levine explained that the organisation's work focuses on issues such as women's rights, children's rights, LGBT rights, refugees and those with disabilities. The fact that Human Rights Watch works on human rights issues in the United States gives it credibility and a certain moral authority to work on human rights issues in other countries. Levine notes that at the time of our podcast, in the early months of the new Trump administration, the United States was at a 'propitious moment' for Human Rights Watch to carry out its work. The anti-rights discourse and agenda of the new administration with respect to the 'Muslim ban', crack down on immigration, refusal of access to refugees and other pronouncements meant that the organisation found itself busier than ever.

The organisation's model of change includes three main areas of work: (1) investigate, (2) expose and (3) change. Like other human rights organisations, Human Rights Watch is dedicated to the careful investigation of human rights abuses using a variety of different sources of information, which are then subjected to a rigorous and robust internal review process to establish the verifiability, legality and credibility of frontline reporting. Interviews with victims, statistics, court records, morgue reports and satellite data are collated, double-checked and verified, and tested to see if the testimony stands up to all possible forms of criticism. Once the facts are verified through these processes, the organisation then decides on the timing and form of release of the information that it has compiled. This timing is agreed to have maximum impact for bringing about change. In the era of 'fake news' and the dismissal of 'experts', Levine was insistent on the need for his organisation to continue to provide a *robust evidence base* (see Chapter 4), to avoid attacks and to provide real human stories based on verifiable facts and data. On the question of measurable change, Levine was more circumspect. The organisation has shared much learning across its different divisions and country locations, but he admitted that it could do much better in closing the loop between the different dimensions of its work, and especially between the exposure of human rights wrongs and real tangible change. It has struggled to demonstrate that its work necessarily led to legal change, parliamentary MPs tabling new bills or the passage of new resolutions at the United Nations Human Rights Council.

He continued by discussing his work in the face of a declining human rights situation in the United States, both in terms of domestic protections and US foreign policy under a Trump presidency. The organisation worked on issues such as criminal justice, Guantanamo Bay, torture, immigration, surveillance, deportation and the effect of the global gag rule, which affected women's reproductive rights around the world. He argued that the media and social media landscape had changed fundamentally during his many years at the organisation, exacerbated during the Trump period. Social media offered both an opportunity for Human Rights Watch to get its message out to a larger and larger audience (e.g. its main Twitter account had 3.2 million followers) and a challenge, as alternative voices and 'alternative facts' were used to undermine a strong human rights message. Overall, he was robust in his defence of the organisation's approach, its work and its continued potential to affect positive change.

Justice and Accountability[27]

Dixon Osburn studied for his Juris Doctor and MBA through a joint degree programme at Georgetown University in Washington, DC, in the late 1980s and early 1990s[28] after receiving his BA from Stanford University. He has worked for a variety of different human rights organisations on issues such as targeted drone killings, torture, Guantanamo Bay and gay rights, with a particular focus on service men and women in the US military. He co-founded and led the Servicemembers Legal Defense Network, which was successful in repealing the 1994 'Don't Ask Don't Tell' policy, a decision in September 2011 that allowed gay, lesbian and bisexual people to serve openly in the US military.[29] For five years between 2014 and 2019, Dixon was the executive director of the CJA in San Francisco, where he worked on a number of high-profile cases against former dictators and military personnel who had committed crimes against humanity.

We discussed with Dixon that at the time of recording the podcast in February 2017, a number of dominant narratives had developed about the limits to the advance of human rights. First, as we set out in Chapter 1, Stephen Hopgood had recently published *The Endtimes of Human Rights*,[30] in which

---

27 This section of the chapter is based on the podcast "Pursuing Justice: What Role for Research Evidence?," The Rights Track, February 7, 2017. http://rightstrack.org/pursuing-justice-what -role-for-research- evidence.

28 Dixon Osburn was a fellow student with author Todd Landman at Georgetown, who was studying for his MA in Latin American Studies (1990). Landman's interest in human rights was galvanised at Georgetown after preparing documentary photographic evidence of the murder of six Jesuit priests in El Salvador in 1989; see T. Landman, "Rigorous Morality: Norms, Values and the Comparative Politics of Human Rights," *Human Rights Quarterly* (2016): 1–26.

29 See D. Osburn, *Mission Possible: The Story of Repealing Don't Ask, Don't Tell* (C. Dixon Osburn, 2021).

30 S. Hopgood, *The Endtimes of Human Rights* (Ithaca: Cornell University Press, 2013). See also D. Lettinga and L. van Troost, eds., *Debating the Endtimes of Human Rights: Activism and Institutions in a Neo-Westphalian World* (The Hague: Amnesty International, 2014).

he criticised the elitist nature of 'Human Rights' (uppercase) discourse and 'sacral' language used in the marble halls of international human rights institutions in Geneva, The Hague and New York. He argues that this discourse is far removed and out of touch with the 'human rights' (lowercase) discourse deployed by grassroots and domestic human rights organisations. The second narrative focused on 'human rights fatigue', which had set in after 40 years of awareness raising and advocacy, where a frequent stream of alarmist imagery, woeful accounts and cases of atrocity lost their critical bite in mobilising people for change. The third narrative was one of the emergence of a 'post human rights' era evidenced by the rejection of rights-based international organisations and multilateralism more generally as a way to address the world's problem. The 2016 referendum on the UK's membership in the European Union and the electoral success of populist and nationalist leaders such as Donald Trump in the United States and Jair Bolsonaro in Brazil brought a retreat from internationalism (or globalism) and a questioning of human rights.

Dixon reflects on these emerging narratives and remains positive and optimistic about what human rights organisations can achieve. His work on service members in the US military began in the same year that the 'Don't Ask, Don't Tell' policy came into effect. At that time in 1994, he believed it would take 20 years or more to repeal the policy. In the end, it took his organisation only 17 years, which he sees as a real achievement. He took this optimism to his leadership of the CJA, which uses a creative and innovative legal approach to bring perpetrators of gross human rights violations to justice. His first example concerns Pedro Pablo Barrientos for his role in the murder of Chilean theatre director, musician and poet Victor Jara in 1973 during the early days of the Pinochet regime. Multiple cases in Chile brought by the Jara family had failed, but then evidence emerged that Barrientos had settled in Florida and had become a naturalised US citizen. The CJA investigated the case and prepared a dossier of documentation on the Jara murder in the national stadium in Santiago in the days after the coup. Since Barrientos was living in the United States, the CJA was able to file a civil case against him under the auspices of the 1992 Torture Victim Protection Act.[31] The CJA won the case, with Barrientos found liable for $28 million in damages to the Jara family. Even though Barrientos was not in the financial position to pay the damages, Dixon argues that the legal outcome was highly symbolic, signalling that perpetrators of human rights violations cannot hide in foreign jurisdictions and that lawyers such as Dixon can use the law in creative ways

---

31 H.R.2092 – 102nd Congress (1991–1992) Torture Victim Protection Act. https://www.congress.gov/bill/102nd-congress/house-bill/2092/text.

to pursue justice. Dixon explained further that 'this is not the end of story', since Barrientos did not declare his role in the Chilean regime at the time of his naturalisation and thus could face further liability for a fraudulent application for US citizenship.

In a second example, the CJA filed a case against the Bashar al-Assad regime in Syria for the 2012 extrajudicial killing of *Sunday Times* journalist Marie Colvin and her colleagues in Homs during the conflict between the government and rebel forces. Since the US government classes the Assad regime as a state sponsor of terrorism, the case was justiciable under the auspices of the 1976 Foreign Sovereign Immunities Act.[32] Like in the case of Barrientos, the CJA collected extensive evidence across many different sources and filed the case on behalf of Colvin's sister in July 2016 with the District Court in the District of Columbia (i.e. Washington, DC), which was heard by a federal judge. The outcome of the case was unknown at the time of the podcast recording, but subsequently Judge Amy Jackson ruled against the Assad regime in 2019 for $300 million in punitive damages, $2.5 million to Marie's sister and $11,836 for funeral expenses.[33]

These two examples are emblematic of the kind of work that the CJA carries out. Dixon explained further that academic analysis of trends, background information, forensic anthropology, statistical analysis and satellite image analysis all help to build legal cases that can be adjudicated under the relevant legal codes within different jurisdictions. The CJA works to advance the rule of law around the world and in those countries with a weak rule of law, it seeks many different and alternative routes to justice for victims of gross human rights violations. For Dixon, the phenomenon of legal incrementalism and slow change are a typical experience in human rights work, where a certain amount of patience is required from activists and advocates. Barrientos did not face justice until 30 years after he murdered Victor Jara, after whom the national stadium in Santiago is now named, while justice in the Colvin case did not come for seven years. Like the examples that Meghna Abraham and Iain Levine provide, the work of the CJA is based on what Iain Levine calls 'doubling down on the facts'; collating and collecting evidence from a variety of sources; and using civil, criminal and human rights law in the pursuit of justice.

---

32 Foreign Sovereign Immunities Act of 1976, Pub. L. 94-583, 90 Stat. 2891, 28 U.S.C. Sec. 1330, 1332(a), 1391(f). https://travel.state.gov/content/travel/en/legal/travel-legal-considerations/internl-judicial-asst/Service-of-Process/Foreign-Sovereign-Immunities-Act.html.

33 O. Bowcott, "US court finds Assad regime liable for Marie Colvin's death in Syria," *The Guardian*, January 31, 2019. https://www.theguardian.com/media/2019/jan/31/us-court-finds-assad-regime-liable-marie-colvin-death-homs-syria.

An Academic Perspective[34]

Amanda Murdie and Shareen Hertel are professors of political science who have been engaged in dedicated quantitative data analysis, in-depth case studies and field missions, and reviews of the vast academic literature on human rights produced over the past four decades. Their work draws general conclusions about the struggle for human rights, and they have dedicated their research primarily to the role of civil society, social movement organisations and human rights NGOs in bringing about positive social change.[35] The academic attention to this issue involves initial observations about the issue at hand, the development of a theoretical framework that yields observable implications, the collection and systematic analysis of data and then the drawing of inferences from these data to address the research questions. In both cases, Amanda and Shareen have shown the variable impact and success of organisations mobilising for human rights.

Amanda's motivation came from dinner table conversations with her father, who at the time was working for the United States Fish and Wildlife Service, where he observed that environmental NGOs were more nimble and could act more quickly than government in addressing environmental concerns. These insights stayed with her through her university years as she honed her work on the effectiveness of NGOs that specialised in the broad area of 'human security', which involves those organisations working on 'freedom from fear' (i.e. civil and political rights) and 'freedom from want' (i.e. economic, social and cultural rights). Her work ranges from single-case studies of individual organisations to large and complex quantitative studies on over hundred countries since the 1980s. She looked at human rights advocacy groups and those that provide frontline services in the areas of food, shelter, water and health. Her analysis shows that the domestic presence or proximate presence of human rights NGOs makes a difference for their effectiveness in changing human rights practices.[36]

---

34   This section of the chapter is based on the podcast "Do NGOs Matter," The Rights Track, January 13, 2016. http://rightstrack.org/do-ngos-matter-1; and the podcast, "Making Human Rights Our Business," published on August 25, 2016. http://rightstrack.org/making-human -rights-our-business.

35   See A. Murdie, *Help or Harm: The Human Security Effects of International NGOs* (Palo Alto: Stanford University Press, 2014); S. Hertel, *Unexpected Power: Conflict and Change among Transnational Activists* (Ithaca: Cornell University Press, 2006); S. Hertel, *Tethered Fates: Companies, Communities, and Rights at Stake* (Oxford: Oxford University Press, 2019).

36   A. Murdie, *Help or Harm: The Human Security Effects of International NGOs* (Palo Alto: Stanford University Press, 2014).

While these findings are what we call 'empirical generalisations', she cautions that organisations are not particularly well coordinated in their efforts, subject to repression and coercion, and often compete against one another for scarce financial support. She argues that for those that cast doubt on the efforts of human rights organisations, their mobilisation in the end is worth it, that they do make a positive impact and that by in large the money they receive for their work is deployed effectively. Her father's observations many years ago have been born out by her systematic approach, where she observes that human rights organisations have been fast to adapt and channel their resources to address some of the world's most pressing problems.

Shareen Hertel comes from a background of working on problems of development, democracy and human rights in Latin America, where the topic of this chapter has much resonance given the region's long period of authoritarianism, patterns of underdevelopment and debt, and transitions to democracy.[37] She globalised her interest in human rights beyond the confines of the region and shifted her attention to economic rights and transnational activism, with a particular focus on business and human rights.[38] Starting from in-depth and participant observation fieldwork in Mexico, Bangladesh and India, much of which she carried out in partnership with UN Women and the United Nations Development Programme (UNDP), Shareen built an understanding of what constitutes 'decent work', including the living wage, job security, access to breaks in the work day, toiletry and hygiene facilities, and maternity leave. Her approach has been to start by listening to what is happening on the ground, collecting structured interview data and recording narratives[39] from workers across a wide range of different geographical areas. She argues that her interview work has to be relatively short, as poor people do not have a lot of time to spare. They are busy with a large number of challenges and do not enjoy many of the modern conveniences that save time. By speaking to a large number of workers, however, she is able to establish a picture of their working experience and conditions, a portrait on which she layers additional data collected from

37 J. Foweraker, T. Landman, and N. Harvey, *Governing Latin America* (Cambridge: Polity Press, 2003); T. Landman, "Democracy and Human Rights: Explaining Variation in the Record," in *Democracy and Its Discontents in Latin America*, ed. Joe Foweraker and Dolores Trevizo (Lynne Rienner, 2016), 133–148.

38 S. Hertel and L. Minkler, *Economic Rights: Conceptual, Measurement, and Policy Issues* (Cambridge: Cambridge University Press, 2007); S. Hertel, *Unexpected Power: Conflict and Change among Transnational Activists* (Ithaca: Cornell University Press, 2006).

39 See T. Landman, "Narrative Analysis and Phronesis," in *Real Social Science: Applied Phronesis*, ed. Bent Flyvbjerg, Todd Landman, and Sanford Schram (Cambridge: Cambridge University Press, 2012), 27–47.

newspaper stories, archives and conversations with other academics working on similar issues. Like the other guests featured in this chapter, Shareen triangulates different sources of qualitative and quantitative data to provide a fuller picture of the many challenges surrounding economic rights.

Sustaining engagement for worker and other economic rights requires allies who provide many different kinds of resources, such as food during meetings and rallies, money for activities, legislative assistance in drafting new labour codes and legal assistance to bring class action suits through the domestic court system. Like our other examples in this chapter, however, Shareen recognises that maintaining collective action from these groups also involves what she calls 'petty rivalries' for control over the issue agenda and for access to scarce resource, where it is important to have open channels of communication across these different groups. She also argues that many of these rivalries are born of the overall philosophy of different groups, where some seek to bring about change by working with state authorities and business stakeholders, while others prefer to engage through more radical forms of social mobilisation.

Shareen took these lessons from the ground and the challenges of collective action that different groups face to frame her systematic analysis of over 6,000 businesses that are part of the data collection provided by the Business and Human Rights Resource Centre.[40] Her analysis of this rich data source revealed that businesses involved in the extractive industries have been more responsive to the worker rights agenda than those in light manufacturing and textiles. The latter two forms of business have far fewer 'sunk costs' and can relocate more quickly than those businesses involved in the extractive sector. Shareen explains that a light manufacturing firm can pack up its supplies and operations, ship them from Mexico to Vietnam in a matter of weeks and then establish new operations in ways that take advantage of the global 'race to the bottom' for cheap labour. In contrast, the extractive industries have much higher sunk costs with their investments in specific locations with high concentrations of raw materials, and thus are more inclined to engage with worker rights movements.

The passage of the so-called Ruggie Principles and the UN Global Compact at the turn of the twenty-first century have established expectations

---

40   The Business and Human Rights Resource Centre has headquarters in London and New York, as well as 18 Regional Researchers around the world who collect data with a view to empowering advocates, strengthening corporate accountability and building corporate transparency with respect to human rights in business operations, supply chains and production processes. See https://www.business-humanrights.org/en/.

for companies to respect human rights, for states to protect individuals from human rights abuse by companies and for individuals to have appropriate remedies for the abuse of their rights. Shareen argues, however, that these emerging business and human rights frameworks, developed alongside a large collection of laws, remain voluntary and require concerted efforts from companies, consumers and workers to realise the mutual gains from respect for economic rights. Her extensive surveys carried out over three years on US consumers during the financial crisis show that more than 50 per cent of Americans are willing to pay higher prices for goods if they have demonstrable evidence that the additional money finds its way into the pockets of the workers engaged in the production of those goods. For their part, there are increasing economic incentives for companies to address their labour issues and to be transparent about the journey their products have taken to reach the market. The incremental change evident in her work comes from multiple stakeholders engaging in making rights claims, demanding change and raising awareness of the business benefits to being more rights protective.

The Making of Human Rights

In this chapter, we have shown that the advance of human rights is not linear, automatic or teleological. Rather, it proceeds in fits and starts, requires unstinting commitment from a variety of stakeholders at many different levels and involves many different kinds of expertise, capacity and organisational dynamics. Lurking throughout our conversations with the guests featured in this chapter is the explicit or implicit articulation of a theory of change and the use of robust evidence. Human rights organisations identify a problem area, scope out its nature and extent, conduct research and investigations, prepare internally and externally reviewed reports and then seek positive social change in light of the evidence that has been obtained. The focused and issue-based work of human rights organisations is complemented by academic research, which is able to take a step back, engage in systematic and comparative analysis of human rights problems and provide actionable inferences that are of use by human rights organisations. It is clear from our discussion that there has been a growth in the number of human rights organisations, some of whom have consolidated their position with financial sustainability and success at prolonged forms of collective action and social mobilisation. We have seen concrete and direct examples of success, such as the civil law suits filed by the CJA; indirect examples of progress, such as the work of Amnesty International and Human Rights Watch; and the broader comparative findings from the academic work carried out by Amanda Murdie and Shareen Hertel.

In a conversation some years ago, the late professor Sir Nigel Rodley, former UN Special Rapporteur on Torture (1993–2001), explained that in his periodic visits to Mexico, he noted that the government had made very little progress in addressing his own report's formal recommendations. He also noted, however, that since his report was in the public domain as a formal UN document, domestic and international NGOs and human rights advocates could use his reports as significant markers around which to organise their continued campaigns for reform. This example from Mexico is illustrative of the many challenges facing human rights advocacy of the kind featured from our podcast guests in this chapter. As we have seen, human rights progress is often incremental and long in coming, where small achievements occur infrequently, but can also be interrupted by larger developments or legal decisions. The diligence and hard work from human rights organisations build a knowledge base, raise awareness and provide an accretion of evidence that can work its way through formal and informal mechanisms that can yield positive change. A casual outside observer may despair at the pace of change and not see the value of extended engagement in human rights issues and cases. Victims and survivors of human rights violations, however, have a much different view as they seek redress and justice.

Chapter 4

HUMAN RIGHTS EVIDENCE

Abstract

This chapter delves into the world of empirical evidence and how it is generated in making the case for human rights. Its point of departure is what Rights Track guest Will Moore calls the 'fundamental problem of unobservability' or the hidden nature of human rights abuses. The chapter's content derives from episodes on how to measure torture, how to count human rights violations, the trends in public opinion and attitudes about human rights, the socio-economic dimensions of human rights and how new forms of data and data analytics can be used to map and explain the nature and extent of human rights problems around the world. The content draws on conversations with Patrick Ball from the HRDAG; James Ron from the Humphrey School of Public Affairs at the University of Minnesota; Sakiko Fukuda-Parr from the New School and former director of the United Nations Human Development Report; Chris Fariss from the University of Michigan; Kevin Bales, Doreen Boyd and Sir Bernard Silverman from the University of Nottingham; and Meg Satterthwaite from New York University.

~

'Statistics are not a silver bullet.'

> – Patrick Ball, Human Rights Data Analysis Group

'The real obstacle is political.'

> – Kevin Bales, Rights Lab, University of
> Nottingham

'Resource is not an excuse.'

> – Sakiko Fukuda-Parr, The New School

'It's a methodology that you can't hide from.'

> – Doreen Boyd, Rights Lab, University of
> Nottingham

Introduction and Background

We saw in our last chapter that a crucial component to successful mobilisation for human rights is the evidence base on which arguments are based and can be advanced. Across our examples and conversations with our various guests, we saw the common and underling theory of change, based on the collation and analysis of systematic evidence. In the absence of such an evidence base, human rights organisations risk being perceived as simple lobbying groups and could have significant questions raised about their authenticity, integrity and credibility. The generation of human rights evidence is grounded in larger debates about ontology (what is to be known?), epistemology (how do we know what we know?) and methodology (how do we know if we are correct about what we know?). Debates around these issues dominate academic conferences and publications across many different disciplines; however, as applied to human rights, there have been many advances in the genesis and use of evidence to demonstrate 'human rights wrongs' in ways that have led to the incremental advance in the promotion and protection of human rights. Through our conversations with world leading and award-winning scholars and activists leading the work on human rights evidence, this chapter demonstrates the many achievements in this work and how it has made a difference. Our discussions range from the use of qualitative case-based analysis of individual victims, perpetrators and survivors to quantitative and aggregate analyses across individuals, groups, sub-national units, countries and regions around the world.

Making the Case[1]

A typical starting point for thinking about human rights evidence centres on the preparation of a case file of alleged human rights abuses carried out against a single individual, where legal proceedings and due process require an evidence base that goes beyond reasonable doubt in ways that a judicial body would be able to make a judgement to convict a perpetrator or perpetrators. This kind of legal work is very much part of the struggle for human rights, as we showed in the last chapter with Dixon Osburn's work with the

---

1 The idea of 'making the case' comes from P. Ball, H. Spirer, and L. Spirer, *Making the Case: Investigating Large-Scale Human Rights Violations Using Information Systems and Data Analysis* (Washington, DC: The American Association for the Advancement of Science, 2000), a seminal resource on human rights and data analysis. The lead author Patrick Ball has been a pioneer in statistical approaches to human rights and is featured in this chapter. In 2021, the HRDAG was awarded the Rafto Foundation Award for outstanding work in advancing human rights.

CJA. Indeed, in the International Military Tribunal in Nuremberg after World War II, case files were prepared to bring charges against the main per-petrators in the Nazi regime.[2] Similar case files have been and are prepared across countless legal proceedings around the world, including the high-profile work of the International Criminal Tribunal for Former Yugoslavia (ICTY),[3] International Criminal Tribunal for Rwanda (ICTR)[4] and the ICC[5] in The Hague. Beyond the preparation of such legal cases, however, human rights evidence is a much broader concept that can scale up from the consideration of single individuals to larger aggregations of people at the subnational, national and international level. As our podcast guests for this chapter will show, there is a large community of human rights scholars and practitioners that use a combination of qualitative and quantitative research techniques across a wide range of different disciplines to provide explana-tions and understanding of broader *patterns* in human rights abuse, including changes over time, significant differences between individuals and groups, and variation across countries.

Hidden in Plain Sight

During the 1970s and 1980s, much of Latin America found itself in the throes of authoritarian rule and conflict, which often included heavy forms of state repression, informal 'death squads' and secret detention centres in urban and rural areas, where individuals were detained arbitrarily, tortured, assassinated and/or 'disappeared'.[6] These practices and modes of operating from state and non-state actors meant that human rights abuses of this kind remained largely undetected and hidden from public view, making their documentation and general knowledge of their occurrence largely unknown.[7] The experience in

---

2   For a gripping account of the work of the International Military Tribunal, see J. Persico, *Nuremberg: Infamy on Trial* (New York: Penguin, 1995). See also P. Sands, *East West Street: On the Origins of Genocide and Crimes against Humanity* (London: Weidenfeld and Nicolson, 2016).

3   For more on the ICTY, see https://www.icty.org/.

4   For more on the ICTR, see https://unictr.irmct.org/en/tribunal.

5   For more on the ICC, see https://www.icc-cpi.int/.

6   See J. Foweraker and T. Landman, *Citizenship Rights and Social Movements: A Comparative and Statistical Analysis* (Oxford: Oxford University Press, 1997); J. Foweraker, T. Landman, and N. Harvey, *Governing Latin America* (Cambridge: Polity Press, 2003); D. Hawkins, *International Human Rights and Authoritarian Rule in Chile* (Lincoln, NB: University of Nebraska Press, 2002); P. Kornbluh, *The Pinochet File: A Declassified Dossier on Atrocity and Accountability* (New York: New Press, 2003).

7   See T. Landman, "Seeing the Unseen World: Human Rights Data Analysis," Keynote Lecture at the Annual Rafto Foundation Human Rights Awards Conference, November 13, 2021, Bergen. https://www.rafto.no/news/the-rafto-conference-2021.

Latin America was and is replicated across many other regions in the world. In terms of evidence, Rights Track guest Will Moore argues that systematic inquiry into such large-scale human rights abuse must confront what he calls the 'fundamental problem of unobservability',[8] which is to say, the very nature of and context under which human rights abuses take place means that a large proportion of them simply remain hidden and difficult to observe. Across many of these different country contexts, diligent work from human rights organisations, international human rights inquiries and official 'Truth Commissions' have variously compiled archives of information, documentation and increasingly sophisticated databases on these kinds of abuses. These groups have also advanced our ability to provide more standardised ways of collecting such evidence and more systematic methods of analysis to understand and explain patterns of human rights abuse.

A helpful way to understand the essence of the unobserved nature of human rights abuse is to consider Figure 4.1. The outer circle represents all possible

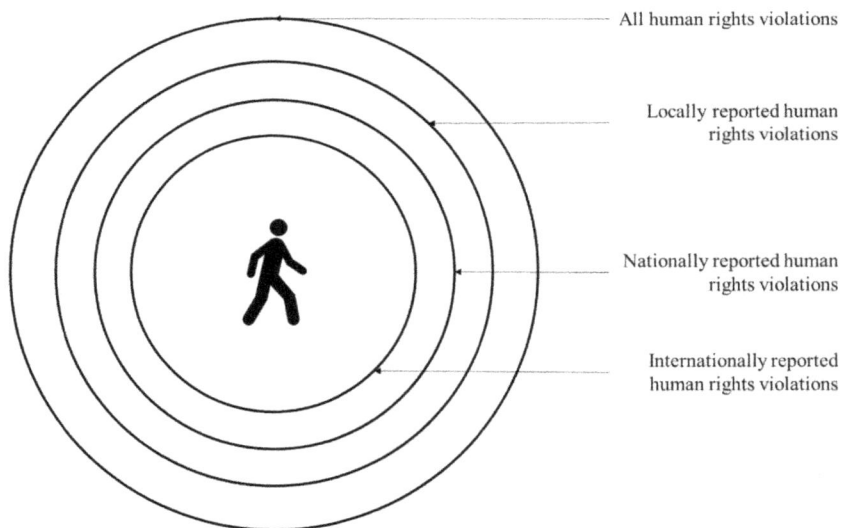

All human rights violations

Locally reported human rights violations

Nationally reported human rights violations

Internationally reported human rights violations

Figure 4.1 Known and unknown human rights violations (levels of reporting). *Source:* Adapted from Bollen, K. (1992) 'Political Rights and Political Liberties in Nations: An Evaluation of Rights Measures, 1950 to 1984', in T.B. Jabine and R.P. Claude (eds) *Human Rights and Statistics: Getting the Record Straight.* Philadelphia, PA: University of Pennsylvania Press, 188–215.

---

8 Will Moore, "How Do We Count Victims of Torture?" The Rights Track, 2016. http://right-strack.org/how-do-we-count-victims-of-torture.

human rights violations that have occurred in a particular context or country over time (known and unknown). The next inward circle represents all human rights violations that have been reported at the local level (known and documented). The next circle represents all human rights violations that have been reported at the national level (known and documented). The innermost circle represents all human rights violations that have been reported at the international level (known and documented). This simple figure illustrates the main challenges associated with gathering evidence of human rights abuse in any given context, where the true universe of violations remains elusive. Each successive circle in the figure is affected by some form of reporting bias—a problem that makes human rights analysis and evidence gathering highly problematic. Our podcast guests, however, have all developed different ways in which to use information known about human rights abuse across a variety of different contexts to make inferences about what is not known.[9] This 'evidence–inference methodological core'[10] lies at the heart of efforts to provide stronger and more systematic human rights evidence.

Evidence and Inference

This idea of the evidence–inference methodological core can be unpacked a little more in order to understand the research and advocacy approach adopted by the kind of human rights scholars and practitioners with whom we spoke as part of the Rights Track. The logic of inference is one that uses information about the world that is known to say something about the world that is unknown, or rather more simply, using a sample of information about human rights to make broader generalisations. The choice of the sample of information is subject to different degrees of randomness and fairness in selection, size of the sample and representativeness of the sample, all of which have an impact on the ability to make generalisations. This relationship between samples and generalisations is nothing new, as our podcast guests Patrick Ball and Sir Bernard Silverman observe in pointing out

---

9 One of the best expositions of the logic of inference and how it applies to social science research of the kind in which our guests engage can be found in G. King, R.O. Keohane, and S. Verba, *Designing Social Inquiry: Scientific Inference in Qualitative Research* (Princeton, NJ: Princeton University Press, 1994). See also G. Almond, "Political Science: The History of the Discipline," in *The New Handbook of Political Science*, ed. R.E. Goodin and H. Klingemann (Oxford: Oxford University Press, 1996); T. Landman and E. Carvalho, *Issues and Methods in Comparative Politics*, 4th ed. (London and Oxford: Routledge, 2017), xvii; 3; 14–16.

10 G. Almond, "Political Science: The History of the Discipline," in *The New Handbook of Political Science*, ed. R.E. Goodin and H. Klingemann (Oxford: Oxford University Press, 1996), 52.

that countries have long sought to estimate the size of their own populations
through the periodic use of the census. Sir Bernard Silverman points out
that such efforts have a deep history by citing the example of the Domesday
Book in England in 1086, which sought to document all land and landhold-
ing as ordered by William I.[11]

There is thus a long history of counting and estimating different dimensions
of society using evidence and inference, and human rights are simply another
such dimension that are subjected to this general approach. Figure 4.2 sum-
marises this idea of evidence and inference graphically. In the obverse of
Figure 4.1, the inner circle in the figure represents some known sample of
information about human rights, while the outer circle represents the inference (or generalisation) made from that sample. The gap or space between
the two circles captures the idea of 'error' (ε), which in statistical terms comes

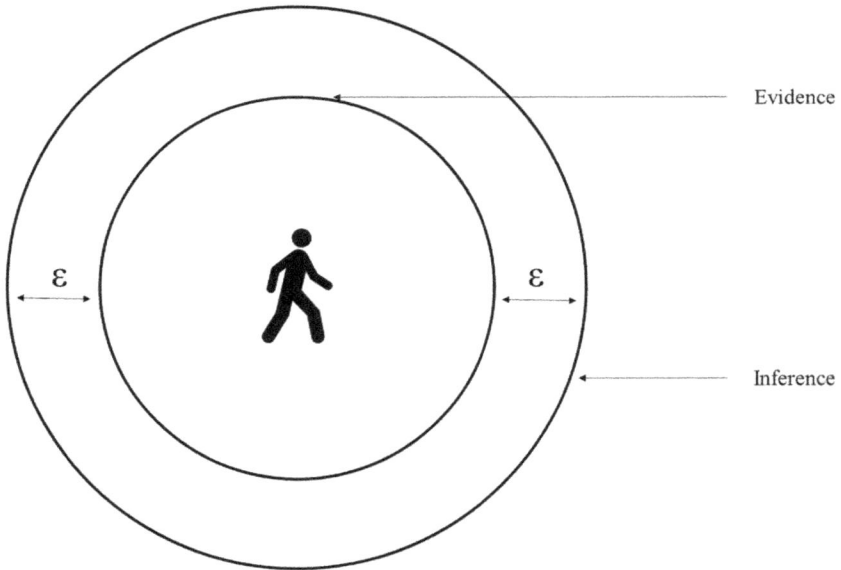

Figure 4.2 Human rights evidence, inference and error (ε). *Source:* Authors.

---

11 In other important historical examples, Landman (2020) shows that nineteenth-century
scholars produced records and maps of chattel slavery in the United States and twentieth-cen-
tury scholars produced quantitative analyses of the French "Reign of Terror" (1793–94). See
T. Landman, "Measuring Modern Slavery: Law, Human Rights, and New Forms of Data,"
Human Rights Quarterly 42, no. 2 (2020): 303–331. See also T. Landman, *Studying Human Rights*
(Oxford and London: Routledge, 2006) and T. Landman and E. Carvalho, *Measuring Human
Rights* (Oxford and London: Routledge, 2009).

with various measures of confidence with which the generalisation can be made. The goal of methodologically rigorous and systematic approaches to human rights is thus to minimise the error and maximise the strength of the generalisations. In addition, there is a trade-off between the authenticity and specificity associated with smaller and less representative samples and the comparability and generalisability of larger samples, the choice of which is defined by the types of human rights issues that scholars and practitioners are seeking to address, and their ability to reach what are known as 'hard-to-find populations'.

Measuring Human Rights

In the context of this chapter, human rights measurement involves the translation of the core content of human rights set out in the international law of human rights into 'systematised definitions' of different categories and dimensions of human rights (see Chapter 1 in this book), which can then be 'operationalised' into indicators, and ultimately 'scores on units'.[12] These units can be individuals, groups of individuals and countries. Since the mid-1970s, academics and NGOs have developed different ways to measure human rights, using what are called: (1) *events-based data*, (2) *standards-based data*, (3) *survey-based data* and (4) *new forms of data* emerging from the ubiquity of the Internet, social media and the application of increasingly sophisticated forms of artificial intelligence, data science and machine learning.[13] This corpus of measurement approaches provides a significant contribution to amassing human rights evidence and features the work of a number of Rights Track guests across all six series of the podcast. The very idea of 'counting and accounting' has been a key theme for us, and in particular, teaching, research

---

12 For the best source for understanding the steps in converting qualitative information of the kind often collected on human rights into quantitative indicators, see R. Adcock and D. Collier, "Measurement Validity: A Shared Standard for Qualitative and Quantitative Research," *American Political Science Review* 95, no. 3 (2001): 529–546.

13 On measuring human rights, see T. Landman, "Measuring Human Rights: Principle, Practice and Policy," *Human Rights Quarterly* 26 (2004): 906–931; T. Landman, "The Political Science of Human Rights," *British Journal of Political Science* 35, no. 3 (2005): 549–572; T. Landman and E. Carvalho, *Measuring Human Rights* (London: Routledge, 2009), 162pp.; T. Landman and L. Kersten, "Measuring Human Rights," in *Human Rights: Politics and Practice*, ed. Michael Goodhart, 3rd ed. (New York: Oxford University Press, 2016); T. Landman, "Human Rights: Quantitative Analysis," in *Human Rights*, ed. Rhona Smith (London and Oxford: Routledge, 2018), 94–113; T. Landman, "Measuring Modern Slavery: Law, Human Rights, and New Forms of Data," *Human Rights Quarterly* 42, no. 2 (2020): 303–331.

and impact work that Landman has carried out on these issues for the last 30 years.

Events-based data and multiple systems estimation

Events-based data approaches are most closely aligned with individual legal case preparation and are often based on narrative accounts offered by survivors of human rights abuse who recount the conditions of their abuse. These accounts are then 'deconstructed' and coded using what Patrick Ball from the HRDAG described to us as the 'who did what to whom' model of human rights events.[14] In this model, any survivor of (or witness to) human rights abuse provides an account that may contain details about one or many abuses they or others may have experienced, one or many perpetrators that may have committed the abuses and the context in which they occurred. The model captures the complexity of any given human rights event, and codes (or counts) the multiple elements of such events, where the violation itself becomes the 'basic unit of analysis'.[15]

To appreciate the scale of this approach, the Truth and Reconciliation Commission in Peru took statements from over 17,000 people who had experienced human rights abuse during the government's conflict with the Maoist *Sendero Luminoso* (Shining Path) revolutionary organisation between 1980 and 2000.[16] These statements were coded into a structured database and cross-referenced with additional sources of information gathered by newspapers, Church organisations and NGOs. Using a statistical technique devised in

---

14 See P. Ball, H. Spirer, and L. Spirer, *Making the Case: Investigating Large-Scale Human Rights Violations Using Information Systems and Data Analysis* (Washington, DC: The American Association for the Advancement of Science, 2000). Landman first met Patrick Ball in Brussels in an EU-sponsored conference on measuring human rights in 2000 and subsequently worked on an assessment of the "who did what to whom" model as it was deployed in various Truth Commissions around the world in 2003 on behalf of the International Centre for Transitional Justice in New York. For more on this model and its applications, see T. Seybolt, J. Aronson, and B. Fishoff, eds., *Counting Civilian Casualties* (Oxford: Oxford University Press, 2013). See also P. Ball, "Human Rights Data Analysis Group (HRDAG)," *Who Did What to Whom?* https://hrdag .org/whodidwhattowhom/contents.html.

15 The unit of analysis refers to the most disaggregated and fundamental countable unit. In the case of human rights, for example, such units may include individual instances of torture, detention, assassination or disappearance. In many case, it is typical for any one victim to suffer one or more such abuses, such that an individual person's account of their abuse will include multiple violations.

16 The official site for the Commission for Truth and Reconciliation in Peru can be found here: https://www.cverdad.org.pe/ingles/pagina01.php.

nineteenth-century Denmark to estimate fish populations,[17] Patrick and his team used these 'multiple sources' to conduct 'multiple systems estimation' (MSE) on these different databases.[18] MSE is based on the ratio of probabilities of any one victim appearing on one or more lists in order to make an estimation of victims that do not appear on any of the lists. In a classic example of 'evidence and inference', the technique uses information on violations that are known and reported (i.e. the lists) to say something about violations that are unknown and unreported (i.e. estimations). The unknown element of the approach is also known as the 'dark figure' and is represented as a statistical estimation with associated margins of error. The original estimation in Peru showed that between 61,007 and 77,552 people died in the conflict, while revised analysis shows a conservative estimate between 56,741 and 61,289 and a more liberal estimate of 61,462 and 75,387.[19] As we shall see, MSE has been used to estimate deaths in other contexts (e.g. Sierra Leone, East Timor and Colombia); the patterns of police violence in the United States (especially in Chicago and Boston);[20] and the prevalence of modern slavery in the UK, the Netherlands and New Orleans.

Patrick Ball is the world-leading statistician of human rights, is executive director of the HRDAG and has worked on data projects for Truth Commissions in South Africa, Haiti, Guatemala, Peru, East Timor and Sierra Leone. He has also testified in the trials against Slobodan Milosevic and General Efrain Ríos Montt in Guatemala, as well as estimated the number of people killed in the Syrian conflict since 2011. In 2021, he and his team received the Rafto Foundation for Human Rights Award for their work on documenting and estimating human rights violations.[21] When we spoke to

---

17 See Y.M. M. Bishop, S. E. Fienberg, and P.W. Holland, *Discrete Multivariate Analysis: Theory and Practice* (Cambridge, MA: MIT Press, 1975), 231–236.

18 See P. Ball, D. Asher, D. Sumont, and Manrique (2003) 'How Many Peruvians have Died?' An estimate of the total number of victims killed or disappeared in the armed internal conflict between 1980 and 2000. Washington, DC: American Association for the Advancement of Science, available at: https://www.aaas.org/sites/default/files/s3fs-public/Peru2003.pdf.

19 D. Manrique-Vallier, P. Ball, and D. Sulmont, "Estimating the Number of Fatal Victims of the Peruvian Internal Armed Conflict, 1980–2000: An Application of Modern Multi-list Capture-Recapture Techniques," 2019. https://arxiv.org/pdf/1906.04763.pdf.

20 K. Lum and P. Ball, *Estimating Undocumented Homicides with Two Lists and List Dependence* (San Francisco: Human Rights Data Analysis Group, 2015), available at: Estimating Undocumented Homicides with Two Lists and List Dependence; see also P. Ball, "Violence in Blue," Granta, 2016. https://granta.com/violence-in-blue/.

21 See https://www.rafto.no/the-rafto-prize/human-rights-data-analysis-group.

Patrick, he told us[22] that statistics are very good for identifying patterns of human rights abuse, comparing levels of abuse across different geographies, different groups of victims and different types of perpetrators. Statistics are not, he says, good for understanding the characteristics of cases of abuse against single individuals, where ethnographies and legal documentation are required to prepare 'case files'. He explains that any given human rights event, such as a 'massacre', is messy, complex and comprised of a network of abuse elements that include violations, victims and perpetrators. Such events can be disaggregated by using the individual violation as the basic unit of analysis to avoid the problem of counting 'the most important violations', which can lead to the undercounting of certain types of violations over others. It is quite typical for human rights violations to progress in a sequence that moves from arbitrary detention to torture to execution. Counting only the killings (the most egregious violation) can undercount the incidence of detention and torture.

This insight is particularly important for those country contexts in which governments change their repressive strategies. We discussed two examples of this: the civil war in El Salvador in the late 1970s and early 1980s, and the Pinochet regime in Chile in the 1970s and 1980s. In El Salvador, President George Walker Bush intervened in the civil war to urge the government to stop killing members of the opposition guerrilla forces. The state stopped the killing, but continued to use detention and torture, which means from a statistical point of view, all violations need to be counted to provide an accurate account of the pattern of abuse over time. In similar fashion, the Pinochet regime moved from a policy of killing opponents of the regime in the 1970s to one in the 1980s, which focused primarily on detention, torture and then release.[23] In both cases, the concentration on the most egregious human rights violations (i.e. killing) would show a downward trend in both countries, while the use of detention and torture may well rise or stay the same over time.

Patrick explained that each of his data projects relies on primary sources such as narrative statements collected by official Truth Commissions, reports gathered by NGOs and newspaper reporting of periods of violence and repression. Using legal frameworks such as the 1948 Universal Declaration of Human Rights, the 1966 International Covenant on Civil and Political Rights, and domestic legislation, each of these accounts is coded using his 'who

---

22 P. Ball, "How Can Statistics Advance Human Rights," The Rights Track, 2016. http://rightstrack.org/how-can-statistics-advance-human-rights.

23 For this change in repressive strategy in Chile, see J. Foweraker and T. Landman, *Citizenship Rights and Social Movements: A Comparative and Statistical Analysis* (Oxford: Oxford University Press, 1997).

did what to whom' model to determine the patterns of human rights abuse that have been recorded. His later work on subsequent Truth Commissions led him to deploy 'MSE' using different source lists and the ratio of probabilities that any one of those lists captured human rights victims. These primary accounts from witnesses and survivors contain relevant information on who was killed, when they were killed, where and by whom. In Peru, his Truth Commission work revealed 17,000 statements, with information on 22,000 named people who died, and when combined with additional lists yielded an estimation of nearly 70,000 people killed. One element of this work showed that reporting of killings carried out by the Shining Path guerrilla movement was reported primarily in Lima, while killings perpetrated by the state were largely reported in the rural areas. Popular perception at the time suggested that the Shining Path was the main perpetrator, while the statistical analysis showed that 46 per cent of killings were carried out by the Shining Path, 30 per cent carried out by the state and 24 per cent by other perpetrators. This difference between popular perception and statistical estimation, Patrick told us, is quite typical in human rights work, where statistics act as a 'counter-intuitive illuminator' of the patterns of abuse, and which involve statistical reasoning as opposed to anecdotal reasoning.

In this way, Patrick argues that 'statistics are not a silver bullet' providing the objective truth of what definitely happened, but, along with many other sources of data, help build an argument about what was likely to have happened. For example, his analysis in Guatemala showed that in the early 1980s, indigenous people were eight times more likely to have been targeted by state security forces, but to conclude that such a finding demonstrates *intentionality* of this violence simply pushed the inference too far. Rather, Patrick argues, statistics can demonstrate the 'gross disproportionality' of violence that is either consistent or inconsistent with an evidence record comprised of legal documentation, ethnographic information, forensic analysis of bodies for 'exceptional savagery' meted out against victims and other forms of evidence. 'Proof' of genocide for Patrick is a legal and subjective judgement, where statistics are but one part of the many elements of an argument linked together.

Drawing on Patrick's work, the Rights Track guests Kevin Bales and Sir Bernard Silverman used MSE to provide the very first estimation of modern slaves in the UK in 2014.[24] For several decades, Kevin has been a

---

24 K. Bales, O. Hesketh, and B. Silverman, "Modern Slavery in the UK: How Many Victims?," *Significance* (2015): 16–21; K. Bales, "Unlocking the Statistics of Slavery," *Chance* 30, no. 3 (2017): 4–12. http://www.tandfonline.com/doi/full/10.1080/09332480.2017.1383105.

world leader in the fight against 'modern slavery' (see Part III of this book), leading the NGO Free the Slaves and then joining academia for research and teaching in this area. Bernard is a mathematician and statistician, who has served in a variety of roles, including the Chief Scientific Officer for the UK's Home Office. Together, Kevin and Bernard joined forces with Olivia Hesketh at the Home Office to estimate the number of enslaved people in the UK. In our conversation,[25] Kevin explained that he worked on the GSI (see below) and noted that the random sample survey approach used in that index was not appropriate for developed countries with a low prevalence of slavery. Drawing on his work in estimating the 'dark figure' of slavery crimes in Europe,[26] which remain hugely under-reported, Kevin and Bernard used six different lists of slavery crimes in the UK, applied MSE to show that, for 2014, there were between 10,000 and 13,000 enslaved people. Kevin reflects that they had to overcome political nervousness about data protection and the possibility of re-identification of victims and survivors in order to carry out the estimation. Bernard carried on with the work to address the problem of 'sparse' overlap between different sources of data and how the modelling had to take this problem into account.[27]

The estimations produced by Kevin and Bernard inspired similar such projects in the Netherlands,[28] the state of Florida and in the city of New Orleans.[29] In the UK, their work was positively received by government as it provided a number from which policy could then be developed and in many ways is credited with making a significant contribution to the passage of the 2015 UK Modern Slavery Act. For Kevin, 'the real obstacle is political' in using statistics to address underlying social problems affecting vulnerable and hard-to-find populations. When, some months later, we spoke to Bernard, he argued that the estimations raised public awareness and led to agenda setting within government to do something about the problem. He said that the

---

25   K. Bales, "Modern Day Slavery: Counting and Accounting," The Rights Track, 2016. http://rightstrack.org/modern-day-slavery-counting-and-accounting-1.

26   M. N. Datta and K. Bales, "Slavery in Europe: Part 1, Estimating the Dark Figure," *Human Rights Quarterly* 35, no. 4 (2013): 817–829.

27   B. Silverman, "Multiple-Systems Analysis for the Quantification of Modern Slavery: Classical and Bayesian Approaches," *Journal of the Royal Statistical Society A* 183, Part 3 (2020): 691–736.

28   J. Van Dijk, P.G.M., Van Der Heijden, and S. Kragten-Heerdink, *Multiple Systems Estimation for Estimating the Number of Victims of Human Trafficking across the World* (University of Southampton Institutional Repository, 2016). https://eprints.soton.ac.uk/399731/.

29   Kevin Bales, Laura T. Murphy, and Bernard W. Silverman, "How Many Trafficked People Are There in Greater New Orleans? Lessons in Measurement," *Journal of Human Trafficking* 6, no. 4 (2020): 375–387. doi: 10.1080/23322705.2019.1634936.

estimate relative to the whole UK population could seem relatively small, but 10,000–13,000 is still 'a lot of people', that 'it is not acceptable for even one person' being in this position, and 'is not trivial'.[30]

We spoke to Will Moore[31] from Florida State University and latterly Arizona State University, who along with Courtenay Conrad from the University of California, Merced produced an events-based data project they call the Ill-Treatment and Torture (ITT) data set, which codes the allegations of torture made across countries between 1995 and 2005. Will argues that other data projects like the Political Terror Scale and the Cingranelli and Richards (CIRI) Human Rights Data Project (see below) code narrative reports from Amnesty International and the US State Department on human rights abuse as if they have a complete record of reported abuse. In contrast, his work has counted the allegations of torture corroborated by Amnesty International to provide raw, incomplete and biased data in need of further statistical modelling. For Moore and Conrad, human rights 'events' are the allegations, which he argues capture an underlying pattern that can be unearthed through secondary data analysis. Will explained to us that he and Courtenay have used the ITT data to show that incumbents, politicians and state actors in democracies are less likely to face accountability for engaging in 'scarring torture', but in those countries with strong judicial powers, the level of 'clean torture' is much higher. Their analysis suggests that public tolerance of human rights abuse in democracies is much higher than expected, while judicial accountability is associated with more hidden and clean forms of torture.[32]

Standards-based data

The second type of quantitative evidence that has been developed over the last several decades includes a wide range of standards-based data, which are comparable scales derived from qualitative reporting on the human rights situation on a country-by-country basis. Raymond D. Gastil developed the 'political terror scale', which codes countries on a 1 (good protection) to 5 (lack of protection) scale for a subset of human rights that include arbitrary detention, torture, extrajudicial killing and disappearance. This scale ultimately migrated to Mark Gibney at the University of North Carolina Asheville and

---

30 B.W. Silverman, "Crunching Numbers: Modern Slavery and Statistics," The Rights Track, 2018. http://rightstrack.org/crunching-numbers-modern-slavery-and-statistics.

31 W. Moore, "How Do We Count Victims of Torture?," The Rights Track, 2016. http://rightstrack.org/how-do-we-count-victims-of-torture.

32 C. Conrad, D.W. Hill, and W. Moore, "Torture and the Limits of Democratic Institutions," Journal of Peace Research 55, no. 1 (2018): 3–17.

now provides updated scores dating back to 1976. The project provides two scales using human rights reporting from Amnesty International and the US State Department. In parallel, the original Gastil idea was then taken on by Freedom House, a NGO, where its *Freedom in the World* reports include two separate seven-point scales on political rights and civil liberties coded from a variety of sources in the Freedom House network of stakeholders. The CIRI human rights data project uses a similar approach but for a wider set of human rights (17 in total) through coding US State Department human rights reports and includes data on all countries in the world from 1980. Finally, the Human Rights Measurement Initiative provides different measures of civil and political rights (33 countries) and economic and social rights (197 countries) based on expert opinion surveys that are then coded into standardised scores for tracking human rights performance. Across all these scales are a series of methodological steps that include (1) the provision of 'systematised' definitions of particular human rights, (2) the selection and use of source material on these rights, (3) the coding frameworks to convert human rights reporting into comparable scales and (4) the variable use of separate coding teams and associated 'inter-rater' reliability tests.

Against this background to the genesis and evolution of standards-based data on human rights, we spoke to Chris Fariss from the University of Michigan on a wide range of issues concerning these kinds of data.[33] Fariss has been principally concerned with the overall level of 'awareness' and a 'rising standard of accountability' of human rights abuse and how these affect human rights reporting as found in the Amnesty and State Department reports, and how these are used to produce the Political Terror Scale. Much commentary suggested that as awareness about human rights increases, reporting of such abuse becomes more complete and extensive, which in turn can lead to the potentially false inference that human rights protection is getting worse in the world. Using a statistical technique known as Item Response Theory, Fariss shows that it is possible to take this raised awareness into account and readjust the scores accordingly. Once this is done, the time series trends in the protection of civil and political rights show that human rights protection in the world has actually improved over the last several decades.[34]

---

33 C.J. Fariss, "Are We Better at Human Rights than We Used to Be?," The Rights Track, 2015. http://rightstrack.org/are-we-better-at-human-rights-than-we-used-to-be.

34 C. J. Fariss, "The Changing Standard of Accountability and the Positive Relationship between Human Rights Treaty Ratification and Compliance," *British Journal of Political Science* 48, no. 1 (2018): 239–272; C.J. Fariss, "Yes, Human Rights Practices Are Improving Over Time," *American Political Science Review* 133, no. 3 (2019): 868–881.

When Chris spoke with us, he used the analogy of standardised testing, such as the SAT or GRE in the United States, where a slate of questions is put to the candidate taking the test from which a standardised set of scores from the pattern of 'right and wrong answers' is derived that capture an underlying concept of aptitude. The 'constellation of right and wrong answers' rates candidates such that the 'smartest' candidate has fewer wrong answers than other candidates who have more wrong answers. This analogy applies to the coders working on human rights reports, and Chris's model takes this variation into account, which not only builds in the changing quality of reporting, but also any biases the coder may have by knowing the name of the country they are coding. Chris argues that overall levels and quality of information on human rights abuse have improved, while his model produces an estimated human rights score with a margin of error that takes into account the uncertainty of our judgements. Beyond his initial findings, Chris continues to work on applying his model to a broader set of human rights than physical integrity rights and going back in history to code human rights abuse since World War II. Our conversation ended with him cautioning us to not 'overreact' to the immediacy of tragic events, such as 9/11 and the terrorist attacks in London, Bali, Madrid and Paris, which though shocking are relatively infrequent and can lead to a false impression that the world is becoming a more dangerous place. For him, the 'rising standard of accountability' is both good for understanding longer-term trends and for holding governments to account.

Survey-based data

Standard social science survey techniques have been developed to address both the *perceptions* and *experiences* of human rights across different countries. Typically such approaches use random samples of country populations and then deploy structured and semi-structured surveys that ask an array of questions about human rights.[35] Large projects such as the World Values Survey have questions on the degree to which human rights are respected across more than eighty countries, and across 65,000 respondents for various years between 1981 and 2017.[36] Over the years, the Pew Research Centre has also deployed

---

35 See, for example, T. Landman and E. Carvalho, *Measuring Human Rights* (London and Oxford: Routledge, 2009), 91–106.

36 The main question in the survey asks, 'How much respect is there for individual human rights nowadays in this country?' There are additional questions on freedom, democracy, freedom of expression, freedom from control and the main actor responsible for guaranteeing human rights. See R. Inglehart et al., eds. *World Values Survey: All Rounds – Country-Pooled Datafile Version* (Madrid: JD Systems Institute, 2014). https://www.worldvaluessurvey.org/WVSDocumentationWVL.jsp.

surveys on human rights around the world[37] while more specifically, the ILO, the Walk Free Foundation and Gallup have used survey instruments across 70 countries to measure the prevalence of modern slavery (see Part III of this book).[38] Other survey projects have been developed for specific communities of people, such as the Physicians for Human Rights work on sexual violence during conflicts.[39]

We spoke to James Ron from the University of Minnesota who carried out a cross-national comparative study about perceptions of human rights in India, Morocco, Nigeria and Mexico using random sample surveys,[40] the results of which appear in his book *Taking Root: Human Rights and Public Opinion in the Global South*.[41] Using national (Mexico) and city (Morocco, Nigeria and India) level representative surveys, Ron found surprisingly high levels of support for the concept of human rights, which belie the many criticisms of human rights as being ethno-centric and Western. Across his surveys, he found that 'hard core' supporters of human rights made up 30 per cent, while for more relaxed understandings of human rights, the proportion increases to 50 per cent. In probing what respondents associate with human rights on a 1 (low association) to 7 scale (high association), he found that people see a higher association between human rights and protection from torture and murder (an average score of 5.2) than between human rights and the protection of criminals and terrorists (an average score of 2.5 and 2.4, respectively). For his measures of trust (on a 0–1 scale), he found greatest trust in religious groups (0.64), followed by human rights groups (0.52) and then politicians (0.31). These findings are further differentiated, where support for human rights is lower for measures of social religiosity (i.e. trust religious organisations and attend services) than for personal piety (i.e. frequency of praying).

Within each of the four countries, James explained he found stark differences in views. In Morocco, there was a strong relationship between support for women's rights and human rights, while distrust of the United States lowers support for human rights. In Mexico, he argued that government support

---

37   See www.pewresearch.org.

38   ILO and Walk Free Foundation, *Global Slavery Index 2018*, 2018. https://www.globalslavery-index.org/resources/downloads/.

39   Physicians for Human Rights. https://phr.org/issues/sexual-violence/program-on-sexual-violence-in-conflict-zones/research/.

40   J. Ron, "A Matter of Opinion: What Do We Really Think about Human Rights?" The Rights Track, 2016. http://rightstrack.org/a-matter-of-opinion-what-do-we-really-think-about-human-rights-1.

41   J. Ron, S. Golden, D. Crow, and A. Pandya, *Taking Root: Human Rights and Public Opinion in the Global South* (Oxford: Oxford University Press, 2017).

for human rights through formal policies and institutions is related to human rights support. In India, support for women's rights was associated with lower support for human rights, while trust in international human rights organisations was associated with stronger support for human rights. Nigeria is a hugely devout country (90 per cent religious identification as Christians or Muslims) with more trust in the US government and deep mistrust in multinational corporations, each of which affects support for human rights. As we wrapped up our episode, James concluded that despite these country-level differences, his work has revealed a gap between what scholars and activists thought what people think about human rights and what people actually think about human rights.

For Kevin Bales, surveys have been a useful way to estimate the prevalence of modern slavery around the world. For a number of years, Kevin has worked with the Walk Free Foundation and the ILO using Gallup household surveys in 'high-prevalence' countries to produce an overall GSI. He argues that more developed countries tend to have lower instances of modern slavery, and thus the use of surveys has concentrated on less developed countries, such as India, which has the highest number of enslaved people in absolute terms, but fewer if understood as proportion of the population. He and his collaborators used the surveys in high-prevalence countries as a first step, and then modelled the prevalence in those countries that did not have surveys based on a series of risk factors, which allowed the GSI to extend to 163 countries. There has been quite a lot of debate about this two-step approach,[42] but there has been great value to the data from surveyed countries for important kinds of secondary analysis.[43]

New forms of data

Widespread access to the Internet in the 1990s has accelerated considerably since then to provide an explosion of new sources of data for human rights evidence. New platforms of data have expanded beyond data sets for download to include 'open source' information that now include social media text

---

42 A. T. Gallagher, "What's Wrong with the Global Slavery Index?," *Anti-Trafficking Review*, no. 8 (2017): 90–112. Alliance 8.7, "Symposium: Modelling Modern Slavery Risk," 2018. https://delta87.org/2018/12/symposium-modelling-modern-slavery-risk/.

43 See, for example, T. Landman and B.W. Silverman, "Globalization and Modern Slavery," *Politics and Governance* 7, no. 4 (2019): 275–290; F. Albornoz, M. Dahm, L. Frones, and T. Landman, "International Trade and Forced Labour," University of Nottingham Working Paper, 2021.

for natural language processing, topic models,[44] corpus linguistic analysis, mobile phone call records,[45] satellite images and other 'earth observation' (EO) data.[46] These data can be combined and triangulated to provide new insights into patterns of direct human rights violations (e.g. mass graves,[47] and forced evictions[48]) and identification of objects and sites related to human rights abuse (e.g. build-up of military forces,[49] brick kilns in South Asia,[50] cobalt mines in the Democratic Republic of the Congo (DRC),[51] palm oil production in Malaysia and deforestation in Brazil).[52] These new forms of data tend to be larger in scale and granularity (or resolution) and can be combined with other forms of data for systematic modelling of trends and relationships relevant to human rights.

---

44 See, for example, Benjamin Lucas and Todd Landman, "Social Listening, Modern Slavery, and Covid-19," *Journal of Risk Research* (2020). doi: 10.1080/13669877.1864009.

45 G. Smith, R. Weiser, J. Goulding, "A Refined Limit on the Predictability of Human Mobility," *IEEE Pervasive Computing (PERCOM)* (2014): 88–94. doi: 10.1109/PerCom.2014.6813948.

46 See, for example, D.S. Boyd, et al., "Slavery from Space: Demonstrating the Role for Satellite Remote Sensing to Inform Evidence-Based Action Related to UN SDG Number 8," *ISPRS Journal of Photogrammetry and Remote Sensing* 142 (2018): 380–388. doi: 10.1016/j.isprsjprs.2018.02.012; G.M. Foody et al., "Earth Observation and Machine Learning to Meet Sustainable Development Goal 8.7: Mapping Sites Associated with Slavery from Space," *Remote Sensing* 11, no. 3 (2019): 266. doi: 10.3390/rs11030266; D. Brown et al., "Modern Slavery, Environmental Degradation and Climate Change: Fisheries, Field, Forests and Factories," *Environment and Planning E: Nature and Space* (2019). doi: 10.1177/2514848619887156; B. Jackson et al., "Remote Sensing of Fish-Processing in the Sundarbans Reserve Forest, Bangladesh: An Insight Into the Modern Slavery-Environment Nexus in the Coastal Fringe," *Maritime Studies* 19 (2020): 429–444. doi: 10.1007/s40152-020-00199-7.

47 Amnesty International, *Burundi: Suspected Mass Graves Revealed in New Satellite Images* (London: Amnesty International, 2018). https://www.amnesty.org.uk/burundi-buringa-suspected-mass-graves-revealed-new-satellite-images.

48 Amnesty International, "Somalia: Satellite Imagery Reveals Devastation Amid Forced Evictions of Thousands Who Fled Conflict and Drought," 2018. https://www.amnesty.org/en/latest/news/2018/01/somalia-satellite-imagery-reveals-devastation-as-thousands-evicted/.

49 American Association for the Advancement of Science (AAAS), *High-Resolution Satellite Imagery and the Conflict in South Ossetia* (Washington, DC: American Association for the Advancement of Science, 2008). https://www.aaas.org/resources/high-resolution-satellite-imagery-and-conflict-south-ossetia-0.

50 See G.M. Foody et al., "Earth Observation and Machine Learning to Meet Sustainable Development Goal 8.7: Mapping Sites Associated with Slavery from Space," *Remote Sensing* 11, no. 3 (2019): 266. doi: 10.3390/rs11030266.

51 C. Brown, A. Daniels, D.S. Boyd, A. Sowter, G. Foody, and S. Kara, "Investigating the Potential of Radar Interferometry for Monitoring Rural Artisanal Cobalt Mines in the Democratic Republic of the Congo," *Sustainability* 12 (2020): 9834. doi: 10.3390/su12239834.

52 T. Landman, "Measuring Modern Slavery: Law, Human Rights, and New Forms of Data," *Human Rights Quarterly* 42, no. 2 (2020): 303–331.

The first attempt to combine different kinds of aggregate country-level data to understand economic and social rights comes from Rights Track guest Sakiko Fukuda-Parr,[53] who led the analysis and publication of the Human Development Index (HDI) at the UNDP. She then went on to create the Social and Economic Rights Fulfilment (SERF) Index,[54] which analyses country-level performance as a function of the overall economic resource available in a county to show whether individual countries are doing better or worse than expected given their underlying levels of resource. She explained to us that the HDI was launched in 1990 to capture country-level progress that moved beyond standard measures of gross domestic product (GDP) per capita. The HDI was based on the work of economist Amartya Sen and his 'capabilities' approach and 'development as freedom' perspective.[55] The HDI combined measures of education, longevity and income, and then ranked countries in a series of annual reports led by Sakiko at the UNDP.

The HDI introduced the idea that human development is correlated with growth, but not perfectly so, and the gap between growth and other indicators fed into her thinking about the SERF index. The main difference for her is the direct reference to states as 'duty bearers' who have the legal obligation to respect, protect and fulfil human rights. For economic and social rights, these obligations require states to oversee the 'progressive realisation' of these rights using the 'maximum available resources' at their disposal. The SERF Index thus contains indicators for education, health and food, and then constructs an 'Achievement Possibility Frontier' through statistical analysis that shows the gap between what is expected of countries given their underlying economic resource and their achievement in these areas. It is thus possible to engage in relative comparisons of countries, such that a country like Tanzania has a higher SERF Index than its neighbouring countries with a similar availability of economic resource, while wealthy countries are further differentiated in ways that show their ability to fulfil their economic and social rights obligations. In our conversation she is optimistic about the pace of change over time and sees the SERF Index as a rigorous way with which to measure progress.

---

53 S. Fukuda-Parr, "Beyond GDP: A Measure of Economic and Social Rights," The Rights Track, 2016. http://rightstrack.org/beyond-gdp-a-measure-of-economic-and-social-rights.

54 S. Fukuda-Parr, T. Lawson-Reiner, and S. Randolph, *Fulfilling Economic and Social Rights* (Oxford: Oxford University Press, 2015). For the latest data, see https://serfindex.uconn.edu/overview-2020/.

55 A. Sen, *Development as Freedom* (Oxford: Oxford University Press, 2001).

Departing from aggregate country-level data, podcast guest Doreen Boyd[56] from the Rights Lab at the University of Nottingham has developed a collection of analytical tools from her environmental research and applied them to the issue of modern slavery (see Part III of this book). Using a combination of EO and remote sensing approaches as they apply to physical geography, Boyd turned her attention to illegal fishing, the production of bricks in South Asia, cobalt mining in the DRC, charcoal production in Brazil, strawberry harvesting in Greece and cotton fields in Central Asia. The pivot to her 'slavery from space' project began initially with work on the UNESCO area of natural beauty known as the Sundarbans in Bangladesh, where its protected status meant there should be no development or degradation of the natural flora and fauna. Working with podcast guest Kevin Bales, she told us how she scanned Google earth images over time and detected emerging infrastructure that with the help of people on the ground confirmed the presence of fish drying racks, where young children were being forced to work.

This initial project led to further work on the 'Brick Belt', an area that is 1.2 million square kilometres and covers parts of Nepal, India, Pakistan and Bangladesh. Brick kilns produce bricks for domestic consumption, where local NGOs estimate that 70 per cent of the workers are in some form of bonded or forced labour. Brick kilns are typically 100 metres by 30 metres with a definitive tall chimney, making them visible through a variety of satellite images. Her initial work involved manually counting these sites across images from a random sample of 320 'geographical cells' and then making statistical inferences to estimate the total number of kilns in the region. She explained how she improved on this initial method by using artificial intelligence and machine learning to trawl through all available images of the kilns over time to build a more complete and accurate picture. While this approach does not count people per se, it does provide a scientific base of evidence of the geospatial distribution of sites, where there is a high probability of forced labour, bonded labour and modern slavery. Like the work of other Rights Track guests featured in this chapter (Part III), her statistical work provides significant evidence that can then be used alongside other kinds of evidence to share with NGOs and government authorities to investigate sites and the practices that are taking place there.

Rights Track guest Meg Satterthwaite[57] is a professor of clinical law at New York University who has been working on access to water in Haiti. This episode

---

56   D. Boyd, "Eye in the Sky: Rooting Out Slavery from Space," The Rights Track, 2018. http://rightstrack.org/eyes-in-the-sky-rooting-out-slavery-from-space.

57   M. Satterthwaite, "Does a Picture Speak a Thousand Words When Advocating Human Rights?" The Rights Track, 2016. http://rightstrack.org/does-a-picture-speak-a-thousand-words-when-advocating-human-rights.

focused on how Meg has used data visualisation techniques in her work to provide a valuable set of tools for raising awareness and securing action from a wide range of development and human rights practitioners.[58] Meg draws on a much longer tradition of visualising data initiated in the nineteenth century, such as John Snow's mapping of cholera deaths in London, Florence Nightingale's use of 'polar charts' on British medical care in Crimea, Charles Minard's work on Napoleon's 1812 Russian Campaign and the work of Ida Wells in the United States on patterns of lynching. These cases for Meg are all examples of 'visual storytelling' that have had a strong impact on different audiences and stakeholders, which inspired her to deploy similar approaches to communicate the results of her work in the case of Haiti.[59] She has been working on gold mining in Haiti and its impact on the right to water, which includes water use, quality, accessibility and availability. She explained how she needed to carry out her own census of the population in order to draw a sample for deploying a household survey, which was designed with local participants to provide local ownership of the data. She also needed to communicate her work to a different set of audiences, where she argues that policy makers and academics are quite happy to look at tables of figures to 'get behind' the data, while for others, she used graphic imagery of the kind found in Edward Tufte's seminal book *Visual Explanations*.[60] In one example, she depicted the relative consumption of water as against WHO guidance using images of toilets to capture the attention of her audience in ways that moved beyond a mere tabulation of 'gallons of water' used for a typical flush of a toilet. In this way, Meg has stressed that her vantage point as a lawyer, scholar and practitioner requires her to understand her different audiences and how to combine quantitative data with narrative text to communicate disparities and inequalities in the enjoyment of different dimensions of the right to water. She is also mindful of the witting and unwitting ways in which data visualisation can mislead audiences, something that all high-quality human rights work must avoid. At the close of our conversation, she makes the case that human rights data projects need trained data analysts, clarity in the

58 M. Satterthwaite, K. Rall, J. Emerson, J. Boy, E. Bertini, A. Pandey, and O. Nov, "Data Visualization for Human Rights Advocacy," *Journal of Human Rights Practice* 8 (2016): 171; M. Satterthwaite, J. Emerson, and A. V. Pandey, "The Challenging Power of Data Visualization for Human Rights Advocacy," in *New Technologies for Human Rights Law and Practice*, ed. M. K. Land and J. D. Aronson (Cambridge: Cambridge University Press, 2018), 162–187.
59 N. Boumba and M. Satterthwaite, "Solidarity in the Fight for Justice: Partnerships to Oppose Extractivism in Haiti," OpenGlobalRights, 2020. https://www.openglobalrights.org/solidarity-in-fight-for-justice-partnerships-to-oppose-extractivism-in-haiti/.
60 E. R. Tufte, *Visual Explanations: Images and Quantities, Evidence and Narrative* (Graphics Press, 1997).

presentation of results and knowledge about the main audiences of the work in generating meaningful yet intelligible visualisations.

Summary and Implications

Human rights evidence is the heart of human rights advocacy and has been one of the founding principles of the Rights Track as it endeavours, episode by episode, series by series to 'get the hard facts about the human rights challenges facing us today'. To achieve this, we have engaged with scholars and practitioners working on assembling human rights evidence using a wide range of methods. All of our guests agreed that the volume and quality of information on human rights has improved over the last several decades. They have also agreed that the methods that have been developed address fundamental questions concerning sources of information, representativeness, samples, inference and bias. Moving beyond single cases to *patterns* of human rights abuse requires deep reflection on all these questions, while each of our guests on the Rights Track developed increasingly sophisticated ways to provide the strongest inferences that minimise margins of error and maximise insight into these patterns. There is still a natural bias towards the measuring and analysis of civil and political rights, but new developments and new forms of data have widened the scope of these efforts to include economic and social rights. The different data approaches (events, standards, surveys and new forms of data) have all provided different and more complete understandings of the patterns of human rights abuse for larger selections of countries over longer periods of time. As in our previous chapter, our guests here recognise the time and effort over many years that need to be dedicated to this work, but all are cautiously optimistic about what their work reveals about the trends in human rights. This optimism, however, should not invite complacency, they tell us, but rather a 'doubling down' on efforts to broaden the scope of inquiry and the continuation of methodological development to provide ever more robust human rights evidence in pursuit of the enhancement of human dignity.

Chapter 5

FREEDOM OF SPEECH, RELIGION, BELIEF AND THOUGHT

Abstract

This chapter takes on the thorny issues surrounding the rights to free speech and freedom of religion, belief and thought, with further references to the human rights values of voice and accountability. Set in the ongoing debates surrounding fake news; media biases; and the challenges to upholding free speech in universities, other large organisations and society, it teases out the many distinctions and parameters that separate free speech from hate speech, and the challenges that arise from freedom of religion, belief and thought. The content of the chapter draws on our conversations with Elisabeth Witchel from the CPJ; Heidi Beirich from the Southern Poverty Law Centre; Akbar Ahmed, former high commissioner to the UK from Pakistan and professor of Islamic studies at American University; and the Rt. Rev. Alastair Redfern, bishop of Derby and former member of the House of Lords.

~

'The web is a gift from God for the hate movement.'
— Heidi Beirich, Southern Poverty Law Centre

'We are reaching a state of civilization of all against all.'
— Akbar Ahmed, Former High Commissioner for Pakistan to the UK and Professor of Islamic Studies, American University

'We are all bound together [...] none of us is morally superior.'
— Rt. Rev. Dr Alastair Redfern, Bishop of Derby

Introduction and Background

In 2005, the Danish newspaper *Jyllands-Posten* published a series of cartoons depicting the Prophet Muhammad, which was deeply offensive to Muslims. Protests against the newspaper and the Danish government spread worldwide, while the newspaper issued an apology as well as asserting its right to publish.[1] Ten years later, terrorists killed 12 people at the headquarters of French satirical magazine *Charlie Hebdo*[2] for publishing cartoons of the Prophet Muhammad as in the Danish case. In August 2017, a 'Unite the Right' rally took place in Charlottesville, Virginia.[3] The night before the rally, khaki-trousered members of the Unite the Right group carried 'tiki torches' through the city chanting 'Jews will not replace us', while as events unfolded the next day, one member of the rally drove his car into a crowd of counter-protestors, killing one of them, Heather Heyer. In 2021, Gavin Williamson, the UK's education secretary announced the creation of a 'free speech champion' to oversee university speaking events and to remain committed to the principle and the law of free speech.

Across these contemporary events and developments are a series of interrelated and significant human rights issues that involve freedom of speech and freedom of religion, belief and thought. These rights are different but fundamental to the protection of human dignity. Their genesis lies in a long struggle between the rise and consolidation of state power on the one hand and the need to protect individuals and groups to express themselves and to hold a plurality of beliefs on the other.[4] In legal and political theory, the right to free speech and expression allows for individual and collective dissent, aggregation of interests and provides one of the fundamental ways in which to hold governments to account. The right to free speech and expression is a fundamental feature of modern democracy, which gives individuals and groups the ability to challenge incumbents and participate in self-government.[5] This

---

1 See Human Rights Watch, *Questions and Answers on the Danish Cartoons and Freedom of Expression: When Speech Offends* (New York: Human Rights Watch, 2006). https://www.hrw.org/report/2006/02/15/questions-and-answers-danish-cartoons-and-freedom-expression/when-speech-offends.

2 BBC, *Charlie Hebdo Attack: Three Days of Terror* (London: British Broadcasting Corporation, 2015). https://www.bbc.co.uk/news/world-europe-30708237.

3 See T. Landman, "Charlottesville, Donald Trump, and the Dark Side of American Populism," *The Conversation*, August 14, 2017. https://theconversation.com/charlottesville-donald-trump-and-the-dark-side-of-american-populism-82459.

4 See J. Foweraker and T. Landman, *Citizenship Rights and Social Movements: A Comparative and Statistical Analysis* (Oxford: Oxford University Press, 1997); T. Risse, S.C. Ropp, and K. Sikkink, eds., *The Power of Human Rights: International Norms and Domestic Change* (Cambridge: Cambridge University Press, 1999); T. Risse, S.C. Ropp, and K. Sikkink, eds., *The Persistent Power of Human Rights: From Commitment to Compliance* (Cambridge: Cambridge University Press, 2013); T. Landman, *Human Rights and Democracy: The Precarious Triumph of Ideals* (London: Bloomsbury, 2013).

5 In his seminal work, *Polyarchy*, political scientist Robert Dahl includes these rights as a fundamental component to a procedural definition of democracy. See R.A. Dahl, *Polyarchy:*

right includes strong legal protections for the exercise of free speech, the presence of a free press and engagement in non-violent protest, which over the centuries have featured an increasing proportion of national-level social protest movements.[6]

The Right to Free Speech

The rights to free speech and expression are now deeply enshrined in international human rights law (see Table 5.1) across a number of instruments and 'general comments' from the Human Rights Committee, the United Nations body that monitors the International Covenant on Civil and Political Rights. Article 19 of the 1948 Universal Declaration of Human Rights states:

> Everyone has the right to freedom of opinion and expression; this right includes freedom to hold opinions without interference and to seek, receive, and impart information and ideas through any media and regardless of frontiers.

As the 1948 Universal Declaration emerged from the horrors of World War II, it affirms a commitment to these freedoms, which to this day vary considerably in their exercise and enjoyment. For example, the NGO Reporters Without Borders produces a Press Freedom Index, which for 2020 shows that of the 180 countries in its index, 14 countries have high press freedom, 32 countries have some limits on press freedom, 62 countries with more restrictions, 46 countries with very strong restrictions and 22 countries with severe restrictions.[7] As our conversation with Elisabeth Witchel revealed there are a 'startlingly high' number of journalists who are targeted, harassed and murdered while doing their job across many countries in the world.

Participation and Opposition (New Haven, CT: Yale University Press, 1971); D. Beetham, E. Carvalho, T. Landman, and S. Weir, *Assessing the Quality of Democracy: A Practical Guide* (Stockholm: International IDEA, 2008); T. Landman, "Democracy and Human Rights: Concepts, Measures and Relationships," *Politics and Governance* 6, no. 1 (2018): 48–59.

6 See C. Tilly, *From Mobilization to Revolution* (Cambridge: Cambridge University Press, 1978); C. Tilly, *Big Structures, Large Processes, Huge Comparisons* (Russell Sage Foundation, 1984); C. Tilly, *The Contentious French* (Cambridge, MA: Harvard University Press, 1986); C. Tilly, *Social Movements, 1768–2004* (London: Routledge, 2004); C. Tilly and S. Tarrow, *Contentious Politics* (Oxford: Oxford University Press, 2006); C. Tilly, *Contentious Performances* (Cambridge: Cambridge University Press, 2008).

7 Reporters Without Borders, 2020 Press Freedom Index. https://rsf.org/en/ranking_table.

Table 5.1 International human rights law and freedom of expression.

Instrument	Provision
1948 Universal Declaration of Human Rights	Article 19
1966 International Covenant on Civil and Political Rights	Article 19
1966 International Covenant on Economic, Social and Cultural Rights	Article 2
1965 International Convention on the Elimination of All Forms of Racial Discrimination	Article 5
1979 Convention on the Elimination of All Forms of Discrimination against Women	Article 7
1971 ILO Convention No. 135, Workers' Representatives Convention	
General Comment 10 [19] (Article 19) of the Human Rights Committee (CCPR/C/21/Rev.1 of 19 May 1989)	Article 19
General Comment 11 [19] (Article 20) of the Human Rights Committee (CCPR/C/21/Rev.1 of 19 May 1989)	Article 20
The public's right to know: Principles on Freedom of Information Legislation. Annex II Report E/CN.4/2000/63	

Source: United Nations Office of the High Commissioner for Human Rights, available at: https://www.ohchr.org/EN/Issues/FreedomOpinion/Pages/Standards.aspx.

Beyond freedom of the press, the right to free speech includes many different forms of speech, including public statements, printed works, art and art installations, and other creative outputs. It is probably safe to argue that at the time of the Universal Declaration, few would have imagined how the phrase 'any media and regardless of frontiers' would now include the Internet and its proliferation of multiple platforms, social media and sources of information and misinformation, which shape our lives, discourses and beliefs on a daily basis.[8] A plurality of views, opinions, statements, facts and fictions are now readily available in real time to anyone with an Internet connection. Coupled with this proliferation of information and commentary, there has been a rise of deep concern over the possible limits and boundaries of free speech. New generations of people are expressing a desire to curb free speech and declare 'no platform' policies for contentious speakers, while 'big tech' firms like Facebook and Twitter have shut down accounts for such prominent leaders and personalities as former president Donald Trump. In the United States and the United Kingdom, there are raging debates about free speech and universities, where particular speakers, such as feminists who are

---

8 For scholarly accounts of how the explosion of social media and digital transformation have affected society, and in particular, democracy and human rights, see D. Coyle, *Cogs and Monsters: What Economics Is and What It Could Be* (Princeton: Princeton University Press, 2021); S. Gilbert, *Good Data: An Optimist's Guide to Our Digital Future* (London: Welbeck, 2021); T. Nichols, *Our Own Worst Enemy: The Assault from within on Modern Democracy* (Oxford: Oxford University Press, 2021).

outspoken about transsexual rights and official representatives of Israel, have had their events cancelled or significantly disrupted by students, which in the UK prompted the government's creation of a free speech champion.[9]

The right to freedom of speech and expression, despite widespread legal protection, continues to be a highly contested issue, as illustrated in the Danish, French, American and British examples described at the start of this chapter. The Danish and French cases illustrate the many challenges of free speech that cause offence and how the right to free speech interacts with freedom of religion. In the United States, two additional examples include the 1987 exhibition of the publicly funded photographic work of Andres Serrano and the 1989 *Texas v. Johnson* Supreme Court case of flag burning. Serrano's work *Immersion* (Piss Christ) features a plastic crucifix immersed in a jar of the artist's own urine to provide a critical commentary on the misuse and abuse of religion. *Texas v. Johnson* involved an anti-Reagan protester at a communist rally in Dallas, who set an American flag on fire. Serrano's work, which has been on show at various art exhibitions since its creation, was partially damaged in an attack in France after causing outrage among Christians. In the *Texas v. Johnson* case, the United States Supreme Court upheld the right to burn the flag, while various attempts to pass a constitutional ban on flag burning have thus far failed. These cases appear extreme, but as we shall see, our conversation with Rights Track guest Heidi Beirich from the Southern Poverty Law Centre reveals precisely these tensions and trade-offs in the 'hard case' of free speech and hate speech in the United States, through her documentation of, and data collection on, extremist groups.[10]

Freedom of Religion, Belief and Thought

There is arguably less protection for freedom of religion, belief and thought in international human rights law (see Table 5.2); however, faith, belief and

---

9 While a student at the University of Pennsylvania in the 1980s, Landman experienced protest from Penn students against the speaking engagement of Louis Farrakhan, leader of the group Nation of Islam, who was ultimately permitted by the university to speak at an event. Nearly twenty-five years later, he experienced students shutting down an event at the University of Essex in 2013 that featured then deputy ambassador of Israel, while at the University of Nottingham in 2017, he hosted an event with then Israeli ambassador to the UK, Mark Regev.

10 See H. Beirich, "Hating the Haters: Tackling Radical Right Groups in the United States," The Rights Track, 2017. http://rightstrack.org/hating-the-haters-tackling-radical-rights-groups -in-the-united-states. See also T. Landman, "Charlottesville, Donald Trump, and the Dark Side of American Populism," *The Conversation*, August 14, 2017. https://theconversation.com /charlottesville-donald-trump-and-the-dark-side-of-american-populism-82459.

Table 5.2 International human rights law and freedom of religion, belief and thought.

Instrument	Provision
1948 Universal Declaration of Human Rights	Article 18
1966 International Covenant on Civil and Political Rights	Article 18
1981 Declaration on the Elimination of All Forms of Intolerance and of Discrimination Based on Religion or Belief	
1951 European Convention on Human Rights	Article 9
1998 Oslo Declaration on the Freedom of Religion or Belief	

Sources: United Nations Office of the High Commissioner for Human Rights, available at: https://www.ohchr.org/en/issues/freedomreligion/pages/standards.aspx; Boyle, K. and Sheen, J. (eds.) (1997) *Freedom of Religion and Belief: A World Report*, London: Routledge; Wehrenfennig, D. (2006) 'The Human Right of Religious Freedom in International Law,' *Peace Review: A Journal of Social Justice*, 18(3): 403–410.

organised religion are a deep and meaningful part of human history and continue to be so in the contemporary world. Religiosity in terms of belief in the divine, the practice of attending regular religious services and praying on a daily basis varies considerably across the world,[11] while nation state legal and institutional arrangements range from the strongly theocratic (e.g. Iran) to the deeply secular (e.g. France). Political and social revolutions in history have led to the formal separation of church and state (e.g. the 1776 United States Revolution and the 1789 French Revolution), the imposition of religious rule (e.g. the 1979 Iranian revolution) or the formal elimination of religion altogether (e.g. the 1917 Communist Revolution in Russia and the 1949 Chinese Communist Revolution). Constitutional monarchies such as the UK still have an official state religion (i.e. the Church of England), while having laws in place that protect freedom of all religions. Even in those secular states with a formal separation of church and state (e.g. the United States), religiosity and religious doctrine find their way into politics, policy and practice on a daily basis, across a wide range of issues such as prayers in school, access to reproductive health services and the display of religious icons in public buildings.

---

11 The main variation in religiosity in terms of the proportion of the population that pray on a daily basis is a function of per capita GDP. Across the world, there is an inverse relationship between religiosity and per capita GDP, such that countries with lower levels of per capita GDP have higher rates of religiosity, where the main outlier country remains the United States, where its rate of religiosity is markedly higher than expected given its high levels of per capita GDP. See National Intelligence Council, *Global Trends 2040* (Washington, DC: National Intelligence Council, 2021), 72.

Article 18 of the 1948 Universal Declaration of Human Rights states:

Everyone has the right to freedom of thought, conscience and religion; this right includes freedom to change his religion or belief, and freedom, either alone or in community with others and in public or private, to manifest his religion or belief in teaching, practice, worship and observance.

The article clearly protects individuals and groups to hold sets of beliefs and the existence of organisations that seek to gather those who share similar beliefs, including well-established religious institutions across all major and minor faith groups. The article also protects the rights of individuals with no faith, or indeed, those who hold atheistic views. There are ongoing tensions between these sets of human rights and other human rights. World history and politics are replete with examples of religious persecution ranging from the Crusades (1095 CE to 1291 CE), to the continued suppression of religious minority groups around the world (see Chapter 6), to the attempts by IS to establish a caliphate in the Middle East.[12] As Rights Track guest Akbar Ahmed, Ibn Khaldun chair of Islamic studies at American University, tells us, the post-9/11 'war on terror' has raised deep suspicion and fear of Muslims, which has fuelled anti-Muslim violence and a curbing of religious freedoms, as well as an under-recognition of the role and contribution of Muslims across different global civilisations.[13]

Moreover, there are conflicting trends and relationships between freedom of religion and the human rights of women and members of the LGBTQ community, while at the same time there is a history of a positive contribution of religion to the genesis and exercise of human rights. Hinduism was at the heart of Mahatma Ghandi's struggle for liberation in India. Protestants in America and the UK were part of the larger movement to abolish transatlantic slavery in the nineteenth century. Catholics in Poland and Lutherans in East Germany were instrumental in challenging authoritarianism in ways that contributed to the collapse of Communism. Ever since the 1968 Second Vatican Council, many Latin American Catholics embraced 'liberation

---

12   See N. Al-Dayel, A. Mumford, and K. Bales, "Not Yet Dead: The Establishment and Regulation of Modern Slavery by the Islamic State," *Studies in Conflict and Terrorism* (2019). doi: 10.1080/1057610X.2020.1711590; A. Mumford, *The West's War against Islamic State: Operation Inherent Resolve in Syria and Iraq* (London: Bloomsbury, 2021).
13   Akbar Ahmed has written a 'quartet' of books on Islam and its relationship to non-Muslim societies around the world. See A. Ahmed, *Journey into Islam: The Crisis of Globalization* (Washington, DC: Brookings Press, 2007); A. Ahmed, *Journey into America: The Challenge of Islam* (Washington, DC: Brookings Press, 2010); A. Ahmed, *The Thistle and the Drone: How America's War on Terror Became a Global War on Tribal Islam* (Washington, DC: Brookings Press, 2013); A. Ahmed, *Journey into Europe: Islam, Immigration and Identity* (Washington, DC: Brookings Press, 2018).

theology' and adopted a 'preferential option for the poor'[14] in addressing systemic poverty and formed 'ecclesial base communities' to provide grass-roots support to the region's most marginalised people.[15] The humanitarian relief NGO Muslim Hands works to address the root causes of poverty and empower local communities, as well as gain access to difficult-to-reach populations in Muslim-majority countries.[16] Catholic sisters in India have engaged in the practice of 'accompaniment' to assist thousands of domestic workers with support from the Arise Foundation.[17] As we discussed with Rights Track guest the Rt. Rev. Alastair Redfern, bishop of Derby, the Church of England has been actively involved in the struggle to end modern slavery through simple acts of kindness, support and the provision of necessities.[18]

Freedom of the Press

We spoke to Elisabeth Witchel, Impunity Campaign consultant with the CPJ about the human rights of journalists and how the CPJ works to protect them.[19] The CPJ collects annual data on the number of journalists who have been confirmed killed, missing journalists and those who have been imprisoned. Between 1992 and 2021, there have been 1,415 journalists confirmed killed, with a low of 18 killed in 2021, a high of 76 in 2009 and an annual average of 47.2 (see Figure 5.1).[20] Elisabeth tells us that the general public are 'not always aware of what journalists are facing' and unaware of the high death rates in the profession. Typically, those journalists most at risk are covering 'criminal activities' and 'corruption' which makes them particularly vulnerable to reprisals, targeting and a state of fear. She claims that in the world 'Mexico is one of the most dangerous places' for journalists to operate and they live in a 'climate of fear and intimidation', where there are 'some topics

14 G. Gutiérez, *A Theology of Liberation: History, Politics, and Salvation* (Orbis Books, 1988); D. Bell, *Liberation Theology after the End of History: The Refusal to Cease Suffering* (London: Routledge, 2001).

15 See S. Mainwaring and A. Wilde, eds., *The Progressive Church in Latin America* (Notre Dame: University of Notre Dame Press, 1989); A. Wilde, ed., *Religious Responses to Violence: Human Rights in Latin America Past and Present* (Notre Dame: University of Notre Dame Press, 2015).

16 See https://muslimhands.org.uk/our-work.

17 Rights Lab, *Beyond the Walls: Microdata on Domestic Workers in Northeast India* (Nottingham: University of Nottingham, 2020). Click here to enter text..

18 A. Redfern, "How Is the Church Leading the Fight against Modern Slavery?" The Rights Track, 2019. http://rightstrack.org/how-is-the-church-leading-the-fight-to-end-modern-slavery.

19 E. Witchell, "Freedom of the Press: How Do We Protect the Rights of Journalists?" The Rights Track, January 2, 2017. http://rightstrack.org/freedom-of-the-press-how-do-we-protect -the-rights-of-journalists.

20 See https://cpj.org/.

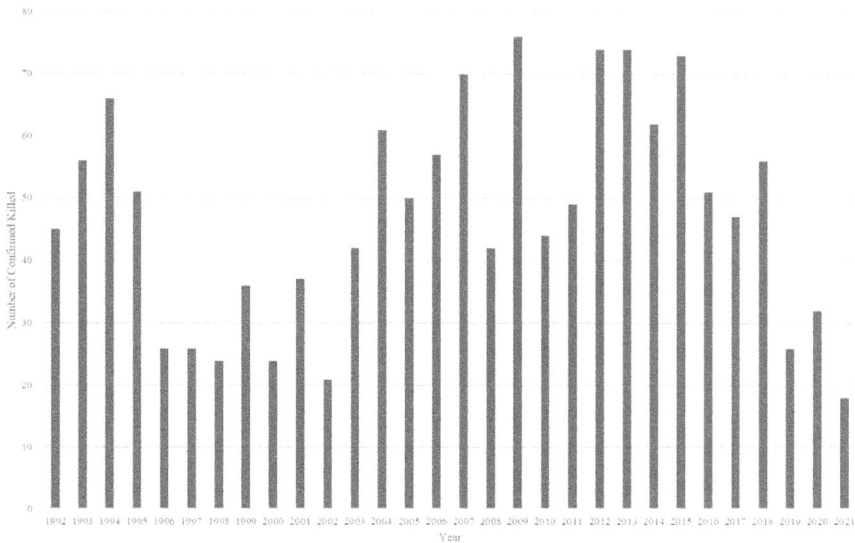

Figure 5.1 Number of journalists confirmed killed, 1992–2021 (Min. = 18, Max. = 76, Mean = 47.2). Data *Source:* Committee to Protect Journalists (CPJ), available at: https://cpj.org/.Data Analysis and Visualisation: Todd Landman and Christine Garrington.

they won't cover'. In both Mexico and Syria, there are a lot of journalists who simply disappear, living in a state of 'fear and encouraging self-censorship', 'exile' or 'stay in hiding', where it is remains 'hard to get information out'. Journalists working under these conditions adopt a variety of different strategies, including 'different systems and different networks' as well as publishing as part of a 'syndicate that does not put any person's name on the reporting'. There has also been an increase, owing to new technologies, in the phenomenon of 'citizen journalism', where 'larger media outlets' have 'vetting systems in place' to 'fact check' stories or where groups are able to have stories 'packaged in exile'. Across all these different strategies, however, Elisabeth reminds us there is a 'heightened amount of risk'.

Elisabeth explains that there is a 'blend' of perpetrators carrying out attacks against journalists, especially in 'conflict' areas, such as Iraq, Syria and Somalia, primarily carried out by 'militant extremist groups', who target journalists under the 'cover of war' and 'cloud of conflict'. In other countries, journalists with a higher probability of attack are working on 'corruption' and 'local politics' or 'working in provincial areas', where they are 'targeted by people in power' such as police, politicians and private sector actors from industry. These journalists are 'uncovering often very important stories' and 'really want to see their communities improve' by exposing a wide range of

practices and activities relating to politics, economics and development. For
Elisabeth, today is 'the best of times and the worst of times'. New technologies
allow for cross-border dissemination of information, which is gathered from
the 'local level', but there has been an 'upsurge of risk', where the 'red line
is very fluid', and where reporting is 'becoming more and more dangerous'.

The 'Hard Case' of the United States[21]

The US Constitution has particularly strong protections for freedom of
speech and expression and freedom of religion, belief and thought. The First
Amendment to the Constitution states:

> Congress shall make no law respecting an establishment of religion,
> or prohibiting the free exercise thereof; or abridging the freedom of
> speech, or of the press; or the right of the people peaceably to assemble,
> and to petition the Government for a redress of grievances.

It is clear that the First Amendment combines protection for both these sets
of rights and embodies the secular motivations of the Constitution that separate church and state, born of the 1776 American Revolution, which fought
against British tyranny and its connected feudal power while at the same
time protecting freedom of religion.[22] In this sense, Americans are often seen
as 'born equal' with this twin set of rights foregrounded in the Bill of Rights
as fundamental to the founding philosophy and law of this new democracy.
The evolution of politics and practice in the United States have tested and

---

21 It is important to note that this section of the chapter includes language and observations that
may offend many groups; however, the content of this language is either the result of objective
reporting of what was said or what was uncovered in the course of the work carried out by our
podcast guests and us as authors. Our inclusion of this content is not an endorsement, but rather
used to illustrate the speech acts and utterances of those individuals and groups we are seeking
to represent in the debate around freedom of speech and expression and the freedom of religion,
belief and thought.

22 It is an important part of American history that the revolution explicitly addressed the divine
rule of kings (i.e. King George III) and severed any links to the feudal order of England. This
founding moment has been characterised as a critical juncture in the evolution of American
democracy and political culture. See L. Hartz, *The Liberal Tradition in America* (New York:
Harcourt Brace, 1955); M. Meyers, "Louis Hartz, The Liberal Tradition in America: An
Appraisal," *Comparative Studies in Society and History* 5, no. 3 (1963): 261–268; B. Moore, *The Social
Origins of Dictatorship and Democracy: Lord and Peasant in the Making of the Modern World* (Boston, MA:
Beacon Press, 1966); D. Rueschemeyer, E.H. Stephens, and J. Stephens, *Capitalist Development and
Democracy* (Cambridge: Polity Press, 1992).

interrogated these rights since the founding. The rights to freedom of speech, expression and assembly have underpinned larger social struggles, such as the expansion of rights through the 1863 Emancipation Proclamation, women's suffrage in the early 1900s and the civil rights movement in the 1950s and 1960s, as well as developments in Constitutional Law. The strong protection of these rights thus makes the United States in the contemporary period a 'hard case' where free speech, hate speech and religious plurality all intersect in tense and often contradictory ways.

Our conversation with Rights Track guest Heidi Beirich from the Southern Poverty Law Centre explored many of these contentious intersections with a focus on free speech and hate speech, where some of the dimensions of our conversation intersected with a discussion of religion. The Southern Poverty Law Centre was founded in the 1970s in the wake of the civil rights movement and the passage of the 1965 Voting Rights Act. It brought a suit against the Ku Klux Klan in the 1980s and set up the 'Klan Watch' intelligence project. Its primary focus today is on collecting quantitative and qualitative evidence (see Chapter 4) on extremist organisations in the United States, with a view to providing an in-depth understanding of their 'views, where they are, and what risks they pose'. Their focus has been on a range of groups, such as neo-Nazis, the Ku Klux Klan, anti-LGBT groups, the Christian Identity movement, armed militia groups and the Nation of Islam.

For Heidi, these are all examples of 'hate groups' since they consider 'other groups of people as lesser' and promote exclusionary and divisive solutions to plurality and diversity in America. The threshold conditions for inclusion as hate groups draw on standards established by the Federal Bureau of Investigation, where the data show between 50 per cent and 60 per cent of the groups are engaged in violence (including against law enforcement officials), the pursuit of separatist policies and strong overlaps with racism. Heidi's work also includes anti-government militias and groups that engage in ideologies of extreme localism, which hold that 'no other entity has authority' over their lives. The Christian Identity movement, Heidi explains, founded its ideology on a 'heretical reading of the Bible', where Jews are seen as the 'spawn of the Satan' and that 'they need to be killed', that the 12 Tribes of Israel were white, that the Tribe of Dan comes from the Danube and that Black people are 'beasts of the field'. She adds that the Nation of Islam, founded in 1930, is also a hate group, which has held that white people are 'blue-eyed devils', and according to her research, espouses views that are racist, anti-Semitic and homophobic.[23]

23 For the Southern Poverty Law Centre's profile of the Nation of Islam, see https://www.spl-center.org/fighting-hate/extremist-files/group/nation-islam.

Heidi discussed with us the claim in recent years that Black Lives Matter and the Ku Klux Klan are equivalent—a claim she dismisses emphatically based on her work documenting the ideas and actions of different extremist organisations. She argues that the Ku Klux Klan is defined by race, is only open to white people, has been classed as the 'first domestic terrorist group' and that it is dedicated to 'ruining the lives of people of colour'. In contrast, Black Lives Matter is a multi-racial organisation, elevates civil rights and challenges the disproportionate use of police violence against people of colour.[24] She argues that similar distinctions can be made between the National Association for the Advancement of Coloured People (NAACP), which is open to white people and the National Association for the Advancement of White People, where 'blacks are not welcome'.

The discussions with Heidi about the terrain of groups that fall within the purview of the Southern Poverty Law Centre's work led us to consider her views on hate speech. In the strong American tradition of freedom of speech, Heidi explains that it is legal to 'scream at a Muslim' and to say 'all the Jews should die', while hate crimes involve actions that range from defacing property to murder, where the intent of such acts is related to bias of the kind seen above. These narrow definitions and conventions mean that hate crimes remain hugely under-reported and under-counted (see Chapter 4), either as they are captured by Heidi and her team, or by the Department of Justice.

With these insights in mind, we turned our conversation to the tragic August 2017 events in Charlottesville, Virginia.[25] For Heidi, these events represent a 'crucible' for a wide range of dangerous elements: (1) a number of disparate far-right groups coming together; (2) open carry gun laws (derivative of the Second Amendment of the US Constitution); and (3) discourses, flags and symbols on display that illustrate the challenges associated with hate speech and free speech. For Heidi, these events 'emboldened the movement', while President Trump was perceived by these groups as a 'glorious leader' and by

---

24   The murders of Michael Brown in Ferguson, Missouri, on 9 August 2014 and George Floyd in Minneapolis Minnesota six years later on 25 May 2020 and the numerous similar murders of Black people in between these two cases have galvanised the Black Lives Matter movement within the United States and across many countries in the world. The statistics on the killing of Blacks in the United States demonstrate the underlying trend of disproportionality. See, for example, T. Landman, "There's No Escaping the Data: African Americans Face Injustice at Every Turn," *The Conversation*, November 20, 2014. https://theconversation.com/theres-no-escaping-the-data -african-americans-face-injustice-at-every-turn-34771. See also M. Alexander, *The New Jim Crow: Mass Incarceration in the Age of Colourblindedness* (New York: Penguin, 2019).
25   See T. Landman, "Charlottesville, Donald Trump, and the Dark Side of American Populism," *The Conversation*, August 14, 2017. https://theconversation.com/charlottesville-don ald-trump-and-the-dark-side-of-american-populism-82459.

Heidi as 'reluctant to denounce extremism'. Her observations led to a wider discussion with us about free speech and the Internet, where she says that 'the web is a gift from God for the hate movement'.

Her organisation has developed a 'hate speech tracker', which reveals widespread use of Internet forums, websites and social media platforms, where hate speech is widely used and shared. One such site is *Stormfront*,[26] which brings together a wide range of right-wing groups and racial identity movements to share their views. Internet provider Network Solutions had removed the site for some time,[27] but it now remains active, while Heidi argues that events in Charlottesville have 'unleashed a racial coarseness' in America. She is encouraged, however, that both the Southern Poverty Law Centre and the American Civil Liberties Union (ACLU) received additional financial support from donors wishing to support their ongoing work to document and challenge hate speech and hate crimes. She ended her conversation with us by observing that by the year 2040, white people will no longer be the dominant group in American society, a fact that is already true for those under the age of 20. These demographic trends in America mean that it is becoming even more of a 'multi-racial and multi-ethnic democracy' and a 'highly diverse society'. Our podcast with Heidi took place three years before the violent insurrection of the US Capitol on 6 January 2021, where many of the groups, discourses and actions she has been documenting had a role to play in the crowds that breached the building (see Chapter 1). It is clear to us that many of her observations and fears had come to fruition with this event.

Islam and the West

On 24 May 2016, Akbar Ahmed, former high commissioner of Pakistan to the UK and the Ibn Khaldun Chair of Islamic Studies at the American University gave a public lecture at the University of Nottingham entitled 'Muslims in Europe: Opportunities and Challenges'.[28] The lecture was extremely well attended with over three hundred and fifty staff, students and the general pub-

---

26 See www.stornmfront.org; see also T. Landman, *Agents of Change: The Impact of Social Movements in Comparative Perspective*, Unpublished PhD dissertation (Colchester, UK: University of Essex, 2000). The dissertation compares the origins, trajectory, strategies and impact of radical right, green, gay rights and women's rights movements in the United States, Europe and Latin America.
27 See J. Biggs, "Another Neo-Nazi Site, Stormfront, is Shut Down," TechCrunch, August 28, 2017. https://techcrunch.com/2017/08/28/another-neo-nazi-site-stormfront-is-shut-down/.
28 For a video recording of the lecture, see https://mediaspace.nottingham.ac.uk/media/t/1 _ssj4rsx5.

lic, and was followed by a formal dinner with representatives of all faiths in the university's iconic Trent Building. The lecture was well received for its balanced view of the importance of Muslims in Europe, the problems of radical elements that misrepresent Islam and the deep suspicion felt towards Muslims across Europe, particularly after the terrorist attacks of 9/11 in the United States, as well as the 2004 Madrid and 2005 London bombings. The gathering after the lecture featured a rich cross-cultural and interfaith dialogue that sits at the heart of Akbar's approach to seeking solutions to many of the current problems in the world. The Rights Track caught up with Akbar to discuss further the content of his lecture and his lifelong work researching and understanding the relationship between Islam and the West.[29]

We began our conversation with him through an exercise in 'myth busting'. We asked him about the two popular myths that (1) Islam is inherently violent and (2) that Islam is incompatible with democracy and human rights. Akbar finds the first myth 'curious, puzzling, and exasperating'. While agreeing that some Muslims (e.g. Isis), like other religious adherents, are engaged in violence, Islam itself is not inherently violent. Rather, throughout the Quran lie the two fundamental principles derived from Allah of *compassion* (Al-Rahman) and *mercy* (Al-Rhamin), both of which are antithetical to violence.[30] He expands on these two commitments in Islam with a third fundamental idea known as 'ilm' or 'knowledge'. This idea goes far beyond the confines of 'book knowledge' to a deeper sense of knowing that includes the knowledge of others, culturally, religiously and with a belief that the power of God is universal. In this sense, he argues, *ilm* is an inclusive term. To illustrate this idea of a transcendent knowledge, Akbar recalls his days at a Catholic boarding school in Pakistan, where he was moved by the following lines from Alfred Tennyson's poem *Ulysses*:

> Yet all experience is an arch wherethro'
> Gleams that untravell'd world whose margin fades
> For ever and forever when I move.
> [...]
> And this gray spirit yearning in desire
> To follow knowledge like a sinking star,
> Beyond the utmost bound of human thought.

---

29   Akbar Ahmed, "Islam and the West: Questions of Human Rights," The Rights Track, March 6, 2017. http://rightstrack.org/islam-and-the-west-questions-of-human-rights.

30   For an accessible and thorough rendering of the Quran, see M. Hussain, *The Majestic Quran: A Plain English Translation, Second Edition* (Nottingham, UK: Invitation Publishing, 2019). Landman has had numerous conversations with Musharraf Hussain regarding Islam, democracy and human rights.

For Akbar, a young Muslim student at a Catholic school, these lines capture the idea of how Islam connects to the rest of the world. He argues that
Muslims are encouraged to travel to China and other parts of the world to
acquire knowledge, to appreciate and understand neighbours and 'those who
are not like you, as well as the divine'. He sees this natural impulse within
Islamic teachings as being countered by current trends, where knowledge is
seen as 'fake news' and the quest to understand 'the other' is being significantly undermined and 'blocked' by those 'not wanting to know the other'.
In the place of these acts of knowledge seeking is a highly reductionist and
fallacious reasoning, which has become linked to acts of violence. Since it
is common for many not to want to know the other, people rely on assumptions, such as 'all Muslims are violent', and 'therefore they should not come to
my country'. Such reasoning for Akbar 'undermines society', 'deprives us of
the capacity to understand' and 'demonises the other'. This logic of othering
leads to acts of violence, Islamophobia, anti-Semitism and mistaken identity,
as in the case of violence towards Hindus, whose style of dress and ethnicity led to them being perceived as 'Iranians' who were legitimate targets for
violence. This reasoning is not exclusive to Muslims alone, as Akbar cites the
proliferation of bomb threats and the desecration of Jewish cemeteries, as
well as the 21 October 2018 attack on the Tree of Life Jewish congregation
in Pittsburgh, in which 11 people were killed. Akbar laments this pattern of
violence, which is well known to Muslims who have been attacked, including
Muslim women in Hijabs. He expresses his worry that 'the state of civilization
has become one of "all against all"', a direct reference to Thomas Hobbes
notion of 'the state of nature' in his seminal work *Leviathan*.[31] His observations
resonate with those of Heidi Beirich, who also sees a connection between the
speech acts of hate groups and the use of violence.

Akbar also addressed our second myth about the incompatibility of Islam
and democracy. He highlights the vision of Muhammad Ali Jinnah, the
founder of Pakistan, who in the 1940s sought to craft a modern democracy
with rights and protections for individuals and groups, including women. In
his work, Akbar has explored this founding vision through a feature film on
the life of Jinnah, a documentary film on Jinnah, an academic book and a
comic book. While he concedes that Jinnah's ideal has not been realised in

---

31   T. Hobbes, *Leviathan. Revised Edition*, ed. A.P. Martinich and B. Battiste (Peterborough, ON:
Broadview Press, 1651/2010); see also The Stanford Encyclopaedia of Philosophy, "Hobbes's
Moral and Political Philosophy," 2002. https://plato.stanford.edu/entries/hobbes-moral/#Bib;
S. Chambers, "Who Shall Judge? Hobbes, Locke and Kant on the Construction of Public
Reason," *Ethics and Global Politics* 2, no. 4 (2009): 349–368.

practice, he argues that there continues to be a strong 'urge' among Muslims towards Jinnah's vision. He argues further that the potential for Islamic democracies should not be judged on the current patterns of political leadership, but rather on a deeper reflection on the philosophy of egalitarianism that runs through Islam since the eighth century CE. He provides the example of the Hajj, the annual Muslim pilgrimage to Mecca, in which kings, prime ministers and common people gather, and where powerful hierarchies are broken down through the homogenisation of dress worn during the event. Through these and other examples, Akbar simply does not see the case for an incompatibility between Islam and democracy.

Our conversation then turned to Islam and human rights, with a particular focus on individual and collective rights found in the international law of human rights. Akbar explains that Islam has a strong and deep emphasis on the role of the individual and his or her responsibility to society. Muslims are expected to give 2.5 per cent of their wealth to charity with a direct allocation of resource and support to the most vulnerable in society, observing that 'the prophet himself [Muhammad] was an orphan'. Individual compassion is directly linked to community compassion, and during Ramadan, all individuals rich and poor are invited to break the daily fast through sharing of food and shelter, where there is a firm commitment of 'reaching out to the stranger'. Mosques and centres of learning throughout Islam's long history have always been welcoming of strangers. While these acts and commitments are not couched in the language of human rights, Akbar sees them as consistent with the ideals of human rights, human dignity and charity.

We asked Akbar to explain the title of his book *The Thistle and the Drone*,[32] which examines the 'war on terror' since 9/11 and the 'fashionable' use of drones in places such as Waziristan and Yemen. Akbar explains that the thistle is a symbol of tribalism ('prickly', 'independent' and 'beautiful') and centuries-old Muslim tribes that extend from Morocco to Central Asia and whose presence transcends, and is often in conflict with, the modern nation state. These tribes are 'poor and impoverished' and 'at odds with central government', which often uses force to 'suppress and dominate' them. The idea of the thistle comes from Tolstoy's *Hadji Murat* in reference to Chechnya, itself a region in Russia that has experienced extended violence and suppression of

---

32   A. Ahmed, *The Thistle and the Drone: How America's War on Terror Became a Global War on Tribal Islam* (Washington, DC: Brookings Institution Publications, 2013). Akbar notes that the book has been reviewed favourably by Noam Chomsky (linguist, philosopher, cognitive scientist and political activist) and the US Central Intelligence Agency for its deep insights into Islamic tribalism.

its Muslim community.[33] Our discussion took us to the political division over the use of the term 'radical Islamic terrorism'. Akbar argues that President Obama was criticised for not using the term, while Trump was lauded for doing so. Drawing on his former role as a commissioner, Akbar says rather than looking at adjectives, the focus should be on 'breaking the law' regardless of who perpetrates it. He saw how Obama's reticence to use the term led to the perception of his 'latent sympathy', while Trump's hyperbolic claim that he would 'wipe radical Islam off the face of the earth' alienated the very people needed to resolve the problem of tribal violence. He notes that 'the main victims of Isis are Muslims' and that solutions to the problem lie in working with allies (e.g. NATO) and fellow Muslims, where Trump's strong forms of speech put the administration into a political 'cul-de-sac'. The situation alienated many Muslims, including the many Iraqi forces fighting Isis in Mosul, who were dying on the battlefield, while the Trump administration declared a 'total shutdown' on all Muslims entering the United States, articulated in the ban on travel from seven Muslim-majority countries in early 2017. Akbar argues that 'there are 1.5 billion Muslims in the world' and growing, while Isis only counts 20,000–30,000 followers and supporters.

Overall, Akbar stresses that solutions to the problems of speech, religion and misunderstanding of Islam require us to return to the idea of *ilm* with which we started our conversation. Akbar believes that the quest for knowledge lies in educating young people, expanding our knowledge of the other and reaching across our different communities, along with the need for this younger generation to go out and 'heal a fractured world'. He sees this as the primary task of all people, Abrahamic and non-Abrahamic alike.

The Church and Modern Slavery

Alongside discussing the relationship between Islam and human rights, we spoke to the Rt. Rev. Alastair Redfern, bishop of Derby and former member of the House of Lords about the role of the Church of England and in particular, the Clewer Initiative,[34] in fighting the problem of modern slavery.[35] Alastair reflected on the theological and organisational dimensions of his

---

33 L. Tolstoy, *Hadj Murat* (New York: Vintage Classics, reprint edition, 2012).

34 For more on the Clewer Initiative, see Rights Lab, *The Clewer Initiative: An Appreciative Inquiry* (University of Nottingham Rights Lab, May 2002). https://iasctoolkit.nottingham.ac.uk/download/the-clewer-initiative-an-appreciative-inquiry/.

35 Alastair Redfern, "How Is the Church Leading the Fight to End Modern Slavery?" The Rights Track, April 2, 2019. http://rightstrack.org/how-is-the-church-leading-the-fight-to-end-modern-slavery.

own work and that of the church. He studied at Oxford and Bristol, where he wrote his doctoral thesis on Samuel Wilberforce, the third son of William Wilberforce, the English philosopher and campaigner for the abolition of transatlantic slavery. It is thus telling that Alastair has become involved in the struggle against modern slavery, which, as we shall see in Part III of this book, involves the denial of agency of a wide group of people engaged in some form of labour or other forms of exploitation. Modern slavery does not involve the claim to property rights as in transatlantic slavery, but it does involve the use of some form of force or coercion in making people either unable or unwilling to leave their exploitative situation. While mobilisation around this topic emerged forcefully in the early 1990s, it has been given new impetus with the passage of the 2015 UK Modern Slavery Act (which Alastair helped draft), anti-trafficking legislation in the United States and Europe and UN SDG Target 8.7.

We began by asking Alastair about the Clewer Initiative, which for him is 'the Church of England's answer to modern slavery'. It works with the Catholic Church, community groups, law enforcement and local government through its convening power and builds powerful partnerships between disparate groups seeking to redress this terrible wrong. His own involvement began with his work across his many parishes, and in particular, the fens of Lincolnshire on food security and food poverty. The Clewer House of Mercy is an order of nuns established in 1848 and was originally inspired to help combat the problem of sexual exploitation and to provide support for the women involved. Today, there are only four nuns left and they see their work on modern slavery as an important 'legacy project'. Alastair explains that the Clewer sisters 'engage with this real issue in real time' across a network of 'people of faith and people of good will'. They build alliances and provide a connection between the 'human face' of this struggle and the institutions established to address it. For Alastair, the Church of England is of course the established church, is hierarchical like the Catholic Church and has an institutionalised presence in British life that is well recognised and valued. Despite this status, he still sees it as often heavily criticised in society and that even though it lacks expertise in this area, it does provide a vehicle and a network of people who will 'listen and work' on this important issue.

The key contribution that the church offers is one of 'love to those who are vulnerable', it 'sits with people, and makes them tea' sharing their burdens and moves beyond just ending a set of bad practices, by dedicating its work to 'rehabilitate brothers and sisters'. In this way, the church is in the words of the Rights Track host 'a warm hug' and not a direct service provider. Rather, it uses its presence across 12,500 parishes to 'convene, enable, and support' directly and indirectly victims and survivors of modern slavery. One of its practical developments has been to work with academics at the University of Nottingham, as well as Chief Constables, the National Crime Agency and the Border Force to develop a phone app to monitor and record attributes and practices across a vast array of largely informal car washes in the UK. Grounded in research on the modalities of the business model underpinning these car washes (see Chapter 10), the application is a platform for collecting data through crowdsourcing and citizen science in ways that provide intelligence and practical support. Alastair stresses that the church's role in this project was not to 'pass judgement', but like other religious efforts to document human rights abuses, to provide a method for generating a new kind of evidence needed in this area that could then be passed onto the authorities.

Like our conversation with Akbar, we asked Alastair to reflect on scripture and human rights, but with a focus on slavery. He conceded that 'the Bible does endorse slavery' but with St. Paul's focus on the 'equal value' of humans[36] followed by the work of William Wilberforce on the abolition of transatlantic slavery, one could see how the position of Christianity has evolved historically to one that opposes slavery in all its forms. In another sense, Alastair cites St. Paul as knowing he was 'a slave to sin' and from this idea claims that 'we are all subject to slavery' and may well 'enslave ourselves'. In this view, there is a contrast between the 'crude materialistic dominating version of slavery' and the temptation for all of us being 'quite close to enslaving others and ourselves'. He cites the example of our demand for and use of mobile phones, the ingredients for which may well involve child labour, which leads him to argue, 'we are all bound together', and that 'none of us is morally superior'. For him, there are no 'perfect answers', but that the issue needs to be 'nudged [...] we need to work at it, and compromise'.

As he reflects beyond personal morality and the interconnectedness of all of us, he does see great promise in business organisations making a difference as a new actor seeking to rid their supply chains of modern slavery. He also sees an ongoing role for such institutions as the House of Lords, which is an unelected legislative body in the UK political system that comprises an array of experts across many different walks of life, business, politics and society who have a role to play in making a positive difference. His own experience in drafting the Modern Slavery Act and on the Select Committee that reviewed its implementation after three years taught him valuable lessons about how this peculiar institution can make a positive contribution. Coming from his

---

36   In Galatians 3:28 Paul says, 'There is neither Jew nor Greek, there is neither bond nor free, there is neither male and female: for ye are all one in Christ Jesus.' See *The Holy Bible: Containing the Old and New Testaments (King James Version)* (Cambridge: Cambridge University Press), 1159.

position of faith and deep reflection, as well as pragmatism, our time with him provides an example of the complex role that the Church of England plays in combatting modern slavery and forging community-based and faith-based networks to advance human rights.

Complex and Enduring Freedoms

Our Rights Track guests shared much about the complexity and interconnectedness of these two freedoms that are fundamental for upholding human dignity. Across these guests lies a significant paradox: freedom of speech and expression as fully protected and exercised does not protect people from the right not to be offended, while the freedom of religion, belief and thought means that there are large communities of people who in the exercise of these rights either offend others or are offended themselves. There is thus a spectrum for both sets of these rights, where there are extreme speech acts and extreme forms of worship, which can lead to lack of understanding of 'the other' and the commission of horrific acts of violence. Reporters and citizen journalists are at high risk of being attacked, 'disappeared' or killed. Through documenting hate speech and hate crime, Heidi Beirich captures elements of this extremism in the context of the United States. Akbar Ahmed and Alastair Redfern show us how collaboration, mutual understanding and the quest for knowledge beyond oneself not only can transcend what are perceived to be fundamental differences, but also provides the networks and epistemic communities necessary for the advancement of human rights. Across all three guests, the lessons we draw demonstrate the need for individuals to recognise the limits of their own subject position (wherever its genesis) and to recognise the value and importance of those who make up our vast and diverse human community.

Chapter 6

MINORITIES, MIGRANTS
AND REFUGEES

Abstract

This chapter discusses a range of different human rights for those considered as 'the marginalised other', a term that emerges from our conversation
with Bill Simmons from the University of Arizona. We explore these issues
through our conversations with Claire Thomas from MRG and Gonzalo
Vargas Llosa, the UNHCR representative to the UK. We then turn to the
issue of Black Americans through our conversations with Karen Salt and
Christopher Phelps from the University of Nottingham; women's rights with
Monica Casper from the University of Arizona; and LGBTQ+ rights with
Richard Beaven, corporate leader and former trustee of Stonewall.

~

'We need to patiently listen to the voice of the other.'
— William Paul Simmons, University of Arizona

'There has been a dramatic retrograde movement in valuing diversity
and what diversity can bring to society.'
— Claire Thomas, Deputy Director, MRG

'Everybody deserves humane treatment.'
— Gonzalo Vargas Llosa, UNHCR

'The hauntings of the past pervade the present.'
— Karen Salt, University of Nottingham and UK
Research and Innovation

'It takes white Americans opening their hearts and their minds and listening, and
then taking action.'

— Christopher Phelps, University of Nottingham

Introduction and Background

In the run-up to the referendum on the UK's membership of the EU in June 2016, the leader of the United Kingdom Independence Party (UKIP) Nigel Farage stood in front of a large billboard depicting a long line of people with the headline 'Breaking Point: The EU Has Failed Us All'.[1] This event took place against the backdrop of Europe's refugee crisis, which in 2015 involved extensive press coverage of a young refugee boy from Syria washed up on a Turkish beach[2] and German chancellor Angela Merkel's announcement that all refugees were welcome.[3] In the United States, the women's march on 21 January 2017 was the largest single-day protest event in the history of the country with between 3.3 and 4.6 million marchers across cities protesting against the newly inaugurated Trump administration.[4] In April 2019, LGBTQ+ protestors gathered outside the Doncaster Hotel in London to criticise its owner, the Sultan of Brunei, for his country's newly passed legislation that made gay sex illegal and punishable by flogging or stoning to death.[5] Between the killing of Michael Brown in 2014 and George Floyd in 2020,[6] the Black Lives Matter movement and its allies have protested the disproportionate ill-treatment of Black Americans by law enforcement officials in the United States. These and other incidents raise to high relief a wide range of human rights issues concerning women's and minority rights and the rights of 'people on the move', such as economic migrants, asylum seekers, internally displaced people (IDPs) and refugees.

The history of the world is one of increasing diversification of the human population through immigration, forced migration, colonial and imperial

---

1   J. Stone, "Nigel Farage's Anti-immigrant Poster Reported to Police Over Claims It Incites Racial Hatred," *Independent*, June 18, 2016. https://www.independent.co.uk/news/uk/politics/nigel-farage-s-anti-immigrant-poster-reported-police-over-claims-it-incites-racial-hatred-a7087801.html.

2   H. Smith, "Shocking Images of Drowned Syrian Boy Show Tragic Plight of Refugees," *The Guardian*, September 2, 2015. https://www.theguardian.com/world/2015/sep/02/shocking-image-of-drowned-syrian-boy-shows-tragic-plight-of-refugees.

3   Reuters, "Welcome Refugees and Reject Racism, Merkel Says after Rallies," Reuters, December 31, 2014. https://www.reuters.com/article/us-germany-merkel-idUSKBN0K90GL20141231.

4   Matt Broomfield, "Women's March Against Donald Trump Is the Largest Day of Protests in US History, Say Political Scientists," *Independent*. Archived from the original on January 25, 2017. Retrieved January 25, 2017; available at: https://www.independent.co.uk/news/world/americas/womens-march-anti-donald-trump-womens-rights-largest-protest-demonstration-us-history-political-scientists-a7541081.html.

5   See BBC, "Brunei LGBT: Protesters at Dorchester Hotel Call for Royal Boycott," 2019. https://www.bbc.co.uk/news/av/uk-47839201. Landman was scheduled to speak at the hotel for a legal conference during the protest, but cancelled his appearance as part of the movement to protest the new law.

6   See BBC, "George Floyd: Timeline of Black Deaths and Protests," BBC, April 12, 2021. https://www.bbc.co.uk/news/world-us-canada-52905408.

conquest, racial miscegenation and other drivers of change. Such natural and unnatural patterns of demographic and geographic change have brought with them a complex politics and law of peoples that has been shaped, contested and changed throughout history in ways that recognise and challenge difference, seek to preserve identities and underpin human dignity with fundamental human rights commitments founded on principles of equality and freedom. The more troubling elements of this history include what Rights Track guest Bill Simmons from the University of Arizona calls 'the marginalisation of the other' in which different types of people and their identities have been 'cauterised' through law and policy structured through power relations in ways that have meant some groups are perceived and treated differently and as if they are not fully part of modern society.[7] The Rights Track guests featured in this chapter share with us their own approaches to mobilising for human rights (see Chapter 3) in ways that focus on the politics of 'the other' (see also Akbar Ahmed in Chapter 5) and that seek to rebalance our treatment of all peoples across the complexity and diversity of the world.

Human Rights and the Marginalised Other

Rights Track guest Bill Simmons is a self-declared 'Eeyore' character in terms of his dour demeanour and style of engagement,[8] but he is a deep thinker and a scholar-activist whose experiential learning travelling the world has led him to challenge dominant discourses and received wisdom about human rights, both within the human rights community and between this community and those communities that challenge it.[9] Our conversation[10] sets the scene for many of the challenges surrounding the human rights of people who are

---

7 W.P. Simmons, *Human Rights Law and the Marginalised Other* (Cambridge: Cambridge University Press, 2011).

8 In his book *Joyful Human Rights*, Bill describes his pessimistic and cautious approach to studying and advancing human rights. See W.P. Simmons, *Joyful Human Rights* (Philadelphia: University of Pennsylvania Press, 2019).

9 Bill has carried out field research and teaching in China, Mexico, Northern Europe and parts of Africa, where he has combined his deep knowledge of philosophy and political methodology to real-world human rights challenges. Over a period of eighteen months, Landman worked with Bill on a project funded by the Norwegian Centre for Human Rights and the Raoul Wallenberg Institute of Human Rights and Humanitarian Law to train Chinese Scholars in human rights research methodologies. See T. Landman, R. Smith, and W.P. Simmons, eds., *Human Rights in Our Time* (Oslo: Norwegian Centre for Human Rights; Lund: Raoul Wallenberg Institute of Human Rights and Humanitarian Law, 2010). The most recent collaboration between Landman and Bill is W.P. Simmons, J. Boynton, and T. Landman, "Facilitated Communication, Neurodiversity, and Human Rights," *Human Rights Quarterly* 42, no. 3 (2021): 138–167.

10 W.P. Simmons, "Human Rights: Reasons to Be Joyful," The Rights Track, October 6, 2016. http://rightstrack.org/human-rights-reasons-to-be-joyful.

treated as lesser human beings (see the section on Heidi Beirich in Chapter 5), who he argues have been 'cauterised' from the rest of society. This word is a strong metaphor drawn from French philosophy and its etymology is rooted in the word 'to brand', literally the physical burning of a mark into someone's skin as was done to slaves during the transatlantic slave trade. Beyond this literal meaning, however, Bill sees the word 'cauter' to apply to the ways in which certain peoples are 'branded as inferior' and 'not listened to', where they are 'sealed off from rights protection' and where the general public therefore no longer cares about them. The Rwanda genocide in 1994, Bill argues, is an example where the Tutsis were branded as inferior, which allowed for their rights to be violated with very few people actually caring about what had happened to them. He sees similar dynamics at play in the migrant crisis in Europe and the United States, where migrants are branded as 'illegal' and thus are denied the protection of their human rights.

This idea of cutting people off from their human rights is combined with an oversimplification and reductionism in the ways that very different groups are seen as being the same and branded through the use of simple and catch-all categories. For example, in the case of Nigel Farage cited above, the UKIP billboard grouped together all people seeking entry into the UK as unwelcome and as not belonging in Britain, while in reality, this diverse group of people may well have included legitimate economic migrants (who at the time were protected through EU mobility laws), asylum seekers with legitimate claims for entry, legal and illegal migrants and other groups. The discursive strategy of 'cauterisation', according to Bill, lumps all these people together and says that they are all the same and that they are bad for Britain. This discursive use of the 'logic of equivalence' is a popular ploy used by political leaders to simplify complex issues in order to garner political support.[11]

Bill sees the same discursive strategy operating in the United States with respect to the US–Mexico border and the Trump administration's ban on travel from Muslim-majority countries. In the case of migrants at the US border, where Bill has carried out extensive research, the flow of people includes a diverse range of nationalities, women who have suffered repeated sexual violence and children. He argues that when Immigration and Customs Enforcement (ICE) agents do not ask migrants about their status, they are branded as 'illegal', which eases the ability for them to be deported. This

---

11 For a fuller explication of this idea of 'the logic of equivalence' and its use in politics, see E. Laclau, *On Populist Reason* (London: Verso Books, 2005). To understand how this plays out in democratic polities, see T. Nichols, *Our Own Worst Enemy: The Assault from within on Modern Democracy* (Oxford: Oxford University Press, 2021).

practice also constructs a simplistic popular narrative against the migrants, such as 'that's what you get, that's what you deserve'. In the broader immigration debates in the United States, Bill sees a similar logic at play and with it, additional complexities. In the 2016 presidential campaign, for example, Donald Trump declared that 11 million people would be deported and that there would be a 'total shutdown' against Muslims entering the country (see Chapter 5), but in practice, the ability to 'cauter' so many people proved very difficult, and soon exceptions to particular groups and countries needed to be made.[12]

Bill also discussed with us how the human rights community can challenge the pervasive practice of 'marginalisation of the other'. For Bill, it involves 'making cracks in hegemonic discourses', where scholars and activists need to push back against these dominant and reductionist attempts to define away large groups of people. He is also clear that the tendency to marginalise the other takes place within the human rights community as well, where he urges that 'we need to patiently listen to the voices of the other', and that only through this kind of deep listening can voices across the world be heard in ways that provide much needed solidarity. This kind of challenge and listening strategy is not a single act, but one that needs to be repeated over time, which, in his view, does lead to moments of optimism, where all people are seen 'as human' and 'deserving of rights'. For the human rights community, Bill worries about a certain 'myopia about the good that it is doing', which neglects the necessary listening and can result in the 'dismissal' of the voices of the marginalised.

As in our conversation with Heidi Beirich in the previous chapter, we asked Bill about his understanding of the Black Lives Matter movement. Bill argues that the movement is 'speaking for itself', in challenging the disproportionality of treatment it experiences, where its strategy is 'hitting in some contexts' but not in others, and where opponents counter the movement with phraseology such as 'all lives matter' and 'blue lives matter' (a reference to police officers). Bill does not see these opposing phrases as problematic, but rather as

---

12   Landman's own experience in the UK as the son of a Dutch immigrant to the United States and now as an immigrant in the UK has included both a questioning of his motivations to settle in the UK and professed acceptance that he is the 'right kind of immigrant,' a coded reference to his white European heritage. He gave a series of public lectures on this topic before and after the 2016 UK referendum to leave the European Union at the Galleries of Justice in Nottingham and the University of Hertfordshire. For the complexities of popular discourses around immigrants in the United Kingdom and the United States, see N. Shukla, *The Good Immigrant* (London: Unbound, 2017); N. Shukla and C. Suleyman, *The Good Immigrant USA* (New York: Little Brown Book Group, 2020).

evidence of success. Indeed, he observes 'the absence of backlash means that we are not doing our job' and that the 'most potential for change is when the backlash happens'. In this way, there is a dynamic and dialectic relationship between claim and counterclaim, while Bill remains optimistic that a resolution to the dialectic over time is possible and that it will ultimately yield an extension of human rights to all.

Minority Rights

Our conversation with Claire Thomas,[13] deputy director of MRG, expanded on Bill's observations as she discussed with us how her organisation seeks to uphold the rights of minority ethnic, linguistic and religious communities around the world.[14] Claire starts with the idea that not only is discrimination experienced by individuals, but there are also significant 'inter-sectional' forms of discrimination (i.e. across different minority attributes), as well as discrimination against whole groups of people. She clarifies that minority rights involve the fundamental rights for people to 'carry out what they wish to do in common', such as speaking a language or engaging in religious practices. Things such as a shared language and belief system (see Chapter 5) involve a deep sense of 'identity, heritage, culture, and community', which in simple terms means 'people doing the same thing at the same time'.

We reflected with Claire on the recent turn towards populist nationalism that has emerged in the United States, Brazil, the UK and parts of Europe, where she argues that we are seeing a 'dramatic retrograde movement in valuing diversity and what diversity can bring to society' with a significant increase in 'hate speech' (see Chapter 5). In line with our conversation with Bill Simmons, Claire observes that such speech and the decline in the

---

13   C. Thomas, "In the Minority: The Right to Identity, Culture and Heritage," The Rights Track, June 13, 2017. http://rightstrack.org/in-the-minority-the-right-to-identity-culture-and-heritage.

14   In 2003–4, Landman conducted an evaluation of nine human rights organisations in receipt of funding from the Ministry of Foreign Affairs of the Netherlands, during which he travelled to Sofia, Bulgaria, to understand better the work that Minority Rights Group was doing with respect to inter-ethnic dialogue, particularly between Bulgarian nationals and the Roma community. Landman worked closely with Claire on their monitoring, evaluation and impact assessment frameworks for their work and of the nine organisations, Minority Rights Group supplied the most robust evidence that demonstrated the effectiveness of their work. See T. Landman and M. Abraham, *Human Rights Organisation Assessment and Performance Evaluation* (Ministry of Foreign Affairs of the Netherlands, 2004). https://minorityrights.org/wp-content/uploads/2015/08/Evaluation-report_EVALUATION-OF-NINE-NON-GOVERNMENTAL-HUMAN-RIGHTS-ORGANISATIONS.pdf.

appreciation of diversity have come not only from popular discourses, but also from political statements based on 'hatred, xenophobia, anti-migrant, and anti-refugee' sentiments. She agrees that a kind of 'Pandora's Box' has now been opened and that people have been 'given licence' or 'permission' to express their resentments towards others. Like Bill, she argues that there has to be significant pushback and challenge to this kind of discourse, and for people to actually call it out when it happens.

The work of MRG thus focuses on advocacy, awareness raising and empowerment in ways that allow for minority groups to 'speak for themselves where possible'. MRG provides financial, logistical and practical support for representatives from minority groups to speak in Geneva to the United Nations human rights bodies, such as those engaged in the Universal Periodic Review process or those monitoring compliance with different human rights treaties.[15] At the grassroots level, MRG works on the ground to document minority rights abuse and discrimination, such as its work in Iraq in setting up an electronic system for groups to submit information in a cost-effective and innovative fashion, which can then be cross-checked and validated. MRG also provides what Claire calls 'old-fashioned support', for example, in combatting attacks on religious minorities in India in order to 'see the totality of what communities are experiencing daily'. Across its many programmes and activities, MRG 'almost never claims to be the sole factor in achieving something'. Rather, through its work, it seeks to get duty bearers of rights to deliver rights to rights holders, which means at a minimum, MRG can share the credit for positive change. In this way, MRG is necessary in its ability to raise awareness in making a case or making an argument, but it does not see itself as 'solely responsible' for the changes that occur. She discusses the example of MRG's work that leads to the passage of a new discrimination law, but is fully aware that discrimination may well continue despite the passage of a law, since key actors will find reasons other than discrimination for why particular outcomes happen.

She shared with us one particularly innovative programme that was implemented across seven different countries in the MENA. In an attempt to move beyond elite advocacy efforts, MRG staged a series of 'street theatre' performances where over 100,000 people engaged with these performances, which were staged in bus stations, markets and other popular locations across the region. MRG learned that 'humour' and 'play' were effective ways to make a connection with their audiences and provide the stimulus for people to think differently about their own sets of attitudes and values with respect

---

15 See https://www.ohchr.org/en/hrbodies/upr/pages/uprmain.aspx.

to different groups in society. This strategy is radically different than formal legal interventions in the halls of power and do not involve 'haranguing' people, but through interactive theatre, provide a set of questions and challenges to dominant ways of thinking that may be significant blockers to progress in the protection of minority rights.

Refugees

We spoke with Gonzalo Vargas Llosa,[16] who at the time was the UNHCR representative to the UK shortly after the peak of the refugee crisis in Europe, which saw thousands of people displaced by conflicts attempt the treacherous journey across the Mediterranean Sea to gain entry into the EU. Gonzalo began with citing some alarming statistics about the refugee problem as of the year 2016, which show that 65.6 million people have been forcibly displaced, 22 million of whom are refugees who leave their countries of origin and over 40 million of whom are IDPs who remain in their country of origin. The scale of the problem, Gonzalo tells us, means that each day 28 people a minute are displaced, where he argues the main drivers for this kind of forced movement of people include 'fleeing persecution in their countries of origin, generalised violence, war, or conflict'. Across this population, 55 per cent come from Syria, Afghanistan and South Sudan alone. The total volume of refugees is the largest it has been since World War II, where Syria has the largest outflows of people (over five million) and South Sudan has the fastest rate of increase in displacement.

We asked him about the media frenzy around the arrival of refugees in Europe, which he concedes had risen dramatically, but he stressed that '85% of refugees live in developing countries', including 'Turkey, Pakistan, Lebanon, Iran and Uganda'. The concentration of refugees in these countries places a burden on already overstretched and under-resourced infrastructure and services. Combined with a reduction in resources, this additional burden created a major driver for Syrian refugees to leave Jordan, Lebanon and Turkey for European countries. Gonzalo says that this 'secondary movement' of refugees could be reduced through additional humanitarian aid to 'meet the minimum basic needs and requirements, such as food, water, and health'. In the absence of this resource and the perception that there is no

---

16 G. Vargas Llosa, "Refugees: Why Hard Times Need Hard Facts," The Rights Track, August 21, 2017. http://rightstrack.org/refugees-why-hard-times-need-hard-facts. Gonzalo is the son of Nobel Laureate and Peruvian presidential candidate Mario Vargas Llosa. Gonzalo is now the UNHCR's representative for EU Affairs, Belgium, Ireland, Luxembourg and the Netherlands.

economic opportunity, refugees are likely to seek out a better life in Europe. He praises the leadership and courage of Angela Merkel in welcoming refugees in Germany, but laments the lack of solidarity from other European countries to uphold their obligations under the 1951 Refugee Convention.[17] This lack of solidarity meant that a large proportion of the refugees (nearly one million) ended up in Germany, when in fact they could have found settled status across a wider collection of countries.

He also criticises the intervention policies of the EU in its efforts to stop ships, boats and dinghies crossing the Mediterranean from sub-Saharan Africa and Libya to countries such as Italy and Greece. For him, the long-term solution should focus on the 'root causes' of refugee movements with increases in humanitarian aid in the regions of origin. He praised the UK as one of the most important donors in offering assistance to Syrian refugees and committed to resettling 20,000 refugees by 2020, as well as 3,000 children at risk from the MENA. Since recording our episode with Gonzalo, however, the UK has made the controversial decision to reduce its foreign aid budget from 0.07 of gross national income (GNI) to 0.05, which in real terms represents more than 50 per cent cut in aid, since GNI itself has also reduced as a result of the economic contractions experienced during the COVID-19 pandemic. The bottom line for Gonzalo, despite the mix of root causes, contested nature of the effects of the refugee crisis and continued attempt to find solutions, is that 'everybody deserves to be treated humanely', and his work with the UN Refugee Agency continues to address this ongoing global challenge.

Black Americans

The African American (or Black American) population in the United States has its roots in the period of transatlantic slavery, which began with the arrival of the first slaves in Virginia in 1619.[18] The coerced and violent history of slavery broke apart Black families and Black communities, subjugated Black people to centuries of violence and abuse, and marginalised them through systematic repression codified in the rule of law and the exercise of property rights. This prolonged and painful period of history

---

17 See the 1951 United Nations Convention relating to Status of Refugees. https://www.ohchr .org/en/professionalinterest/pages/statusofrefugees.aspx.

18 See J. Lepore, *These Truths: A History of the United States* (New York: Norton, 2018). The 1619 Project, run by the *New York Times*, takes its name from this significant date, which marks the starting point for the history of slavery in the United States. See also M. Sinha, *A Slave's Cause: A History of Abolition* (New Haven: Yale University Press, 2016).

has had lasting effects on the lived experiences of Black people to this day (see Chapter 7). Despite the end of slavery in the nineteenth century, the implementation of Jim Crow laws and the legal success of the civil rights movement, the persistence of systemic and institutionalised racism has been manifested in disproportionately harsh treatment of Black people from law enforcement officials; excessive sentencing from the judicial system; high probabilities of young Black men spending prolonged periods of time in prison; and structural inequalities in employment, education and career progression for many Black Americans.[19] These and other issues affecting the Black community have given rise more recently to the Black Lives Matter movement, which has not only galvanised American politics, but also has received solidarity in countries outside the United States in the wake of the murder of George Floyd in Minneapolis. A recent Pew Research report shows that 49 per cent of Americans feel that there has not been enough progress in achieving equal rights for Black people, while there is a much higher and growing proportion of Black (86 per cent versus 78 per cent) and Hispanic (57 per cent versus 48 per cent) people who think more needs to be done to achieve equality.[20]

In international human rights law, the UN system promulgated the 1965 International Convention on the Elimination of Racial Discrimination, where Article 1 defines 'racial discrimination' as

any distinction, exclusion, restriction or preference based on race, colour, descent, or national or ethnic origin which has the purpose or effect of nullifying or impairing the recognition, enjoyment or exercise, on an equal footing, of human rights and fundamental freedoms in the political, economic, social, cultural or any other field of public life.[21]

While this definition provides clarity on what racial discrimination means, its coming into force and the pattern of increasing state ratification since 1965 have not eliminated the very kinds of discrimination it seeks to address.

---

19   For a stark assessment of the status of Black Americans, see the 2016 country visit report of the United Nations Working Group of Experts on People of African Descent on its Mission to the United States of America. https://undocs.org/en/A/HRC/33/61/Add.2.

20   Pew Research Centre, "Amid National Reckoning, Americans Divided on Whether Increased Focus on Race Will Lead to Major Policy Change," October 6, 2020. https://www.pewresearch.org/social-trends/2020/10/06/amid-national-reckoning-americans-divided-on-whether-increased-focus-on-race-will-lead-to-major-policy-change/.

21   See International Convention on Racial Discrimination (CERD). https://www.ohchr.org/en/professionalinterest/pages/cerd.aspx.

Our Rights Track episode with Karen Salt and Christopher Phelps[22] from the University of Nottingham framed its discussion of these issues around the idea of the United States needing a Truth Commission, much like that which was held in post-Apartheid South Africa[23] and other countries in order to understand the underlying patterns of experience of Black Americans, coupled with their stories about life as Black people in the United States. Karen Salt is an African American academic who has worked on transatlantic slavery and Haiti,[24] and who is now working on equality, diversity and inclusion (EDI) as deputy director of Research, Culture and Environment for United Kingdom Research and Innovation. Christopher Phelps is a white American academic who works on labour movements, social protest movements, American literature and authoritarianism, and the politics of race in America.[25]

We began our conversation around the statistical evidence of the disproportionality of treatment of Black people (see Chapter 7), and how a Truth Commission would allow America to pause for a few years, conduct deep and methodologically sound epidemiological studies of violence in general, gun violence in particular, and combine this analysis with a moment of reflection, as well as one to hear testimonies and carry out in-depth case studies on the lived experiences of Black people. We also note that the UN Working Group of Experts on People of African Descent had just published its findings, where Recommendation 88 in the report asks for a human rights commission to be established with a specific and dedicated division to work precisely on this issue.[26] Karen responds by asking 'what sort of discourses need to happen?' since 'the hauntings of the past pervade the present' and how there is a real 'need to reshape how we talk to each other'.

For Karen, there has been a 'loss of trust' both within and between communities. She believes that we need to bring about 'reparative trust' and to

---

22 K. Salt and C. Phelps, "Does America Need a Truth Commission?" The Rights Track, October 31, 2016. http://rightstrack.org/does-america-need-a-truth-commission.

23 See T. Landman, *Studying Human Rights* (London: Routledge, 2005), 44–45; T. Landman and E. Carvalho, *Measuring Human Rights* (London: Routledge, 2009), 45–63; P. Hayner, *Unspeakable Truths: Transitional Justice and the Challenge of Truth Commissions*, 2nd ed. (London: Routledge, 2011); T. Landman, *Human Rights and Democracy: The Precarious Triumph of Ideals* (London: Bloomsbury, 2013), 97–112.

24 K. Salt, *The Unfinished Revolution: Haiti, Black Sovereignty and Power in the Nineteenth-Century Atlantic World* (Liverpool: Liverpool University Press, 2019).

25 C. Phelps and M. Shactman, *Race and Revolution* (London: Verso, 2003); C. Phelps, *Radicals in America* (Cambridge: Cambridge University Press, 2015); C. Phelps, "The Novel of American Authoritarianism," *Science and Society* 84, no. 2 (2020): 232–260.

26 See United Nations Working Group of Experts on People of African Descent on its Mission to the United States of America. https://undocs.org/en/A/HRC/33/61/Add.2.

'rebuild a set of relationships' in order to move forward. She argues that any such process will take time and that single events, such as the election of Barack Obama as the first Black president, cannot be seen as 'panaceas' since there is a much longer history of 'encoding' of racism that will not disappear with one individual. She believes that Obama was cast as a 'Moses politician' in whom far too many expectations were vested, and that somehow Americans believed that the country had suddenly become 'post-racial'. These high expectations put incredible pressure on him (as he now has written in the first volume of his memoirs[27]), while at the same time almost set him up to fail, leading to the claim that 'Obama didn't do anything' or even more harshly, 'there was no racism in America until Obama was elected'. She thus agrees with the idea that a Truth Commission in America would offer the opportunity for not only a 'reckoning with the statistics' but also for Americans to see the 'value of testimonials'. In echoing the language of Bill Simmons, she says that we need to listen to people and allow them to 'tell their stories'.

Christopher agrees with Karen that after centuries of slavery and the period of Jim Crow laws America had 'come far enough to elect a Black president'. But against this backdrop of progress, he also sees deep-seated structural inequality and 'flagrant racism in political discourses'. He explains that the 1967 Kerner Commission was a Truth Commission of sorts that sought to understand a period of particularly acute civil disorder and violence in Newark, Detroit and neighbouring communities. The final report reached a damning conclusion: 'Our nation is moving toward two societies: one black, one white – separate and unequal.'[28] In the spirit of this commission, Christopher sees that a Truth Commission in America would perform a useful role in the supply of information as even today, there is not a national database on violence in America, either from citizens, for gun-related violence or for police violence (see our discussion with Patrick Ball in Chapter 4).

Karen accepts this idea of a 'two-nation' society in reflecting on her own childhood, where her hometown was an urban area partly disconnected from the main city. In her view, her community had been 'intentionally forgotten', and as such had to create its own 'shadow government' to provide basic services as it could not depend on the formal government to do so. She argues that this was a different story from a typical 'urban ghetto' or the poor towns of rural Alabama or Mississippi. Rather, she saw 'redlining' and districting that 'cut off' her community from the rest of the city, but that over time, a 'thoroughfare' emerged that partially re-established a connection. Christopher

---

27 See B.H. Obama, *A Promised Land* (London and New York: Penguin Random House, 2020).
28 See *Report of the National Advisory Commission on Civil Disorders*. http://www.eisenhowerfounda-tion.org/docs/kerner.pdf.

reflects on Karen's experiences and agrees that 'structures of social inequality dovetail with structures of political inequality', and that what is truly required is for 'white Americans opening their hearts and their minds and listening, and then taking action'. He concedes, however, that in contrast to the case of South Africa, this is 'a lot to ask'. In the South African case, a political revolution had dismantled Apartheid, and after the publication of the report of the Truth and Reconciliation Commission, white South Africans had 'to come clean'. No such public reckoning of this kind has taken place in America (see our conversation with Heidi Beirich in Chapter 5).

We moved beyond consideration of the domestic political context and discussed whether and in what way an international perspective would help in addressing these issues. Christopher quoted at length from a 1947 pamphlet produced by the NAACP. He was particularly taken by the introduction to the pamphlet written by civil rights activist W. E. B. Dubois:

> a discrimination practiced in the United States against her own citizens and to a large extent a contravention of her own laws, cannot be persisted in, without infringing upon the rights of the peoples of the world and especially upon the ideals and the work of the United Nations. This question then, which is without doubt primarily an internal and national question and will in the future become more and more international, as the nations draw together.[29]

Here, Christopher argues, is an example of a direct link between discriminatory practices in the United States and an appeal to international and universal human rights, articulated just two years after the founding of the United Nations and one year before the Universal Declaration of Human Rights. This appeal issued by the NAACP is part of a much longer lineage in Christopher's mind of different efforts to invoke universal human rights, to use international human rights law to criticise the United States and to use 'human rights as a lever' to bring about positive change.

Karen returns to her childhood experiences to suggest that in addition to such formal appeals to human rights, the mere survival and presence of Black people is a form of 'resistance'. She grew up in a poor area, but Black people

---

29   W.E.B. Dubois, "An Appeal to the World: A Statement of Denial of Human Rights to Minorities in the Case of citizens of Negro Descent in the United States of America and an Appeal to the United Nations for Redress," National Association for the Advancement of Coloured People, 1957, p. 14. https://www.aclu.org/sites/default/files/field_document/appeal_to_the_world.pdf. In his freshman year in 1984–85 at the University of Pennsylvania, Landman lived in the W.E.B. Dubois House, which was a student accommodation facility dedicated to advancing Black students at Penn and which included a diverse set of students in that year.

formed families, had babies, fought hard against the system and continued 'to resist by existing'. She reflects on her own education and her love of the poet Langston Hughes who inspired her to believe that 'I can be part of this world, and demand more from it'. In this way, the politics of presence for Black people she sees as 'good trouble' or 'necessary trouble,'[30] such that the election of Black politicians to long-standing political institutions 'troubles' some people, and represent some sign of progress. This 'troubling' contributes to the kind of awareness raising and consciousness raising that is much needed to understand and overcome the deep divisions in America. Both Karen and Christopher see the current state of despair in American politics, but they both know that in the near future, the demographic shifts taking place in terms of societal diversity and the generational shifts taking place with respect to values of young people both offer significant signs of hope.

Women's Rights

Quantitatively, women are not in the minority, but there are many factors; demographic changes; and changes in economy, society and polity that mean women as a group have been and continue to be disproportionately worse off. Across different dimensions, women on average work for less money, often work for no money (especially in domestic contexts) and experience many different forms of discrimination in terms of access to education, healthcare and employment, as well as suffer different forms of gender-based violence and sexual exploitation, both within the home and as part of wider societal conflicts. In the Global North, political movements for women's rights extending from the suffragette mobilisations in the late nineteenth and early twentieth centuries through to the different 'waves' of feminism in the latter part of the twentieth century have secured a number of significant advances in legal protections and progress, but women remain socially unequal. In the Global South, women's movements in Latin America have made positive strides and have used gender quotas for elected offices, while in the case of Rwanda, women in its national legislature make up a majority. These positive indicators of progress, however, must be seen against broader patterns of continued gender discrimination.[31] Even in the human rights community, there

---

30 Karen is referring to former US representative from Michigan and civil rights activist John Conyers who frequently invoked the term 'good trouble' and Jennifer Jaffe's book *Necessary Trouble: Americans in Revolt* (2016), Nation Books.
31 For more on the status of women around the world, see UN Women. https://www.unwomen .org/en.

are some human rights lawyers who argue that since international human rights law applies to all human beings, no special instruments or provisions are needed for the explicit protection of women's rights.[32] The lived reality for millions of women, however, suggests that there is a strong case for such protections.

Our conversation with Monica Casper[33] from the University of Arizona took place shortly after the election of President Donald Trump and before his inauguration and the women's march in January 2017, where there was great concern among women's organisations about the emerging policy landscape of the new administration. Monica expressed her great worry over women's healthcare, reflecting on Donald Trump's declaration to 'repeal and replace' the Affordable Care Act (ACA), which would have a deleterious effect on women's reproductive health, their ability to care for their families, access to child health insurance, access to contraception and increasing levels of maternal mortality, especially in the case of women of colour, who are 'four times more likely to die than white women'. She tells us that despite the desire to repeal and replace the ACA, no alternative model had been proposed. We now know that one never emerged during the Trump administration and that the ACA has not been repealed. She worries further about the call to 'defund Planned Parenthood', which contrary to popular opinion, focuses '80% of its activities on preventing unplanned pregnancies' and is not focused solely on providing safe access to abortion services.

In terms of women in employment and in the workplace, she argues that trends in corporate America have turned away from 'equal opportunity and equal pay', and not been 'friendly toward issues, such as labour law enforcement and sexual harassment'. While she accepts that Trump ran his campaign on the economy, he offered little in terms of 'policies that would benefit women', particularly single women and women of colour. Moreover, despite appeals to a new electoral coalition that propelled him to office, he offered few concrete policies that would benefit the working class, which is 'not fully

---

32 From 1997 to 2005, Landman was part of the EU-funded European Master's Degree in Human Rights and Democratisation, a multinational educational programme hosted in Venice for half the year and participating universities for the other half of the year. On numerous occasions, some of the academic staff on the programme argued this point that there is no need for explicit instruments or protections for women's rights. This claim is at odds with the fact that the international law of human rights includes the 1979 CEDAW. See https://www.ohchr.org/en/professionalinterest/pages/cedaw.aspx.

33 M. Casper, "Women and Trump: A Question of Rights?" The Rights Track, January 20, 2017. http://rightstrack.org/women-and-trump-a-question-of-rights. Monica is now dean of the College of Arts and Letters at San Diego State University.

white.' The promise of trade protection and the use of tariffs meant to keep jobs in America, would weaken the working class with insecurity of contracts and health benefits, developments that Monica sees have also been problems under previous Democratic administrations.

At a cultural level, Monica argues that the political discourses and behaviours during the 2016 presidential campaign 'gave permission to speak as openly as possible about race and gender', with appeals to white nationalism, hidden forms of racism and sexism that were 'firmly on the table'. She knows from her own work that it continues to be hard for women to come forward and tell their stories, and that her own two daughters 'are worried about the world they are going to inherit'. She sees a much larger picture of the complex relationship between power and gender relations and that the signalling from the new administration is not positive in this regard. In her own state of Arizona, she worries for women and undocumented students in face of an increase in xenophobic language, particularly around the chants of 'build that wall' and Trump's claim that Mexico would 'pay for the wall'.

She shared her thoughts with us on the upcoming inauguration and women's march. For the inauguration she argued that 'any legitimacy afforded to this administration is a problem', that in her view, 'it is the most hostile administration to human flourishing I have ever seen' and that 'there is something about his dismissal of basic human decency' that is 'offensive to people on the left'. While these observations appear overly partisan and ideological, she is quick to say that she has been troubled by former administrations, such as that of President George Bush, but she has enhanced concerns over a Trump presidency that goes 'beyond politics'. The women's marches scheduled for the day after the inauguration are being joined by her own scheduling of 'teach-ins' in which she hopes to promote discussions that are not anti-Trump per se, but that help students understand how to craft 'a vision of a democratic America'. For her, the marches are a 'moment to stand up and resist' what many people think is an illegitimate 'white misogyny'. The essence of the marches is grounded for her in the statement 'we are here and we are marching'.

She explained that the composition of the marches are not uncontested, since many women complained that elements of the organisation of the marches did not fully address the issue of intersectionality, and that it remained unclear who had organised the marches and who was meant to participate. These complexities featured across the more than four hundred and fifty marches that were organised, and in the case of Portland, Oregon, women of colour pulled out owing to the absence of a broader set of demands around their rights. In her home city of Tucson, for example, organisers wanted to link the women's march to larger issues of immigration and race, since Arizona is a state that shares its border with Mexico. The combination of a national march on Washington and locally organised marches, for Monica, represents 'an overarching sense of trying to show strength'.

We ended our conversation with Monica about the international dimension of the marches and the struggle for women's rights more generally. Across Europe and other parts of the world, there was evidence of solidarity from women's organisations and the need for vigilance. We also discussed one of the most famous examples of women's resistance Las Madres de la Plaza de Mayo in Argentina, which challenged the authoritarian regime in the late 1970s and early 1980s for the widespread 'disappearance' of men during the so-called dirty war. We discussed the idea that women's 'subject position' as mothers offered a degree of protection and safety in opposing the regime and its strategic use of repression at the time. As a mother herself, Monica has concerns about the path being taken by America and the possibility for political violence. She hopes that the marches will be 'a democratic moment' where 'people have the right to show up and disagree with us', but is equally clear that they do not have the right to engage in violence. In the event, the marches proceeded with large rates of participation across the United States with no reports of violence.

Gay Rights

Like women's rights movements and civil rights movements, the gay rights movement has made progress in the legalisation of gay sex, the recognition of civil partnerships and other rights protections for the LGBTQ+ community, which is defined by questions around sexual orientation and gender fluidity. Its progress, however, as in the case of women and the Black community, has varied by country and over time, where it is still illegal in some countries to engage in same-sex relationships, while the rights of transsexuals remain highly contested with opposition coming from more conservative elements on the political spectrum, as well as from some feminists who challenge the distinction between biological sex at birth and gender identity claims made by transsexual individuals. Rights Track guest Richard Beaven[34] is a corporate leader in the insurance industry and for many years was a member of the board of trustees for Stonewall, an LGBTQ+ advocacy group and NGO founded in 1989 whose name is taken from the famous Stonewall gay bar in Greenwich Village in New York City, which was the site of a police raid and

---

34 R. Beaven, "Gay Rights: How Far Have We Come?," The Rights Track, December 10, 2016. http://rightstrack.org/gay-rights-how-far-have-we-come.

subsequent riots. He was married with children and then came out as a gay man and has been an ardent advocate of gay rights, equality and inclusion in his professional and public life.

We began by asking Richard in the context of the UK, what the signs of progress have been for the advance of gay rights in the broader struggle for human rights. He feels that 'if laws are oppressive then people will be oppressive', and thus welcomes many of the legal changes that have taken place, where he argues that 'when law is embracing and compassionate', then society as a whole may become more accepting of difference. The Marriage (Same Sex Couples) Act 2013[35] is one such example of legal change that for Richard represents a major positive step for the country in recognising and legalising marriage as an institution for gay couples. He is also pleased that at a cultural level, the 'pride' festival in London and other areas of the UK celebrates 'diversity and inclusion' with a raised awareness about the identity and lifestyles of those making up the gay community. Against these and other positive developments, however, Richard worries 'how much has the progress we've made buried homophobia or racist ideas?' He notes that after the UK referendum to leave the EU there was 'appalling racism' and 'a rise in homo- phobic hate crime', which he attributes to the rise of a certain type of political leader who 'stands up, lies a lot, uses minority factions' to define 'the other as the enemy'. He argues further that 'picking on minorities is a common way for leaders to get elected' and that in the era of 'post-truth' politics, it matters less what someone says than if they say it in a way that makes them 'just sound convincing'. He reflects on this strategy historically and says that leaders have variously declared that 'Jews, gays, Blacks, Asians' and others are a 'threat to you' and have used this to come to power.

He is also critical of internecine struggles within the gay community, how- ever, where he has seen a rise in racism between gays, for example, a rise in anti-Asian racism and two separate events for Pride celebrations: 'London white pride' happens on one day and 'London Black pride happens on another day'. This angers and puzzles him since it means 'if you are a Black person, you think there are two gay prides going on [...] one for whites and one for Blacks'. This phenomenon for him simply 'doesn't feel inclusive'. In reflecting on this split in the gay community and drawing on Monica's obser- vations about the women's march in Washington, we ask if there is a similar 'elite white feminism' in the UK as has been seen in the United States with the ascendency of Hillary Clinton. From a corporate perspective, he recalls

---

35 See Marriage (Same Sex Couples) Act 2013. https://www.legislation.gov.uk/ukpga/2013/30 /contents/enacted.

a presentation from a successful white woman executive who said her career development meant that she now requires 'two nannies' in order to carry out her role in the company. Other women see this and think 'this is not for me', 'she is not a role model' and 'I don't feel inspired by this kind of woman'.

We then asked about what sort of progress has been made in corporate Britain in terms of the larger EDI agenda. He believes that 'large organisations are trying very hard indeed to be much more inclusive' where some appear a bit more 'lip service' while others are 'going much further and deeper'. He has been very impressed with Lloyds Bank, where EDI has now become part of 'its DNA'. For Richard, the EDI agenda is about 'talent'. He is firm that organisations should provide equal rights, but ultimately the success of a firm is about 'talent and inclusivity', where the 'most talented get on and get up'. He recalls a programme of inclusion at the company EY that was not successful. He felt their use of unconscious bias training only made employees aware of their inherent biases, but did not ultimately change their behaviours. Richard sees special training programmes for women as simply shifting the perception of male employees to it being 'a women problem' and nothing to do with men. As a leader in the insurance industry, he reflects that only 1 per cent of recent graduates consider insurance as a career path, and only 0.1 per cent of gay graduates think so. For him, the industry is still very much 'pale, male, and stale' and he knows of cases of gay men 'going back in the closet' once they have joined the industry.

On reflection, though, Richard remains hopeful. He celebrates all the achievements that have been made and says, 'The hope for me comes through my own children. They don't see the world like some of the people that are racist and homophobic at all.' He was very supportive of the Stonewall 'laces' campaign, which sought to raise awareness about the LGBTQ+ community within Premier Football. While he concedes that the campaign attracted strong negative criticism on social media, the negative comments from 'trolls' were not just 'left hanging there', but were challenged openly through well-considered, positive and supportive comments. The laces campaign and other campaigns aimed at the roots of homophobia, in schools, for example, are well targeted. His sense of hope in the face of progress, setback and challenge for the gay community leads him to say that the Brexit and Trump electoral outcomes, and the many complex issues that have surfaced in their wake, should be seen as a 'blip' in the history of gay rights, and to all of us, 'Let's keep going!'

Bringing the Other Back In

Diversity is a mainstay feature of the human population and will continue to be so. The major economic and demographic changes in the world over the next several decades mean that this diverse population will interact at an ever-increasing rate, while major drivers of change will continue to mean that a proportion of this population will be on the move. As the complexion of countries continues to change, popular attitudes, policies and norms will need to adapt accordingly. Resistance to this adaptation will inevitably lead to contestation and conflict over identity and difference as more and more people from a variety of backgrounds interact with one another. In his book *Behave: The Biology of Humans at Our Best and Worst*,[36] biologist and neurologist Robert Sapolsky demonstrates that there is a natural and inherent tendency for humans to engage in 'Us/Them' dichotomies of the kinds that we have seen through the eyes of our Rights Track guests in this chapter. For him, 'in-group parochialism' tends to focus on a core set of shared values and 'inflating the merits of arbitrary markers', while 'people with the strongest negative attitudes towards immigrants, foreigners, and socially deviant groups tend to have low thresholds for interpersonal disgust'.[37] In his view, 'Thems are frequently viewed as simpler and more homogenous than Us'.[38] Our Rights Track guests featured here have each in their own way sought to alert us to the human rights consequences of this cognitive tendency to construct Us/Them dichotomies.

There is thus a conflict between the ever-increasing diversity and interactions between different groups in the world, and this simplifying and reductionist cognitive tendency. Human rights laws, norms and principles provide a guiding framework and moral compass for navigating this contested terrain of identity, difference, equality, exclusion and inclusion. The fundamental commitment to human rights and the principle of non-discrimination provide a bedrock for the ways in which societies will need to be organised and the ways in which the faultlines between different groups can be transcended. In each of their own ways, the Rights Track guests included in this chapter have shown us the roots of the problem and the different ways in which their own forms of human rights advocacy have sought to address it. The key lesson from our conversations across such a variety of work on different groups of people is that the future hope of the world rests on our ability to bring 'the other' back in to our discourses, policies, programmes, systems of governance and rule of law. In contrast to the claims of 'social Darwinism',[39] the true

---

36 R. Sapolsky, *Behave: The Biology of Humans at Our Best and Worst* (New York: Penguin Random House, 2017).

37 Ibid., 395, 399.

38 Ibid., 399.

39 H. Spencer, *The Principles of Biology, Volumes I and II* (General Books LLC, 2012/1864).

strength in Darwin's theory of evolution[40] lies in diversity and adaptation, not 'cauterisation' and separation. From Bill's use of this idea of cauterisation through the many advances achieved by the gay rights movement, the Rights Track guests included here have all challenged the reductionism and simplification of human diversity and call for a human rights-based approach to identity and difference, which emphasises the recognition of our common humanity and how human rights protection can help us all flourish.

---

40 C. Darwin, *The Origin of the Species and the Voyage of the Beagle* (Everyman Library, 2012/1859).

Chapter 7

HUMAN RIGHTS AND COVID-19

Abstract

This chapter explores the many different ways in which the COVID-19 pandemic has had a profound impact on numerous human rights. The chapter begins by situating COVID-19 in the larger context of ecology, a healthy planet and its relationship with healthy people, drawing on our conversation with award-winning nature photographer Garth Lenz. We then turn to the impact of COVID-19 on human rights in general with Alison Brysk (University of California Santa Barbara), followed by many conversations with our guests about its impact on different groups of people. We discuss women's rights with Nina Ansary (UN Women), people of African descent with Dominique Day (member of the UN Working Group of Experts on People of African Descent), prisoners in the United States with David Fathi (American Civil Liberties Union) and refugees in Malaysia with Mahi Ramakrishnan (Beyond Borders Malaysia). We then explore the value of a human rights-based approach to the existential threats posed by terrorism and COVID-19 with Thomas Parker (journalist, consultant, educator and counterterrorism expert). We conclude with a consideration of COVID-19, democracy and migration with David Owen (University of Southampton) and Arlene Tickner (Universidad del Rosario in Colombia).

'COVID-19 has only exacerbated the hardships on Iranian civil society.'
– Nina Ansary, UN Women

'Have you solved the problem if you have not solved it for everyone?'
– Dominique Day, Chair of the UN Working Group
of Experts on People of African Descent

'Prisons house people who are disproportionately vulnerable to become very sick or die if they contract the virus because of pre-existing medical conditions.'
– David Fathi, American Civil Liberties Union

'We were shocked to see the kind of hate and backlash and xenophobia against the Rohingya.'

– Mahi Ramakrishnan, Beyond Borders Malaysia

'COVID made apparent to us how far we are from the ideal of democracy.'

– David Owen, University of Southampton

Early Warning

As early as 2005, President George W. Bush expressed his concerns about the emergence of a global pandemic as he issued a call to develop a global warning and response system in the event of an outbreak. These concerns were shared by President Barack Obama, who, in 2014, asked for US politicians to set aside their partisan differences in order to develop a plan to respond to a potential pandemic of the kind the world has witnessed since early 2020. Across a number of events, including his now famous Ted Talk in 2015 and the Munich Security Conference in 2017, Bill Gates, the former CEO of Microsoft, argued that the main threat to the world in the near future was not nuclear destruction, but a global pandemic.[1] In Munich, he warned:

> Whether it occurs by a quirk of nature or at the hand of a terrorist, epidemiologists say a fast-moving airborne pathogen could kill more than 30 million people in less than a year. And they say there is a reasonable probability the world will experience such an outbreak in the next 10 to 15 years.[2]

Bush, Obama and Gates all shared similar concerns not only over an outbreak itself but also how unprepared the world was to respond to such an eventuality. Indeed, the Obama administration had to contend with outbreaks of swine flu (H1N1), Ebola and the Zika virus. As the COVID-19 pandemic unfolded during 2020–21, many of Obama's fears and those of Gates and Bush were realised with tremendous variation in the pace and spread of the pandemic and the different ways in which governments around the world responded to it. Scientific advice suggests that COVID-19 is likely to be with us for some time (as evidenced by the Omicron variant emerging in late 2021),

---

1   B. Gates, "The Next Outbreak? We're Not Ready," *Ted Talk*, 2015. https://www.youtube.com/watch?v=6Af6b_wyiwI.

2   B.Y. Lee, "Bill Gates Warns of Epidemic That Could Kill over 30 Million People," *Forbes*, February 19, 2017. https://www.forbes.com/sites/brucelee/2017/02/19/bill-gates-warns-of-epidemic-that-will-kill-over-30-million-people/.

while it remains a real possibility that other similar viruses will emerge in the future. COVID-19 has had a profound effect on the economy, society and politics, coupled with the new era of rapid and diffuse mass communications technologies that have provided scientific and unscientific information to the world's population desperate for answers and solutions. Across many different countries, the pandemic has become politicised and involves many trade-offs between liberty, the power of the state, the economy and society.

In stepping back from the specific concerns that Bush, Obama and Gates expressed, we were struck by the prescience and timeliness of similar observations expressed through our conversation with nature photographer and activist Garth Lenz.[3] Lenz produces large, high-resolution photographs of the natural world and its relationship to the human world. He has won numerous awards for his images of the destruction wrought by the development of the Tar Sands oil fields in Canada, which capture the vastness of the surface oil excavation and its impact on the natural environment and indigenous populations.[4] In his conversation with us, he argued that based on his work 'you tend to have healthy human communities when you have healthy ecosystems' and that 'we are part of the ecosystem'. These observations can also relate to the phenomena of 'zoonotic' pandemics or the link between the spread of viruses through the human consumption of animals and the intensification of wildlife farming, as well as the consumption of wild species, particularly as practiced in China.[5] COVID-19 and its predecessors such as SARS and MERS are zoonotic pandemics. While the precise origins and initial transmission of COVID-19 are a topic of intense study, Lenz's general observations about the ways in which the human and natural world are all part of the same ecosystem provide an excellent starting point for our conversations on the human rights dimensions of the pandemic. We were also struck by how

---

3 G. Lenz, "Picture This: Using Photography to Make a Case for Environmental Rights," The Rights Track, August 31, 2017. http://rightstrack.org/picture-this-using-photography-to-make-a-case-for-environmental-rights.

4 See G. Lenz, "The True Cost of Oil," *Ted Talk,* 2011. https://www.ted.com/talks/garth_lenz_the_true_cost_of_oil.

5 See D. Cao, "To Avoid More Pandemics, We Need to Stop Eating Wild and Factory-Farmed Animals," LSE Festival 2021, London School of Economics, 2021. https://blogs.lse.ac.uk/covid19/2021/03/05/lse-festival-2021-to-avoid-more-pandemics-we-need-to-stop-eating-wild-and-factory-farmed-animals/. See also A. Whitfort, "COVID-19 and Wildlife Farming in China: Legislating to Protect Wild Animal Health and Welfare in the Wake of a Global Pandemic," *Journal of Environmental Law* 33, no. 1 (2021): 57–84; J.S. Mackenzie and D.W. Smith, "COVID-19: A Novel Zoonotic Disease Caused by a Coronavirus from China: What We Know and What We Don't," *Microbiology Australia* 41 (2020): 45–50. https://www.publish.csiro.au/ma/pdf/MA20013.

many of the themes we had been discussing with our guests during the first five years of the Rights Track were being played out in stark relief during the pandemic, reinforcing the lessons around discrimination, disproportionality, the politics of the other, and the status of free speech and how it intersects with science and policy making.

A Pathway Out of the Pandemic

Our conversation with Alison Brysk revealed a number of complex and cross-cutting impacts of the pandemic on human rights.[6] Alison is the Mellichamp Professor of Global Governance at the University of California Santa Barbara, and she has spent her entire academic career working on human rights. A descendent of Jewish immigrants who fled Europe, Alison has spent decades researching human rights violations in Argentina and Latin America, democratic responses to global terrorism, the politics of the globalisation of the law, global norms and governance, human rights foreign policy, global civil society and a human rights-based approach to combatting human trafficking and modern slavery.[7] Being based in California has provided Alison with a rich tapestry of experiences of the many different dimensions that characterise the impact of COVID-19 on human rights. In a state that is so large, diverse and complex, Alison has been reflecting on government response to the pandemic, the ideological spectrum of voices for or against COVID-19 mitigations and the disproportionate impact the pandemic has had on the many different communities that make up the state.

In looking out from California to the world, Alison argues that the pandemic has 'intensified dynamics' that have long been in play, where she sees a significant 'citizenship gap' that separates those people who belong and those people who are 'out of place', leading to problems and questions around the 'status of displaced people'. For Alison, COVID-19 has 'incredibly intensified the vulnerability of refugees, migrants, internally displaced people, pandemic patriarchy *vis-à-vis* women, indigenous people and minorities, having the greatest vulnerability and incidence', while at the same time, 'being subject to the greatest surveillance and tracking' in ways that have been 'injurious to their human rights'.

In drawing on the idea of the 'interdependence' of human rights, she sees increasing empirical evidence that 'people who are vulnerable are now

---

6 A. Brysk, "Do Human Rights Provide a Pathway Out of the Pandemic?" The Rights Track, April 7, 2021. http://rightstrack.org/do-human-rights-provide-a-pathway-out-of-the-pandemic.
7 See http://www.alisonbrysk.org/research.

chronically disadvantaged in social rights in a way that has now been securitised'. For others, she sees 'genuine civil rights threats, threats to property', and 'economic' activity with a 'selective attention to certain kinds of rights over others'. Differential access to healthcare for vulnerable groups, particularly 'cross-border' groups and other vulnerable populations, intersects with the pandemic in ways that mean the virus has had a negative differential impact on their health. For example, despite the fact that women suffer lower morbidity and mortality effects of the virus, two-thirds of all frontline workers and 80 per cent of healthcare workers are women, which raises their susceptibility to transmission and probability of contracting the virus. In turn, she sees that for women, government response to the pandemic, particularly among those ruled by 'populist authoritarian' governments, has also included 'marked reduction' in women's 'reproductive rights' and 'access to abortions'.[8]

She also argues that the 'flow of migrant domestic workers' has left many 'trapped, expelled, exposed, and dependent', and that 'across every region' of the world, there has been an 'estimated increase of 25% to 45% in domestic violence' against women. For these women, there has been 'differential impact' of 'lockdowns on domestic violence' and 'lack of access to supportive institutions'. These and other impacts of the pandemic, for Alison, require creative and lateral thinking about the kinds of alternative institutions, groups and mechanisms other than the state that need to be mobilised to provide much needed support. In two examples, she describes how in France and Spain, local reporting protocols have been developed for women in vulnerable domestic circumstance to report their abuse in 'groceries' and 'pharmacies', which are seen as natural locations where women are outside the home and can access much needed support. As the pandemic continues unabated, Alison argues (as do many of our guests in this chapter) that 'rights framing is helpful in managing public health and other security crises', providing a much needed 'pathway out of the pandemic'.[9]

---

8 It is very telling that some months after this episode of the Rights Track, the US Supreme Court did not overturn a Texas state law that bans all abortions after the first six weeks of pregnancy even in the cases of rape or incest. The law further delegates 'enforcement of the prohibition to the population at large'. In keeping with Alison's understanding of 'interdependence' of human rights, the ruling will have a disproportionate impact on poor women and women of colour who may not have the financial means to seek health support outside the state. See US Supreme Court, *WHOLE WOMAN'S HEALTH ET AL. v. AUSTIN REEVE JACKSON, JUDGE, ET AL.*, 594 U.S_(2021), No. 21A24. https://www.supremecourt.gov/opinions/20pdf/21a24_8759.pdf.

9 This final phrase 'pathway out of the pandemic' is from Landman as host of this episode and was used in his closing remarks.

COVID-19 and Groups

Michelle Bachelet, a doctor, former president of Chile, former political prisoner, survivor of torture and UN High Commissioner for Human Rights has been deeply troubled, but not surprised, by the disproportionate impact COVID-19 has had on many different and marginalised groups in the world. Against a backdrop of historical discrimination, Bachelet argues that these groups were 'overexposed to the contagion', 'under-protected' and 'structurally less able to isolate themselves', where the pandemic 'kept making all these factors worse'.[10] Across our conversations on the Rights Track, our guests agree with these observations from Bachelet, all arguing that COVID-19 exacerbated pre-existing forms of discrimination across different groups of people, including women, African Americans and people of African descent, prisoners, refugees and children.

Women

The status of women across the world has been one of 'glacial' advance according to our guest Nina Ansary.[11] Nina is an award-winning Iranian American author, historian and women's rights advocate. As a UN Women Global Champion for Innovation, she presents her work on the transformative role women are playing in global affairs at multilateral conferences and universities in the United States and the United Kingdom, including Columbia, Harvard, Oxford, Cambridge and the London School of Economics and Political Science.[12] Nina's birth country Iran was hit particularly hard in the early months of the pandemic and the WHO reports that Iran has had over five million cases and over 100,000 deaths.[13] We asked Nina about the experiences with COVID-19 in the 'patriarchal society' of Iran, which during the

10	United Nations Office of High Commissioner for Human Rights, "Addressing the Disproportionate Impact of COVID-19 on Minority Ethnic Communities," November 24, 2020, Geneva: Office of the High Commissioner for Human Rights. https://www.ohchr.org/EN/NewsEvents/Pages/DisplayNews.aspx?NewsID=26541&LangID=E. For more on Bachelet, see T. Landman, *Human Rights and Democracy: The Precarious Triumph of Ideals* (London: Bloomsbury Press, 2013), 145–148.
11	N. Ansary, "COVID-19 and Women's Rights: What Impact is the Pandemic Having?" The Rights Track, December 10, 2020. http://rightstrack.org/covid-19-and-womens-rights-what-impact-is-the-pandemic-having.
12	See https://www.ninaansary.com/about.
13	Since the outbreak of COVID-19, Iran has experienced three waves of the virus, with the first in November 2020 with 94,941 cases, the second in April 2021 with 166,637 cases and in August 2021 with 369,975 cases. See https://covid19.who.int/region/emro/country/ir.

pre- and post-pandemic periods implemented 'a stringent crackdown' against protestors in general and women in particular, who are in many cases unable 'to retain a lawyer' and access justice effectively. Nina believes that the 'regime is threatened by powerful women, women who have a voice, women who have excelled despite the circumstances'. It has made a 'concerted effort to enact discriminatory policies and laws against women', which have not 'derailed women from pushing the boundaries and trying to challenge the status quo', but which have 'come at a high price'. In terms of COVID-19, the country 'was already in turmoil' with an 'economic downturn' and 'high unemployment', as well as under increased external pressure from international sanctions. For Nina, 'COVID-19 has only exacerbated the hardships on Iranian civil society' and the regime has 'continued to intensify its crackdown on Iranians who are advocating for more social freedoms and engagement with the West'.

For women outside Iran, Nina argues that in the pre-pandemic period, there has been 'legalised discrimination', and 'invisible barriers' for women's advancement that manifest themselves in various and 'insidious forms'. There is discrimination against 'women in STEM,[14] entrepreneurial fields, the workplace, wage discrimination, paid maternity leave', a 'gender gap in the political arena' and 'violence, child marriage, and inadequate access to education', all of which 'hold half the population from reaching its potential'. Against this backdrop, Nina argues that COVID-19 has 'magnified the disparities with the system', where 'women-dominated industries have unfortunately been hit the hardest and women are losing jobs at a disproportionate rate'. The pandemic has 'deepened pre-existing inequalities' and 'exposed vulnerabilities, not only in the social but the political and economic systems as well'. For Nina, in reflecting on the 25 years since the 1995 Beijing Declaration and Platform for Action issued at the Fourth World Conference on Women,[15] COVID-19 has simply exacerbated 'long standing inequities and decades of discriminatory practices which have really led to unequal trajectories' for women, and that the world needs to 'minimise these setbacks'.

People of African descent

The discrimination against African Americans and people of African descent is well known and well documented, while in the time since the murder of

---

14 STEM is an acronym for academic disciplines in Science, Technology, Engineering and Mathematics.

15 See https://www.un.org/en/events/pastevents/pdfs/Beijing_Declaration_and_Platform _for_Action.pdf.

George Floyd, the full nature and extent of this discrimination and what should be done about it have received renewed attention (see Chapters 1 and 6). We spoke with Dominique Day about this history and how COVID-19 exacerbated the plight of people of African descent in the United States and around the world.[16] Dominique is founder and executive director of the Daylight Collective, which seeks to fill the space between the status quo and substantive justice with creativity, diverse voices, and multi-sector approaches and understandings. She is also chair of the UN Working Group of Experts on People of African Descent. Dominique cites her own work and that of others to assert that there have been 'massive racial disparities in who gets COVID-19, who has access to healthcare, who gets severe illness, and who dies'. She is keen to point out that this differential impact on peoples of African descent is neither accidental nor a surprise. Rather, she argues that this impact is a function of much longer historical trends and trajectories dating back to the advent and effect of the period of transatlantic slavery:

> Policy decisions continue to be grounded in the legacy of systemic racism and the trade and trafficking in enslaved Africans, in colonialism in the ways that we have seen black and brown bodies as there for exploitation, available for service, available to exploit opportunities.

For her, the world faces an 'important moment to think about [...] our commitment to human rights and the ways that systemic racism are global, and not local in their manifestation'. We discussed the idea of intentionality and larger structural reasons for systemic racism with Dominique. She concedes that in the world, there are people who hold overtly racist and white supremacist views, but that across many policy domains, 'systemic racism proceeds through individual decision making by people with subjective amounts of power and subjective perspectives' whose decisions are 'informed by what people are used to'. For example, she cites the idea of 'medical bias', and the context of 'doctors under stress', particularly during the early days of the pandemic. Under these conditions of stress and the need for quick decision making, she says that 'doctors default to biased decision making that disadvantages people of African descent'. In this way, there has been 'decision making by one person with a limited amount of power operationalising systemic racism', or 'operationalising the root of these racial disparities', such

---

16 D. Day, "COVID, Race, and Inequality: Why It's Time to Hold Tight to Human Rights," *The Rights Track*, January 21, 2021. http://rightstrack.org/covid-race-and-inequality-why-its -time-to-hold-tight-to-human-rights.

that pre-pandemic practices have been replicated. Such doctors are, according to Dominique, 'not filled with racial animus', but their decisions are based on individuals and their data and affect in a profound way 'whose lives matter, whose lives don't'.

She cites one example of Robert Femia, head of the Department of Emergency Medicine at New York University's Langone Health. His email to staff appeared in the *Wall Street Journal* during the early days of the pandemic effectively stating 'we're not going to have the luxury of time, data, or committees to make decisions about who gets ventilated, who gets access to care'.[17] Femia instructed his staff that they had 'sole discretion' to place patients on ventilators and that they had institutional backing to 'withhold futile intubations'.[18] Dominique appreciates the pressure such doctors were under, but makes the observation that 'kinetic decisions were made quickly without benefit of review'. Extant hospital protocols come with expectations of data and the convening of committees to inform decision making; however, owing to the volume of patients during the crisis, following such protocols was simply not possible. Rather, doctors and administrators had to 'rely on instincts' and 'rely on bias', which effectively meant that hospital staff were operating with a 'blank check'. It is within this delegated discretion and instinctive decision making that Dominique sees the operation of systemic racism and the resultant racial disparities in impact that emerged from the progress of the pandemic.

We turned our conversation with Dominique to the question of vaccination, both in terms of its distribution and take up. At a global level, Dominique asks, 'Can you solve the problem of COVID-19 without providing an equally viable solution on the continent of Africa?'[19] Or more generally, 'Have you solved the problem if you have not solved it for everyone?' Her answer to these questions is a resounding 'no' where she is concerned that thus far, science has found 'a solution for a highly developed and resourced society that is a decision about whose lives matter, whose lives are there to be exploited'. On the distribution of the vaccine, Dominique says that there have been a 'lot of concerns', that 'distribution is a huge problem' and that key stakeholders in

---

17   This quotation is from Dominique Day as she recollects the case.

18   The quotations in this sentence are taken from the email communications that appeared in *The Wall Street Journal*. See S. Ramachandran and J. Palazzolo, "NYU Langone Tells ER Doctors to 'Think More Critically' About Who Gets Ventilators," *The Wall Street Journal*, March 31, 2020. https://www.wsj.com/articles/nyu-langone-tells-er-doctors-to-think-more-critically-about-who -gets-ventilators-11585618990.

19   Dominique's question was extremely prescient given the future emergence of the Omicron variant, the cause of which has been partially attributed to very low vaccination rates in Africa.

the United States have 'failed to step into our best and most resourced selves'. In 'struggling to be excellent', she argues that we need to 'think about race' more explicitly with reference to 'home health aides', 'drivers' and 'grocery personnel', all of which are important roles, and disproportionately held by Black and brown people. Dominique urges that we 'need to explicitly think about race in this vaccine response', otherwise we run the risk of 'reifying and rejuvenating forms of systemic racism'.

On the issue of 'vaccine hesitancy' among people of colour in the United States, Dominique argues that 'a lot of people don't trust the vaccine', which for her is 'absolutely rational decision making in the face of atrocities from the past', where she cites the now famous case of the 1932 Tuskegee research project on syphilis among Black men.[20] The research did not have appropriate protocols for consent, withheld medicine and created ethically unjustified levels of risk for what have been described as meagre scientific results. For Dominique, this research in the name of science, coupled with other historical patterns of practice and mistrust (including the persistence of police violence), has led to 'concern based in the history of science', where 'people's fears may be legitimate'. In the COVID-19 crisis and the rollout of the vaccine, 'this is not scepticism that comes from ignorance; this is scepticism that comes from history'.

Prisoners

The United States has the highest incarceration rate in the world across a 'mixed economy' of public and private prisons operating in multiple and complex jurisdictions at the state and federal levels.[21] Prisons are confined spaces, and their conditions vary considerably across institutions, making them particularly susceptible to the spread of COVID-19. Prisons are also disproportionately populated by people of colour, owing to the operation of the US justice system, sentencing practices and a long history of government response to criminal activity perpetrated by African Americans and other people of colour. David Fathi is director of the ACLU National Prison Project, and we spoke to him about the plight of prisoners in a highly disaggregated

---

20 For a full time line on this research, see https://www.cdc.gov/tuskegee/timeline.htm.

21 Incarceration in the United States is the highest in absolute numbers (over two million people) and in per capita terms, making it five times the rate for countries such as Canada, England and Wales and China. The number of prisoners per 100,000 people in the United States is 737, in Russia is 615, in Ukraine is 350, in South Africa is 334, in Poland is 235, in Mexico is 186, in Brazil is 193 and in China is 118. See http://news.bbc.co.uk/1/shared/spl/hi/uk/06/prisons/html/nn2page1.stm.

and varied system that poses increased risk of COVID-19 for prisoners and raises significant questions over the administration of vaccines to this population of people.[22]

David tells us that the current system in the United States is run across 51 different jurisdictions, one for each state and one for the federal system, where the use of 'private for profit' prisons varies from an average of 10 per cent to a maximum of 40 per cent of all prisons affecting over 100,000 people. He says that this mixed system means that particularly among the private prisons there is 'lack of oversight', and such prisons are 'not subject to the same democratic control and oversight' as public prisons. David welcomes that the Biden administration has now returned to the policy of the Obama administration in stipulating that the 'federal prison system will no longer use private prisons' since there have been 'troubling findings about the quality of services that are provided by private prisons' across programmes and activities, as well as the 'level of safety and security'. Like Dominique, David sees a longer history behind the growth in incarceration in the United States, such that 'you can't talk about incarceration in the United States without talking about slavery and Jim Crow', as well as 'structural racism'.[23] He argues that in the period immediately after the Civil War, there was a 'deliberate strategy to incarcerate the black population in the South to establish slavery by another name, so that the ruling class could once again benefit from the free labour of the black population'. This history in part explains why 'people of colour and black people in particular are grossly over-represented', where Black people are 'six times as likely to be incarcerated as white people' even though they do not commit six times as many crimes.

In addition to the over-representation of people of colour in prisons, he also explains that the prison population is an aged one, since the United States has the longest sentences for equivalent crimes in the world, including the use of solitary confinement, life imprisonment and the death penalty.[24] These and other factors mean that 'prisons are the ideal environment

---

22   D. Fathi, "COVID and Incarceration: How If the Pandemic Affecting Prisons and Prisoners?" The Rights Track, May 4, 2021. http://rightstrack.org/covid-and-incarceration-how -is-the-pandemic-affecting-prisons-and-prisoners.

23   For an in-depth study of this history and its contemporary manifestations, see M. Alexander, *The New Jim Crow: Mass Incarceration in the Age of Colourblindness* (New York: The New Press, 2012). See also E. Hinton, *From the War on Poverty to the War on Crime: The Making of Mass Incarceration in America* (Cambridge, MA: Harvard University Press, 2017).

24   For a comprehensive study of prisons, prison conditions and variation in incarceration, see D. Van Syl Smit and C. Appleton, *Life Imprisonment: A Global Human Rights Analysis* (Cambridge, MA: Harvard University Press, 2019).

for the rapid and lethal spread of COVID-19'. Prisons have 'large numbers of people in close quarters' with '100s or 1000s in a single facility' with 'poor ventilation' and 'poor sanitation', and which 'house people who are disproportionately vulnerable to become very sick or die if they contract the virus because of pre-existing medical conditions'. This combination of the demographics of the prison population 'make[s] incarcerated people sitting ducks, just waiting for the virus to rip through their prisons'. Although data collection has not been systematic, David says that the 'general thrust of the data is unquestionable, prisoners have suffered disproportionately from COVID-19', prisons are COVID-19 'hotspots' and have very high case rates, such that 'one in every five has tested positive'—a case rate that is 'four times higher than rest of population'. Even more troubling, prisons are not collecting robust COVID-19 data, which allow for a breakdown of cases and deaths by race or ethnicity, despite such demographic data being collected at the point of imprisonment. David can only infer from COVID-19 data collected on the general population that it is very likely people of colour are disproportionately affected by the pandemic in prisons. He also speculates that failure to collect the relevant demographic data 'can be nothing other than intentional'.

The conditions and outcomes with respect to COVID-19 transmission in prisons are also present in other detention centres across the country, including pre-trial detention centres and immigration detention centres. David and his organisation have 'filed over fifty lawsuits trying to protect incarcerated people' across 'prisons, jails, and immigration detention facilities', where he argues the 'problems are similar' but in immigration facilities there is 'more churn' of people, a factor to his mind that may make COVID-19 transmission even worse. The ACLU has had some success in its legal challenges, as David explains that for 'ICE detention cases',[25] there has been 'quite a bit of success', with 'a thousand people' being released 'as a direct result of litigation'. For those in prison for 'criminal charges, pre-trial detention, and convicted prisoners', these efforts have been 'unsuccessful'. In further work on COVID-19 mitigation measures around testing and masks, there has been more success, but this success varies across the 51 different jurisdictions. In terms of vaccination, David and his team need to fight 'state by state', and 'county by county' across which there remain significant differences, where 'some states' and the 'federal government' have started to deliver vaccines, while other states continue to be 'holdouts and outliers'.

---

25   ICE stands for the US Immigration and Customs Enforcement, see https://www.ice.gov/.

Refugees

Before the pandemic, conflicts and the turn towards authoritarianism created multiple areas and dire conditions for so many people in the world that fuelled the interrelated problems of internally displaced populations, refugee flows and asylum seekers. One stark example of these phenomena occurred in Myanmar and the Rohingya people in Rakhine state, who are not formally recognised by the government and who found themselves at the mercy of scorched earth policy. In 2017, more than 740,000 Rohingya either fled or were moved to refugee settlement areas primarily in Bangladesh, and further groups of Rohingya migrated to Malaysia. The combination of the push factors for these refugees and the outbreak of COVID-19 increased risk for this community of people, which was coupled with xenophobia, suspicion and inadequate support from the Malaysian government, which itself has used a series of 'Movement Control Orders' to try to stem community transmission of the virus. Mahi Ramakrishnan is a refugee rights activist and runs a non-profit organisation, Beyond Borders Malaysia,[26] which works to promote and protect the rights of refugees and stateless persons in Malaysia. In our discussion with her, we covered the history and a wide range of contemporary issues facing this group of people, with larger insights around the impact of the pandemic on refugees and migrant workers in general.[27]

Our conversation with Mahi echoed many of the themes raised in our Rights Track episode with Gonzalo Vargas Llosa (see Chapter 6) in terms of the 'push' and 'pull' factors for refugees and migrants, as well as the policy responses required to protect and enhance the exercise of human rights for this vulnerable population of people. To put things into context, Mahi tells us that there are five hundred thousand refugees in Malaysia alone, where two hundred thousand Rohingya make up the largest proportion of this group, alongside refugees from 'Syria, Palestine, Somalia, Sri Lanka, Sudan, and Pakistan'. Currently, 'these refugees do not actually have the legal status to be here', since the Malaysian government has not ratified the 1951 UN Refugee Convention. They have 'no right to work', 'no rights to education, no rights to healthcare', in addition to suffering from 'immigration raids' and 'police raids'.

For the Rohingya in particular, Mahi's experiences in Burma/Myanmar demonstrate that there is a 'lack of racial unity' there, and where 'Rohingya

---

26 See https://beyondbordersmalaysia.org/.
27 M. Ramakrishnan, "COVID and Refugees: Protecting the Rights of the Other," The Rights Track, April 19, 2021. http://rightstrack.org/covid-and-refugees-protecting-the-rights-of-the-other.

are stateless in their own home country' since the Burmese government considers them formally as Bangladeshi and revoked their citizenship several decades ago. The Rohingya have been migrating to Malaysia since the 1970s, so there are now three to four generations in Malaysia, where 'they have forgotten their culture' and 'occupy the lowest stratification in Malaysia'. In addition to this social status, the Rohingya are characterised by 'deep-seated patriarchy' that leads to expectations about women's role in society, the phenomena of trafficking, child marriage and a situation where young women and girls are 'in a very vulnerable position'.

With respect to COVID-19, Mahi tells us 'from last year March–April [2020] we were shocked to see the kind of hate and backlash and xenophobia against the Rohingya', which 'spread out to other refugees and migrant groups', that was 'so well planned and so well coordinated'. She feels that Malaysia 'itself is such a xenophobic racist society', which she finds 'completely appalling'. She explains, 'amongst the three major groups – Malays, Indians, and Chinese – there is a lot of dissatisfaction', which means an 'already difficult situation' has been made even more difficult by the presence of the refugee community. This dissatisfaction led to 'backlash and xenophobia' against the Rohingya. COVID-19 case rates and death rates are 'largely amongst the migrant communities', in which Mahi sees a certain 'karma' and 'poetic justice', since for years she had been working on improving the living conditions for the Rohingya, which are 'beyond appalling' with 'human bodies piled up on top of one another' in very close quarters, making it 'impossible for social distancing'. Like David, she has also seen 'high rates of infection in immigration detention quarters', as well as in prisons, jails and other holding facilities. Outside these facilities, refugees and migrants are 'forced to work in very difficult situations', within a dense network of 'middlemen' and 'enforcement authorities', characterised by 'rampant corruption'. Many of these people have 'become undocumented in Malaysia', where those who were 'already victimised, keep being victimised'. These developments during the pandemic have fed a 'narrative that already exists: all migrant workers are bad people'.

Mahi is concerned that simply not enough has been done to address the multifaceted challenges faced by these groups: 'we have not seen a comprehensive healthcare policy that includes everyone that make up the fabric of Malaysian society'. Government and society have not recognised the basic understanding that 'in order for me to be fine, the other person has to be fine'. From her perspective leading a refugee rights NGO, 'the Government is really difficult to work with', but she and her organisation raise awareness, advocate on behalf of refugees and 'push for the existing legal framework' to be used 'in a more effective and efficient manner' since ratification of the UN Refugee Convention will 'take a long, long time'. International organisations, including the WHO, the UNHCR and the ILO 'are having ongoing conversations with the Malaysian government', but Mahi explains, 'we are not privy to these conversations'.

Children

While children on balance have not been as susceptible to the severe effects of the virus, concerns over community transmission in schools have led many countries around the world to close schools for prolonged periods during 2020–21. Economic downturns and readjustments of national budgets have also decreased available resources for children across many different dimensions, while prolonged periods at home with much reduced social interaction have led to many concerns over children's mental health. To address these and other relationships between COVID-19 and children's rights, we spoke to Aoife Nolan.[28] Aoife is professor of International Human Rights Law, co-director of the Human Rights Law Centre in the School of Law at the University of Nottingham and vice-president of the Council of Europe's European Committee of Social Rights. As in our conversations about other groups, Aoife highlights to us that pre-existing inequalities, injustices and disproportionalities with respect to children and the exercise of their rights were exacerbated by the pandemic.

She tells us that there have been a 'wide range of issues globally' during COVID-19, with 'school closures, interruption in education, reduced access to food in places where there is heavy reliance on school meals', a 'global mental health crisis' and 'terrifying evidence of increased levels of child abuse and domestic violence both during and after lockdown'. Lockdowns themselves have led to the 'enforced constant company of children with adults in highly pressurised and often substandard housing conditions'. There has been 'poor housing', 'loss of social and play opportunities', an 'impact on survival' and with the turn to remote learning, an unforeseen increase in 'online harm'.

These different issues and areas of impact, for Aoife, 'map onto the rights of children' and the 'obligations' and 'the duties that states have with regard to giving effect to those rights' as found in the 1989 UN Convention on the Rights of the Child (see Chapter 1). These rights include the 'right to the highest attainable standard to children's physical and mental health', 'the child's right to live free from violence', 'the child's right to a standard of living

---

28 A. Nolan, "Promoting and Preserving Children's Rights after COVID: What Needs to Happen?" The Rights Track, May 11, 2021. http://rightstrack.org/promoting-and-preserving-childrens-rights-after-covid-19-what-needs-to-happen.

adequate for their development' as well as rights to the family and play. Like other groups, Aoife cites evidence that shows that 'not all children have been affected equally' by the pandemic, which has 'absolutely entrenched inequalities' for 'poor, disabled, and minority children'. Through her work, she is keen that the world is able to avoid the situation where the 'unequal impact of the pandemic is perpetuated'.

With respect to government response and the measures used to mitigate the worst effects of the virus, Aoife says that existing human rights law allows for 'permissible state limitations' on certain rights protections in order to 'protect public health', but 'such restrictions must be imposed only when necessary, be proportionate, and only for limited periods of time'. Globally, there has been a 'diversity of measures', where 'in the UK', Aoife observes 'we see very positive measures' alongside 'major shortcomings', including the 'provision of food and other support to families'. She is worried that there are 'examples of the government to instrumentalize the crisis to push forward agendas', to 'relax obligations to certain groups of children' and 'weaken the protections required under statute', particularly with respect to 'social care'. The UK implemented 'new social care regulations' that relaxed 'local authority legal duties with regard [to] education, health, and care needs assessments', but these 'have now expired and been reversed' as a result of 'assertive campaigning' from children's rights advocacy groups. In light of pre-pandemic 'mass de-regulation', of social care, Aoife believes that 'Covid is an excuse, as a cover' for policy changes. Even though the government 'had already changed direction', the UK Court of Appeal ruled that the 'secretary of state for education acted unlawfully', and has a 'duty of consultation' with key stakeholders in social care for children, which had not happened. Aoife is concerned that children's rights have either been 'deliberately disregarded, or more likely, they are being misunderstood'.

Outside the UK, Aoife sees similar problems with the disproportionate impact of COVID-19 on children in the United States, South Africa and India. In the United States, a country that has not ratified the UN Convention on the Rights of the Child, she sees 'significant change' in direction between the Trump administration and the Biden administration, which has moved the country from policies 'strongly driven by state approaches', to one that sees a greater 'level of federal intervention'. In the absence of international human rights obligations on children's rights there are 'education rights provisions in state constitutions', which do provide access to legal remedies through state courts. In South Africa, there have been 'key problems' that 'amplify pre-existing inequalities' as well as the impact of the 'digital divide' during lockdown that have affected disadvantaged children. Aoife argues, however, that there has been 'so much advocacy and political discussion' addressing 'long-term shortcomings' in the provision of 'adequate infrastructure' to support children. Now that 'schools are largely open again' there remain challenges around addressing these pre-pandemic issues. In India, which saw a massive spike in cases in late April and early May of 2021, Aoife is sure that 'as absolute numbers go up, they go up among children as well'. The absence of measures and support for children were only made worse during the pandemic.

In the face of the many challenges affecting children and the exercise of their rights, Aoife is impressed with the community of children's rights advocates, whose work has 'made very clear how strong and how resilient the discourse of children's rights discourse is'. She echoes the words of the UN Secretary General in saying that children are 'not the face of the pandemic, but they risk being among its greatest victims', but she is certain that children have not become 'invisible', and that the children's right agenda has 'traction'. For Aoife, 'if we are serious about ensuring that we come out of COVID and come out of the pandemic, shall we say, in a more child rights friendly world', then we need to ensure that 'children's rights are put at the heart of the COVID recovery effort', including 'law making, policy making, and budget making'. One key part of this recovery effort must be including the 'voices' of children, inclusion of their views and the articulation of 'intergenerational solidarity' as well as embracing the interdependence of different human rights across different groups in society.

COVID-19, Terrorism and Human Rights

The international human rights framework has provisions and mechanisms in place for states to 'derogate' from their human rights obligations if a determination is made that the country faces an existential threat. Both terrorism and COVID-19 can be argued to be examples of such an existential threat. As Aoife reminds us, state response to threats such as these must, however, be *proportionate* and *temporary*, and the determination of an existential threat *carefully considered*. The 'war on terror' since the 9/11 attacks on the United States has involved this kind of determination and the strengthening of terrorism legislation that puts limits on the protection and exercise of certain human rights and fundamental freedoms (see Chapter 1). Government response to COVID-19 has been of a similar character, as states across the world have implemented a variety of restrictions with the aim at reducing community transmission of the virus. Policies to combat terrorism and COVID-19 have been highly contested on the grounds of the nature of the threat, the proportionality of the response and the duration and phasing of measures. Our conversation with Tom Parker sought to tease out these many different dimensions of response with a view to understanding how a human rights approach to both these issues is both appropriate and effective.[29] Tom is a prominent counterterrorism practitioner who has consulted for the EU, the UN, Amnesty International and MI5 on post-conflict justice, security sector reform and counterterrorism. He is the author of *Avoiding the Terrorist Trap: Why Respect for Human Rights Is the Key to Defeating Terrorism.*[30]

Tom joined us from Abuja, Nigeria, to share his thoughts on the dual threats of terrorism and COVID-19 and their direct and indirect relationships with human rights. After such a long career and after years of conducting research for his book on 150 years of terrorism, Tom is keen to point out that there is 'no one profile of a terrorist' and that 'it is very difficult to predict who is or who will become a terrorist'. Given that terrorists come from a variety of social, economic, political, religious and family backgrounds, terrorist acts are always uncertain and 'always a minority activity'. In light of this uncertainty, Tom advocates for a human rights-based approach. He says that 'if you respond to terrorism within that human rights framework, you are less likely to fall into the trap that each terrorist groups sets for its opponents, which is [an] over reaction'. Terrorists, in Tom's experience, are dedicated to 'stripping the mask of the state' in its response to 'see the harsher reality' underlying state structures, institutions and attitudes. For him, it is 'hard-wired into terrorism' to 'provoke the state' in order to 'open a political dialogue through the use of violence'.

Consistent with Aoife's view on children's rights, 'human rights law doesn't prevent states from taking actions to protect themselves from terrorism', and that it is 'quite permissive' with a variety 'techniques' that states can deploy, as long as they are used 'lawfully, proportionally' and have a commitment to 'get back to the *status quo ante*'. The 'assumption that human rights get in the way', or that such an approach 'ties the hands of the state', for Tom, is a 'false assumption'. Tom is clear: 'I don't think there is actually a tension between effective counter terrorism and human rights observance.' For him, 'terrorism does pose an existential threat', but more importantly, 'the threat is how we respond to terrorism'. He is thus supportive of the temporary nature of anti-terror legislation as was used in the UK before 9/11; however, he now worries that countries in the West have 'built a security architecture' that was never meant to be temporary.

He applies this same thinking to the state response to COVID-19, which he sees as 'a silent killer' that 'does not discriminate', but a threat that has been

---

29 T. Parker, "Tackling COVID-19 and Terrorism: The Need for a Human Rights Approach," *The Rights Track*, July 12, 2021. http://rightstrack.org/tackling-covid-19-and-terrorism-the -need-for-a-human-rights-approach.
30 T. Parker, *Avoiding the Terrorist Trap: Why Respect for Human Rights Is the Key to Defeating Terrorism* (London: World Scientific, 2019).

given a special 'privilege' in the West that has not been accorded elsewhere. From his perspective working in Nigeria, COVID-19 sits alongside other significant threats, such as malaria, where 'not many people in Nigeria are taking COVID as serious as in the West'. In the West, however, there has been considerable debate over the necessary and appropriate responses, which for Tom also require a human rights approach, where human rights law 'anticipates that you may need to curtail freedoms out of a concern for public health', an idea that is 'hard-wired into the International Covenant on Civil and Political Rights'. We reflected on the many approaches taken around the world, and in particular to those followed in the United States and the United Kingdom, which have been captured by research at the Blavatnik School of Government at Oxford University, which tracks government response with its 'stringency index' (see Figure 7.1). In both countries, there have been significant restrictions on movement, the size of gatherings and the ability for family members to see one another. Tom argues that this kind of state response 'isn't *per se*, a threat to human rights, so long as the measures taken are lawful, reasonable, and necessary to prevent the harm that you are seeking to avoid'.

His worry, however, concerns the degree to which these measures are permanent or temporary, since it is typical for governments to fall into the problem identified in political science called the 'iron law of bureaucracy'.

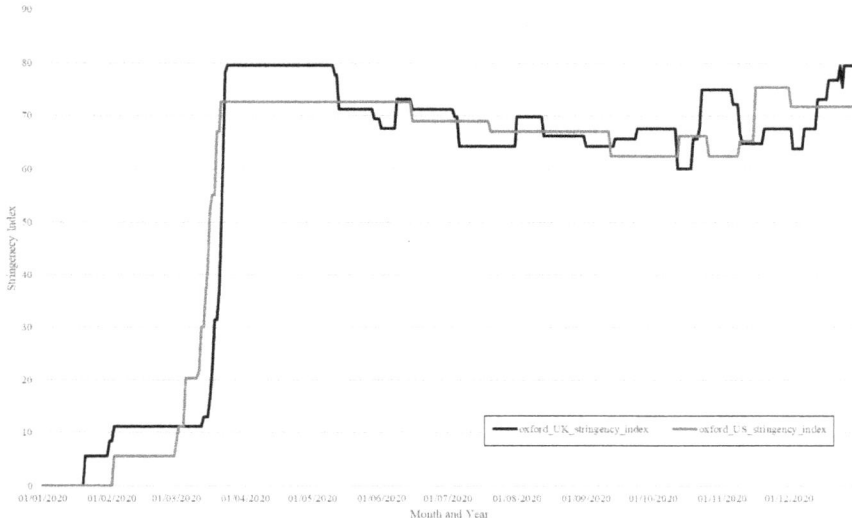

Figure 7.1 COVID-19 stringency index, January–December 2020 (the United States and United Kingdom). *Data Source:* The Blavatnik School of Government, University of Oxford: https://www.bsg.ox.ac.uk/research/research-projects/covid-19-government-response-tracker. Data analysis and visualisation: Todd Landman and Benjamin Lucas, University of Nottingham.

Tom characterises this law as 'once you establish a bureaucracy, it will seek to strengthen and enlarge itself', or 'once you build a wall, it will be very difficult to take it down'. He is worried that 'we will likely live with the measures that have been put in for a very long time'. For example, the 'shoe bomber' Richard Reid tried to sneak an explosive device onto an airplane in his shoe in 2001, and now it is a common feature in all airports for passengers to remove their shoes as part of standard security protocols, more than twenty years after the event. Tom argues that the main reason for the prolonged nature of such polices is political: 'no one politician wants to take responsibility' for changing the policy because of the risk of a future event, leading such policies to 'stay around years, even decades, after their utility is evaporated'. In terms of COVID-19, Tom worries that 'you can imagine very easily a society in ten or twenty years' time where you are being surveilled passively wherever you go' and 'that generally free public space will shrink considerably'.

In the event that COVID-19 declines in its intensity and impact, Tom tells us that 'terrorism has not gone away' and that 'threats have been multiplying', especially from right-wing terrorists, who represent an 'internal threat'. He argues that 'Islamist terrorism is still a significant threat around the world', particularly in Africa, the Middle East and Central Asia, a prescient observation in light of the developments in Afghanistan from August 2021 with the withdrawal of the United States and other forces. He adds that in the face of its deteriorating socio-economic conditions, left-wing terrorism may return to Latin America. He believes that 'COVID has had a mitigating effect on terrorism', since it made its coordination and delivery slightly harder, but the 'underlying reasons' for terrorism have not disappeared. Tom reminds us that 'counter terrorism is hard, public health is hard', where there will be 'strong dissenting voices to any sensible public policy that you propose'. In the end, however, 'the beauty of a human rights based approach is that it is designed to resist specifically the goals that terrorist organisations are seeking to achieve'. 'Human rights are designed to stay, contain, and measure state strength', and they are 'purpose-built to ensure a more effective response to terrorism'. In this way, Tom 'absolutely' upholds the view that a human rights approach remains the best way for states to respond to the kinds of threats represented by terrorism and COVID-19.

COVID-19, Democracy and Migration

Grounded in a commitment to freedom of speech, deliberative legislative chambers and the need for the electoral survival of political leaders, the experience of the democratic response to COVID-19 has been highly contested and controversial. Mass publics and freedom of information, coupled with long-held experiences of liberty and freedom more generally have led to different coalitions within civil, economic and political society that have variously contested scientific evidence and government advice on how best to prevent community transmission. Failing democracies, such as those in Colombia and Venezuela alongside severe case rates in the Latin American region, have put additional pressure on internal displacement and cross-border migration. To discuss these and other issues facing democracies during the pandemic, we spoke to Arlene Tickner and David Owen.[31] Arlene is a professor of international relations in the School of Political Science, Government and International Relations at the Universidad del Rosario in Bogotá, Colombia. David is a professor of social and political philosophy at Southampton University.

David begins by observing that 'COVID made apparent to us how far we are from the ideal' of democracy and liberal democratic institutions. It 'has done three things that have put into question the everyday ideal of democracy'. The first question concerns issues 'within states', where 'different people are treated unequally', for example citizens and non-citizens, and those who can work from home and those who cannot. He is somewhat surprised that those employed in 'low skilled jobs' are now classed as 'essential workers', a status that has increased their risk of infection. The second question is the 'depth of global inequalities', concerning things such as access to health and 'disease exposure' in regions such as Africa. The third question for David is how 'radically interdependent we all are, both within states and between states'. He agrees that we all share responsibility for addressing climate change, but COVID-19 has been 'more rapid than climate change' in terms of its effects and revealed the true 'weakness of global systems'. This suggests that problems in one part of the world can affect other parts of the world, demonstrating that these are 'threats to all of us'.

Arlene agrees with his assessment and that what she has witnessed 'not only [for] Colombia, but Latin America *writ large*' such that 'democracy has been questioned by the general public' for its failure to deliver. The pandemic has 'worsened different forms of inequality' and led to 'different treatment of distinct sectors', and 'has put this into staunch relief'. Latin America has a very high concentration of COVID-19 cases and deaths, with '35% of all deaths concentrated' in the region. In terms of vaccination, 'most countries have been very slow to obtain vaccines or apply them' in contrast with the

---

31 A. Tickner and D. Owen, "Sowing Division: COVID-19, Democracy and Migration," The Rights Track, July 20, 2021. http://rightstrack.org/sowing-division-covid-19-democracy-and-migration.

United States and the United Kingdom. In both respects, 'Colombia represents top of the list', which for her demonstrates the 'limitations of democracy' in response to COVID-19 and to the ability in general to protect human rights.

In Colombia, the pandemic and government response has been coupled with widespread and violent social protests. Arlene explains that Colombia 'doesn't have a long history of social protest' after a 'half century war'; however, ever since the August 2016 Peace Accords, there have been 'waves of protest'. The most recent protests were fuelled by 'tax reform being proposed at a very inopportune time'. Colombia is the only country to have proposed such a reform, which 'would have affected the middle class', in the 'midst of a pandemic'. The reform 'did not propose raising taxes on the wealthy', which 'sparked protest'. In addition, the 'lack of effective implementation of the peace accords', 'discontent with education', 'frustration with the government's efforts to combat the pandemic', 'deteriorated health infrastructure', 'the lack of dignified work', failure to protect 'pensions' and to 'protect the environment' have all been 'sources of grievance and discontent'. The 'use of excessive police force' has not helped and the 'offer of dialogue has been an empty offer', which is 'worsening of the situation'.

The worsening conditions in Colombia are coupled with a massive influx of migrants from neighbouring Venezuela, which Arlene calls a 'political crisis and a humanitarian crisis'. US sanctions against Venezuela during the Trump administration have worsened the socio-economic conditions, which have led to the flow of 2,000,000 Venezuelan migrants into Colombia. Arlene explains that 'countries of the region itself have been unable to agree upon a joint strategy to address the situation', but the Colombian government, since January 2021, has given these migrants 'temporary protection status'. The combination of this 'influx' and the pandemic has placed an even larger strain on Colombia's economic capabilities. The Colombian government continues to put pressure on the Venezuelan government to make it comfortable for the migrants to return home.

Like Colombia, there have been recent waves of protest and large events in the UK. These include 'Black Lives Matter' protests, violence against women protests, anti-lockdown and anti-mask protests and the Euro 2020 football matches in London. These protests and events involve what David calls 'the balance between public health and public security' and debates over what is 'permitted and unpermitted'. He is thus concerned about the trade-offs between 'security and public health' on the one hand, and 'public health versus the right to protest' on the other. He is also concerned with the 'use of culture as a way of provoking and intensifying social division', with an 'appeal to small-c cultural conservatism', where 'culture and cultural identity becomes a key battleground for the kind of democracy that you want'. He has witnessed 'two very different visions of England', as opposed to the whole of the UK. The first vision represented by the English football team is one of diversity, difference, equality and inclusion. The second vision is one of 'division and generating division and ruling through division'.

These reflections from David and Arlene raise significant questions about the future of democracy. For David, the period of the pandemic has shown that for 'most European democracies', there has been 'massive visibility of inequality', which may lead to a call for a 'move back to social democracy'. The case of Portugal stands out in his mind as a positive example of extending health rights to migrants, but no such access has been granted in other European countries, and for other sectors in society, the pandemic has 'made the inequalities more starkly visible'. From Arlene's perspective, there are not 'many success stories', with 'profound types of inequality in Latin America', a 'crisis of democracy and state institutions' and 'deficiencies in public health'. She believes that there must be 'some degree of reckoning on the part of political and social actors to address issues', which have been 'compounded by the pandemic'. She asks, 'who is the *human* in human rights?' 'What are human rights?' 'How broadly or limited are they defined?' For her, 'without a hard and long reflection' on the limitations of democracy during this period and the lessons learned, the sources of hope tend to be reduced.

Holding on Tight to Human Rights

It is very clear from our conversations in this chapter that the many inequalities and disproportionalities that pre-date the pandemic have been made worse by COVID-19. When the virus eventually recedes, these problems will still be there and, in many cases, will have been enhanced. Across groups such as women, Blacks, prisoners, refugees and children, the post-pandemic world poses continued and significant challenges for human rights. In the absence of significant structural change and social justice for these groups, enhanced hardships will continue. The post-pandemic world will once again turn its attention to the ever-present threat of terrorism from many different quarters in society. Democracies have not demonstrated the most effective response to the threat of COVID-19, and in the era of enhanced nationalism, populism and scepticism over who belongs and who does not belong within countries, the post-pandemic world does not bode well for the millions of 'people on the move' who are refugees, migrants, IDPs or asylum seekers. Across all of our guests, however, there is a strong view that only by holding on tight to human rights we will be able to curb the worst forms of our own behaviour.

Part III

MODERN SLAVERY

Part III of *The Rights Track* focuses on the problem of modern slavery and represents the collective wisdom we gathered from our conversations with a wide array of scholars, practitioners and activists over three years between 2017 and 2020. In 2017, the University of Nottingham made a multi-year and multimillion-pound investment in a new Research Beacon of Excellence called the Rights Lab. Since its launch, the Rights Lab has built a globally recognised research platform dedicated to ending modern slavery. It has over 100 academics drawn from all five faculties in the University of Nottingham, has raised millions of pounds in external funding, produced over 300 publications, numerous 'impact case studies' as part of the UK's Research Excellence Framework and published over 100 policy reports and briefings. It has a network of over one hundred and fifty active policy, NGO and business partnerships, and incubated the Survivor Alliance, the world's first NGO designed by and for survivors of modern slavery. In many ways, the work of the Rights Lab has successfully created a new and thriving 'epistemic community' dedicated to ending modern slavery.

Over Series 3, 4 and 5 of the Rights Track, we spoke to researchers in the Rights Lab and a wide range of stakeholders in its network across many different topics and issues related to modern slavery. Our conversations include discussions on conceptions of 'freedom from slavery', 'survivor voices', perpetrators of modern slavery, legal frameworks, the role of international governmental organisations, transparency of supply chains and the economics of modern slavery, forced marriage and fighting slavery on the ground, which includes the idea of how to understand local government resilience to slavery to create 'slavery free cities'. Throughout our conversations, like our other human rights conversations, we learned a great deal about the unstinting commitment of a community of people working together to address this significant global challenge, and how these efforts draw on transdisciplinary approaches to research and transcend the boundaries between academia and the wider community of anti-slavery stakeholders.

Chapter 8 'Slavery Past and Present' uses the concept of 'the useable past' to look at the continuities and discontinuities between the anti-slavery movements of the past and the anti-slavery movement today. The chapter draws on our in situ conversations with David Blight (Yale University), author of the award-winning biography of Frederick Douglass and John Stauffer (Harvard University), who has worked on African American history. The chapter then moves on to consideration of modern slavery through our conversations on conceptions of freedom with Juliana Semione (Rights Lab and Salvation Army), anti-slavery legislation with Katarina Schwarz (Rights Lab) and Laura Dean (Millikin University in Illinois) and the role of international institutions such as the United Nations with James Cockayne (Rights Lab). These different elements of slavery past and present are then brought together through our conversation with Zoe Trodd about her idea of the 'Freedom Blueprint' for ending modern slavery.

Chapter 9 'Perpetrators and Survivors' focuses on the primary relationship between perpetrators and survivors of modern slavery, and how this is embedded in family, community, national and international structures. We spoke to Austin Choi-Fitzpatrick (Rights Lab and San Diego University) about slaveholders in India; Andrea Nicholson (Rights Lab), who has developed qualitative methods for interviewing survivors of slavery; and Minh Dang (Rights Lab and Survivor Alliance), a survivor-scholar who works to empower survivors and to rebuild their lives. Chapter 10 'Business, Economics and Modern Slavery' considers business models and the global economy as drivers for modern slavery. We set the scenes with Genevieve LeBaron (University of Sheffield) and John Gathergood (University of Nottingham) on the business and economics of modern slavery. This is followed by our conversations with Baroness Lola Young of Hornsey (House of Lords and University of Nottingham) who has been leading reform to transparency laws, Alexander Trautrims (Rights Lab) on how having a slavery free supply chain is good for business, Siddharth Kara (Rights Lab) on cobalt mining and technology and Hannah Lerigo-Stephens (Rights Lab) on business and modern slavery. We conclude with our conversation with Elaine Mitchel-Hill (Marshalls plc) and Arianne Griffiths (Rights Lab) on how some businesses are 'walking the supply chain' in their efforts to combat slavery.

Chapter 11 'Fighting Slavery on the Ground' is our final chapter in Part III and focuses on the grassroots efforts to combat modern slavery where it happens in the world. We discuss bonded labour in India with Pradeep Narayanan and Anusha Chandrasekharan (Praxis); forced labour in Vietnam, Uganda and Albania with Patricia Hynes (University of Bedfordshire) and Patrick Burland (International Organisation for Migration (IOM)); interventions in 'slavery hotspots' with Dan Vexler (Freedom Fund); the pursuit of perpetrators with David Westlake and Steven Webster (International Justice Mission); collective public health and modern slavery in Brazil with Luis Leão (Federal University of Mato Grosso); forced marriage and women's rights with Karen Sherman (Akilah Institute) and Helen McCabe (Rights Lab); and the idea of how to achieve a network of 'slavery free cities' with Alison Gardner (Rights Lab).

Chapter 8

SLAVERY PAST AND PRESENT

Abstract

This chapter uses the concept of 'the useable past' to look at the continuities and discontinuities between the anti-slavery movements of the past and the anti-slavery movement today. The chapter draws on our in situ conversations with David Blight (Yale University), author of the award-winning biography of the former slave and abolitionist Frederick Douglass and John Stauffer (Harvard University), who has worked on African American history. The chapter then moves on to consideration of modern slavery through our conversations on conceptions of freedom with Juliana Semione (Rights Lab and Salvation Army), anti-slavery legislation with Katarina Schwarz (Rights Lab) and Laura Dean (Millikin University in Illinois) and the role of international institutions such as the United Nations with James Cockayne (Rights Lab). These different elements of slavery past and present are then brought together through our conversation with Zoe Trodd (Rights Lab) about her idea of 'the freedom blueprint' for ending global slavery.

'[Frederick Douglass] is the best prior example of a person with more to say on these issues than anyone.'

– David Blight, Yale University

'History is the activist's muse.'

– John Stauffer, Harvard University

'[Anti-slavery requires] multiple different pieces of the governance puzzle fitting together.'

– Katarina Schwarz, Rights Lab

'We need for this to be global.'

– Zoe Trodd, Director of the Rights Lab

Introduction

After eight years of sexual slavery and forced domestic servitude, Mende Nazer, a Nuba tribe member from war-torn Sudan, organised her own route to freedom from the home of a Sudanese embassy official in London in 2000.[1] Her harrowing escape, aided by the local Sudanese community, involved several additional years of legal battle to have her 'leave to remain'[2] confirmed by the UK government. Her story is moving, and in many ways incredulous, as today the problem of modern slavery has emerged as a significant human rights problem and global challenge. Mende expresses her own incredulity about her escape to freedom:

> Despite the fact that I escaped, I still can't believe it's true. I just keep fearing they'll come and capture me again and take me back there. I really can't believe I'm free, even though I'm living it and experiencing it.

Our conversations that form the content for this chapter centre on key questions around slavery in the past and slavery in the present, the concept of freedom and the role that law and institutions, and academic research play in ending modern slavery. Long thought to be a thing of the past, scholars and practitioners variously working on forced labour, human trafficking, sexual exploitation and forced marriage have drawn together common themes and attributes under the overall rubric of 'modern slavery'.[3] The United Nations has embraced this term, which is formally articulated in SDG Target 8.7, which demands that states:

> Take immediate and effective measures to eradicate forced labour, end modern slavery and human trafficking and secure the prohibition

---

1 See M. Nazer, *Slave: The True Story of a Girl's Lost Childhood and Her Fight for Survival* (London: Virago, 2004). This book featured as part of the University of Nottingham's annual reading programme, where the university provided free copies of the book to students and organised a year of guest lectures and discussions on the topic of modern slavery.

2 Leave to remain or 'indefinite leave to remain' are the formal terms the UK government uses to refer to individuals who acquire full settled status in the country. See https://www.gov.uk/settle-in-the-uk.

3 K. Bales, *Disposable People: New Slavery in the Global Economy* (Berkeley: University of California Press, 2004); K. Bales, *Understanding Global Slavery: A Reader* (Berkeley: University of California Press, 2005); K. Bales, *Ending Slavery: How We Free Today's Slaves* (Berkeley: University of California Press, 2007); K. Bales, and R. Soodalter, *The Slave Next Door: Human Trafficking and Slavery in America Today* (Berkeley: University of California Press, 2009); K. Bales, Z. Trodd, and A. K. Williamson, *Modern Slavery* (Oxford: Oneworld, 2009); A. Choi-Fitzpatrick, *What Slaveholders Think: How Contemporary Perpetrators Rationalize What They Do* (New York: Columbia University Press, 2017); J. Mende, "The Concept of Modern Slavery: Definition, Critique, and the Human Rights Frame," *Human Rights Review* 20 (2018): 229–248.

and elimination of the worst forms of child labour, including recruitment and use of child soldiers, and by 2025 end child labour in all its
forms.

This SDG target can be seen as the culmination of many different efforts in
line with the idea of the 'social construction of human rights',[4] where a history
of consensus building since the advent of the 1926 Slavery Convention has
sought to develop the core content of human rights instruments that address
the problem of modern slavery (see Chapter 3). Evidence submitted to the
UN Special Rapporteur on Contemporary Forms of Slavery, Its Causes and
Consequences shows that between 62 per cent and 90 per cent of countries
in the world have ratified the core international instruments on slavery and
forced labour, while 47 per cent of countries have 'no provisions criminalising
slavery or the slave trade'.[5] This variable legal commitment to the problem is
also reflected in great variation in the practice of modern slavery across the
world, where there is a persistent gap in the implementation of laws prohibiting slavery.

The term 'modern slavery' references a much longer history of slavery that
has existed for nearly 4,000 years as a common practice across many different
societies and systems of government.[6] In addition to the prevalence of slavery
among ancient civilisations, the most commonly known form of slavery took
place during the transatlantic and imperial periods between the early 1600s
and the late 1800s. These overt forms of slavery based on the protection of
property rights were finally abolished when Brazil declared the end to slavery
in May 1888.[7] Less than forty years after the Brazilian abolition of slavery,
the world saw the first purportedly universal treaty prohibiting slavery (and
the slave trade) emerge with the 1926 Slavery Convention. Article 1(1) of the
Convention defines slavery as 'the status or condition of a person over whom
any or all of the powers attaching to the right of ownership are exercised'.
This convention, characterised as the 'first true international human rights

---

4 J. Donnelly, "The Social Construction of International Human Rights," in *Human Rights in
Global Politics*, ed. T. Dunne and N. Wheeler (Cambridge: Cambridge University Press, 1999),
71–102.
5 United Nations Office of the High Commissioner for Human Rights (OHCHR), "Delta 8.7
Consultation: Addressing Tomorrow's Slavery Today," p, 5. Click here to enter text..
6 F. Braudel, *Civilization and Capitalism* (New York: Harper and Row, 1981–1984); S.E. Finer, *The
History of Government, Vol. I: Ancient Monarchies and Empires* (Oxford: Oxford University Press, 1997).
7 R. E. Conrad, *Children of God's Fire Children of God's Fire: A Documentary History of Black Slavery in
Brazil* (Princeton: Princeton University Press, 1983), xxviii, 515; P. Winn, *Americas: The Changing
Face of Latin America and the Caribbean* (Berkeley: University of California Press, 2006).

treaty',[8] gives primacy to the ideas of *ownership* and *property*. Further developments in international human rights law and international humanitarian law have articulated more fully the definition of slavery.[9]

Provisions on slavery and other related forms of exploitation are also set out in other international instruments and norms. Article 8 of the 1966 International Covenant on Civil and Political Rights and Article 7 of the 1998 Rome Statute of the ICC have provisions. Slavery is part of the 1945 Charter of the International Military Tribunal (Art 6(c)) and in the Statute of the International Criminal Tribunal for the Former Yugoslavia (Article 5(c)), where enslavement in qualifying circumstances is defined as a crime against humanity. The ILO has provisions in its 1930 Forced Labour Convention (No. 29), 1957 Forced Labour Convention (No. 105), 1999 Worst Forms of Child Labour Convention (No. 182) and 2014 Forced Labour Protocol addressing forced or compulsory labour, and slavery and related exploitation of children. The various regional human rights instruments for Europe, the Americas, Africa and the Arab region all have provisions addressing the problem of slavery, servitude, forced labour and/or traffic in women, as well as dignity, respect and free choice of work.

Participation in this international legal regime has varied considerably across the different core instruments. A simple tabulation of participation in core instruments is shown in Figure 8.1, where it is clear that some instruments enjoy stronger commitment than others. The 1999 Worst Forms of Child Labour Convention enjoys 94 per cent participation, a similar ratification record to the 1989 Convention on the Rights of the Child (see Landman 2005).[10] In contrast, the 1926 Slavery Convention enjoys only 63 per cent participation even though it is the first core instrument established after the wave of nineteenth-century abolitionism.

Alongside these legal definitions, scholars and practitioners working on modern slavery have developed through consensus the Bellagio-Harvard Guidelines on the Legal Parameters of Slavery (2012), which focus on the right to ownership, the powers attached to the right of ownership and the notion of possession. In focusing on these elements as foundational to slavery, the guidelines emphasise the notion of control and lack of agency for victims

---

8 P. Sieghart, *The International Law of Human Rights* (Oxford: Oxford University Press, 1983).

9 These legal instruments include (1) the 1956 Supplementary Convention on the Abolition of Slavery, the Slave Trade and Institutions and Practices Similar to Slavery (Article 7a); (2) the 1998 Rome Statute (Article 7.2.c); (3) the International Tribunal for the Former Yugoslavia (Article 5c); (4) the 2000 United Nations Palermo Protocol on Trafficking in Persons and (5) the 2005 Council of Europe Convention on Action against Trafficking in Human Beings.

10 T. Landman, *Protecting Human Rights: A Comparative Study* (Washington, DC: Georgetown University Press, 2005).

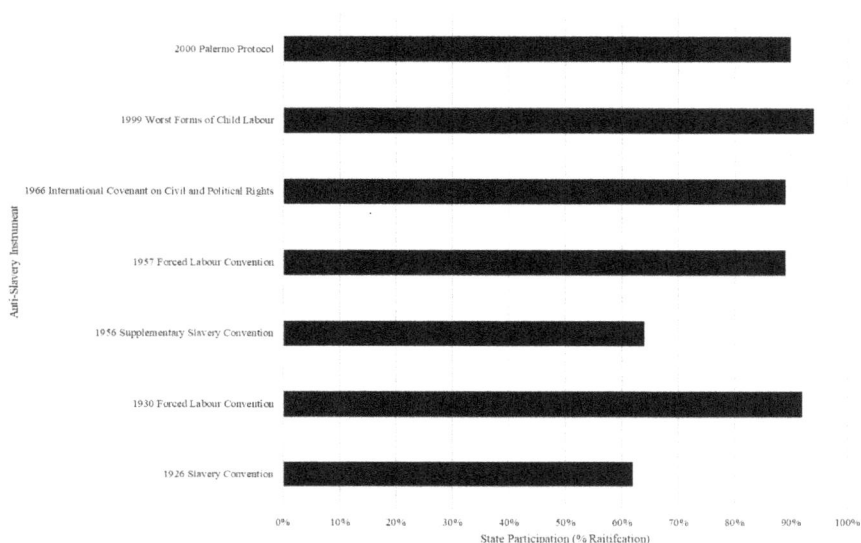

Figure 8.1 States party participation[†] in core international instruments on slavery. *Source:* United Nations Office of the High Commissioner for Human Rights (OHCHR) (2019) 'Delta 8.7 Consultation: Addressing Tomorrow's Slavery Today', p, 5.; Landman (2020: 310). [†]Participation includes only those countries that have signed and ratified the instruments.

of slavery, where different forms of coercion maintain power over individuals.[11] The key phrase from the guidelines with respect to ownership, also at the heart of the concept of modern slavery, asserts that it constitutes

> control over a person in such a way as to significantly deprive that person of his or her individual liberty, with the intent of exploitation through the use, management, profit, transfer or disposal of that person.

This notion of ownership is then linked to possession, which is an extreme form of control that goes far beyond any understanding of reasonable labour relations and management of workers.

Like other human rights abuses, the practice of modern slavery is a phenomenon that is 'hidden in plain sight' and one that has the same 'problem of unobservability' (see Chapter 4 in this book), since much of the activity

---

11 J. Cockayne, N. Grono, and K. Panaccione, "Slavery and the Limits of International Criminal Justice." *Journal of International Criminal Justice* 14, no. 2 (2016): 253–267; A. Choi-Fitzpatrick, *What Slaveholders Think: How Contemporary Perpetrators Rationalize What They Do* (New York: Columbia University Press, 2017).

and its impact on individuals remain elusive and evade detection. Victims and survivors of slavery make themselves known through testimonies, narratives, survey-based data projects and other forms of data used to track and estimate the temporal and spatial distribution of the objects and sites associated with slavery. In 2018, the ILO and the Walk Free Foundation, a human rights organisation based in Australia, published its latest version of *The Global Slavery Index*, which estimates that 40.3 million people in the world are in some form of modern slavery (see Chapter 4 and the section with Kevin Bales).[12] This number represents the largest number of enslaved people in the history of the world, but as a proportion of total global population, the smallest number. The relative size of this population of affected people encourages anti-slavery activists to assert that the world is 'at a tipping point' for ending modern slavery. Our conversations with anti-slavery scholars and practitioners explore these and other issues surrounding this persistent and evolving human rights problem.

The Useable Past[13]

To situate the global human rights challenge of ending modern slavery, we begin by framing the work on modern slavery through the lens of history with award-winning historians David Blight from Yale University and John Stauffer from Harvard University.[14] By speaking with them,[15] we hoped to understand better the continuities and discontinuities between historic and modern forms of slavery and what can be learned from their work on Frederick Douglass, an escaped slave from Maryland and arguably the world's most famous abolitionist. Through his Pulitzer Prize-winning work on Frederick Douglass,[16] David argues that Douglass was indeed a 'prophet of freedom', understood in

---

12   International Labour Organisation and Walk Free, *The Global Slavery Index*, 2018. https://www.globalslaveryindex.org/.
13   The idea of the 'useable past' is found in V.W. Brooks, "On Creating a Usable Past," *The Dial*, April 11, 1918, pp. 337–341; see also C.R. Sunstein, "The Idea of a Useable Past," *Columbia Law Review* 95 (1995): 601.
14   D. Blight and J. Stauffer, "The Useable Past: What Lessons Do We Learn from History in the Fight to End Slavery?" The Rights Track, November 12, 2018. http://rightstrack.org/the-useable-past-what-lessons-do-we-learn-from-history-in-the-fight-to-end-slavery.
15   Landman had the good fortune of sitting with David Blight at the Gilder Lehrman Centre for the Study of Slavery, Resistance, and Abolition at Yale University, and with John Stauffer at Harvard University in October 2018 as part of a human rights and modern slavery mission to the United Nations and anti-slavery organisations in New York, as well as a conference at Yale, and further meetings with research centres working on modern slavery at Harvard.
16   D. Blight, *Frederick Douglass: Prophet of Freedom* (New York: Simon and Schuster, 2018).

the Old Testament sense of prophet, such as 'the prophets Jeremiah, Isaiah, Amos, and Ezekiel'. For David, Douglass was a 'genius with words', 'a master of language' who could 'explain a catastrophe, a pivot in history, and victories and triumphs in history'. Through his various writings, Douglass was able to 'capture what's happening in America, what's happening with the slavery crisis, what's happening with emancipation, what's happening with the aftermath of emancipation, what's happening with lynching towards the end of his life'.

David is keen to point out that a prophet is not one who predicts the future, as is sometimes assumed, but one who 'can speak words that stun us', 'that shatter us'. In this way, prophets 'trouble us', showing us 'the depths of our condition, and the depths of our tragedies'. They warn us that we are 'about to be destroyed before we can be renewed'. In referencing Old Testament scholar Abraham Heschel,[17] David explains that a prophet is a 'person who can find words and speak words *one octave higher than the rest of us actually understands*'. For David, Frederick Douglass was one such person and his prophetic language expressed through his speeches, his biographies and his other writings has significant resonance for human rights and the struggle against slavery today. For example, David says Douglass's words apply to issues such as 'birth right citizenship, the nature of equality and inequality, equality before the law' … 'the carceral state in America, as a form of slavery' (see the David Fathi section in Chapter 7 of this book). His writings offer a primer for these issues, and Douglass represents in David's view, 'the best prior example of a person with more to say on these issues than anyone'. He is the kind of leader who started from the position of radical outsider 'who through time find partial or complete victories', such as we have witnessed with leaders including Nelson Mandela in South Africa and John Lewis, the great civil rights leader in the United States. This transformation from radical outsider to political insider occurred in Douglass, who became a Republican Party functionary, who 'lives that trajectory from outside radicalism always beating down on the doors and never inside of power through an Armageddon of a Civil War that leads to emancipation, [and who] experiences the victory of his cause, or seems to, in his forties'. Over the next 30 years into the 1890s, however, Douglass 'sees those victories slowly erased and betrayed'. By the end of his life, Douglass gives one of his greatest speeches about the problem of lynching, which he wonders might constitute a new form of slavery,

---

17   Abraham Heschel (1907–1972) was a professor of Jewish mysticism at the Jewish Theological Seminary of America, wrote a number of books on Jewish philosophy and was a leader in the civil rights movement.

a 'neo-slavery' coupled with systems of sharecropping, the imposition of Jim Crow laws and the terror and violence of the age. Douglas lived through the 'Fugitive Slave Law,[18] the Dred Scott decision,[19] emancipation, black exodus, and Reconstruction'. Through these experiences, he 'left us with prophetic language' about 'slavery, race, and their afterlives'.[20]

We asked David of the many millions of words from Douglass, what are the key words that he left with us that are of relevance today in the struggle against modern slavery. David shared two important passages. First, in his second autobiography *My Bondage and My Freedom*,[21] Douglass writes, 'without struggle there is no progress, there never was, there will never will. Power never concedes anything without a demand, it never did, and it never will'. David notes that Douglass wrote this passage in the 1850s, 'in the midst of the political crisis over slavery and its expansion' while its message transcends this period into the future. Second, David shares with us the last sentence of this book, 'as long as heaven allows me to carry on this work, or to fight this fight, I will fight with my voice, my pen, and my vote'.[22] These three things – voice, pen and vote – are signs of the learning that took place within Douglas,

---

18   The Fugitive Slave Law was passed by the US Congress in 1850, which was part of a compromise between Northern 'Free Soilers' and Southern interests in slavery. It required that all escaped slaves, if captured, had to be returned to their owners and did not have a right to a trial. See J. Lepore, *These Truths: A History of the United States* (New York: W.W. Norton, 2018), 261.

19   *Dred Scott v. Sandford* [1857] was a Supreme Court case in which the majority ruled that the rights of American citizenship did not extend to Black people, who the court considered were inferior to white people. The decision was important as it applied to both slaves and free people and meant that the protections of the US Constitution did not apply to them. See J. Lepore, *These Truths: A History of the United States* (New York: W.W. Norton, 2018), 289.

20   In his June 2019 testimony on reparations to the United States House of Representatives, Ta-Nehisi Coates, American author and journalist, said, 'It is impossible to imagine America without the inheritance of slavery.' See Ta-Nehisi Coates, "Read Ta-Nehisi Coates's Testimony on Reparations," *The Atlantic*, June 2019. https://www.theatlantic.com/politics/archive/2019/06 /ta-nehisi-coates-testimony-house-reparations-hr-40/592042/.

21   F. Douglass, *My Bondage and My Freedom. Part I. – Life as a Slave. Part II. – Life as a Freeman* (New York: Miller, Orton & Mulligan, 1855).

22   The full quote from Douglass is 'believing that one of the best means of emancipating the slaves of the south is to improve and elevate the character of the free colored people of the north I shall labor in the future, as I have labored in the past, to promote the moral, social, religious, and intellectual elevation of the free colored people; never forgetting my own humble orgin [*sic*], nor refusing, while Heaven lends me ability, to use my voice, my pen, or my vote, to advocate the great and primary work of the universal and unconditional emancipation of my entire race'. See F. Douglass, *My Bondage and My Freedom. Part I. – Life as a Slave. Part II. – Life as a Freeman* (New York: Miller, Orton & Mulligan, 1855), 406; see also D. Blight, "What America Owes Frederick Douglass," *New York Times*, November 5, 2018. https://www.nytimes.com/2018/11/05/opinion/ what-america-owes-frederick-douglass.html.

who by the end of his life had become a 'political abolitionist' whose message is powerful for young people today. Both of these quotations, in David's view, have universal applicability and sit at the heart of all social movements, and for us, resonate both for the general struggle to advance human rights (see Chapter 3) and for the specific struggle against modern slavery.

We caught up with John Stauffer at the Barker Centre at Harvard to discuss his own views on how the lessons of history with respect to slavery are relevant today. Our conversation with John echoes that with David focusing on the idea of 'voice', and why this is so important for the struggle against modern slavery. He starts by saying that 'slavery is about dehumanising, or the attempt to dehumanise another human being', and that, 'slavery does not exist without violence or the threat of violence'. In the face of this violence or threat of violence, John argues that 'voice, whether it is orally, or written, or an image that can circulate, has extraordinary power'. Historically, John says that *The Liberator*,[23] an abolitionist newspaper established by William Lloyd Garrison in 1831, became the most influential periodical of its time. Garrison sought to disseminate it as far and wide as possible, deep into the South and across America. It so threatened the pro-slavery lobby that John C. Calhoun sought to prohibit its circulation and prohibit any imagery produced by abolitionists, effectively resulting in a gag rule passed by Congress to put limits on freedom of speech (see Chapter 5 in this book).

We turned our conversation to the idea of the authenticity of voice in the anti-slavery struggle. We asked John if this voice was from slaves themselves or from people speaking on behalf of slaves. He says that 'it could be both', and that the abolitionist struggle was 'thoroughly integrated' with Blacks and whites, slaves and free people, men and women. For him, it was the 'first civil rights movement and the first human rights movement' that 'treated every human as equal'. Blacks were very much part of this movement and 'important members' who could 'speak truthfully about their experiences'. Such lived experiences, for John, were 'powerful' voices.

In the face of these powerful voices, we asked John how the abolitionists at the time maintained momentum for the movement, especially since at that time it did not benefit from the ubiquity of social media and the almost instantaneous communications technology available today. Indeed, as we have discussed in Chapter 3 of this book, maintaining collective action is challenging given the costs and benefits that any single individual incurs or receives through his or her participation, a problem in the current period

---

23 For more on this publication, see the digital archives held by the Smithsonian Institution, available at: https://transcription.si.edu/project/11766.

that has been mitigated in part by what has been called 'the logic of connective action'.[24] For John, the abolitionists of the nineteenth century were in the 'golden age of oratory', where speaking events were hugely popular, 'akin to pop concerts and hip hop concerts' today. An abolitionist orator, in John's view, 'had to hold a crowd', and the best and most popular orator was Frederick Douglass. He tells us that not only was Douglass the most photographed American of the nineteenth century, but in making reference to David's book on Douglass, more Americans 'saw Douglass speak than any other figure'. These kinds of events, led by a relatively small number of abolitionists, did not necessarily convert everyone into an abolitionist, but certainly turned the tide against slavery.

We asked John what then are the linkages between historical abolitionism and the struggle against modern slavery, and whether there is a misappropriation in using the word slavery today, or if there are any limits to these linkages. He says that 'there are very few if any limits [...] virtually no limits'. For him, 'history is the activist's muse [...] if we don't learn from the past and use the past, it will come back to haunt us'. He sees direct connections between historical slavery and modern slavery with respect to violence and the denial of voice. He repeats that 'without violence, or the threat of violence, slavery cannot exist', an observation that is still true today, since 'violence, and the threat of violence against another person, being held against their will, and forcing them to work for no pay' is just as much part of modern slavery as it was part of historical slavery. He is concerned by the denial of voice to enslaved people today, but argues that 'if you give them voice, you are not going to keep them', where 'silence is the great weapon of the slave holder, then and now'. The key for the modern abolitionist movement is thus giving voice to enslaved people, 'bearing witness to these atrocities', and 'the more you bear witness, that collective voice will mobilise government, at the national and local level, to end it'.

Our conversations with David and John very much align with the idea of the useable past, where past struggles and the learning that comes with them carry strong lessons for the future. Rather than making a strict demarcation between the slavery of the past and the slavery of the future, our conversations reveal certain important continuities. Slavery as a practice has been a dark part of human history for millennia, while the transatlantic and American periods of slavery between the early 1600s and the 1880s show that social

---

24   See W. L. Bennett and A. Segerberg, *The Logic of Connective Action: Digital Media and the Personalisation of Contentious Politics* (Cambridge: Cambridge University Press, 2013).

struggle, moral suasion and in certain cases, violence[25] have yielded one form of emancipation. Other struggles for emancipation have mirrored those in the United States across Europe, Africa, Latin America and the Caribbean.[26] The legal emancipation of African American slaves, however, was replaced with what David alludes to as 'neo-slavery', where new forms of control and coercion in the absence of explicit claims to property rights have ceded way to more informal methods of enslavement through patterns of voter suppression, sentencing, incarceration, police violence and access to social and economic rights.[27] If David is correct, and we believe that he is, this neo-slavery is evident around the world across many different forms, and despite the legal prohibitions that have come into force, the practice of slavery continues.

Freedom and Modern Slavery

If Douglass is the 'prophet of freedom' and his writings capture what freedom means historically in a 'voice that is an octave higher' than the rest of us, we were keen to gain further insight into conceptions of freedom and what it means for the contemporary period and struggle against modern slavery. We spoke to Juliana Semione,[28] who has worked for the Salvation Army, the main agent with responsibility for the National Referral Mechanism (NRM)[29] that provides assistance and support to survivors of modern slavery as part of the 2015 UK Modern Slavery Act.[30] Juliana has also finished her doctoral research on conceptions of freedom *after* slavery, which moves beyond mere theorising and uses what is known as 'Q Methodology' to probe how sur-

25 For a fascinating history of Black violence and emancipation, see K. C. Jackson, *Force and Freedom: Black Abolitionists and the Politics of Violence* (Philadelphia: University of Pennsylvania Press, 2020). For white violence and abolitionism, see J. Stauffer and Z. Trodd, *The Tribunal: Responses to John Brown and the Harpers Ferry Raid* (Cambridge: Harvard University Press, 2012).

26 See S. Drescher, *Abolition: A History of Slavery and Anti-Slavery* (Cambridge: Cambridge University Press, 1989); see also V. Brown, *Tacky's Revolt: The Story of an Atlantic Slave War* (Cambridge: Belknap Press of Harvard University Press, 2020).

27 This incomplete or partial emancipation also appears in Stanley Harrold's book, *American Abolitionism: Its Direct Political Impact from Colonial Times into Reconstruction* (Charlottesville and London: University of Virginia Press, 2019); see also M. Alexander, *The New Jim Crow: Mass Incarceration in the Age of Colourblindness* (New York and London: Penguin, 2019).

28 J. Semione, "Life after Slavery: What Does Freedom Really Look Like?" The Rights Track, October 13, 2019. http://rightstrack.org/life-after-slavery-what-does-freedom-really-look-like.

29 See https://www.gov.uk/government/publications/human-trafficking-victims-referral-and-assessment-forms/guidance-on-the-national-referral-mechanism-for-potential-adult-victims-of-modern-slavery-england-and-wales.

30 See https://www.legislation.gov.uk/ukpga/2015/30/contents/enacted.

vivors, service providers and law enforcement individuals in the United
Kingdom and the United States think about freedom. This method, she
says, is 'the science of subjectivity', which 'measures what people think'. Her
research involved establishing a 'concourse' of over 700 words and phrases
most commonly associated with freedom and then transferred a reduced set
to cards, which she then sorted by different respondents according to the
degree to which they represent their own understanding of freedom. She was
keen to uncover conceptions of freedom from lived experiences across these
three different groups involved in the area of modern slavery. Her analysis
allowed her to compare across these groups and countries, as well as within
the two countries.

Juliana chose to select the United States and the United Kingdom since
they have shared principles and similar forms of anti-trafficking and anti-
slavery legislation, as well as a 'self-made identity about being leaders' in this
issue area. She sees the three groups in her study as being responsible for
'actuating freedom', certainly with respect to survivors of slavery, but also service providers and law enforcement officials who provide help and support for
survivors. While the individual respondents did not know each other personally, these three groups for Juliana have a lot of overlap, given their identities
and their function, in ways that she acknowledges 'interact with each other'.
She identified these groups in seven different cities and in the end used over
seventy respondents to take part in her formal 'Q-Sort' process.

Juliana's 'concourse' included words and phrases that come from text,
images, popular culture and other elements of public discourse on freedom.
From this initial representation of freedom, she then selected a smaller sample of phrases that (1) addressed the question around freedom from slavery
and (2) that covered a variety of common themes and categories. In the end,
she used 49 statements that she printed onto cards, which the respondents
then sorted on a specially prepared mat. Juliana explained that the mat had
a grid in the shape of an upside-down pyramid printed on it. At one side of
the grid, respondents placed the two cards with which they agreed the most,
while at the other side of the grid they placed the two cards with which they
disagreed the most. They then sorted the rest of the cards onto the remaining
parts of the grid, effectively forming a normal distribution of cards represent-
ing conceptions of freedom. This sorting process allows for statistical analysis
of the different importance of each of the statements and the frequency of
where the respondents placed them on the grid.

Her analysis shows that it was quite rare for the different groups to disagree fundamentally on these words and statements, but they would 'prioritise
them differently'. Almost all the respondents agreed on the idea that freedom
means that an individual is 'free from coercion, having free will to do as you

wish without being forced, pressured, coerced to act in a certain way'. We discussed whether they were more interested in the notion of 'freedom from' something or 'freedom to' something. Julian discovered that her respondents had a much lower ranking for 'freedom from' statements than 'freedom to' statements, where one of the strongest statements in terms of priority was 'having the ability to defend yourself against those who might try to limit your free will'. In her view, this idea of freedom should be seen as 'a capability' and a 'freedom to' something. The second most ranked statement was that 'freedom is a process of adjustment to no longer being enslaved', followed by 'being healed from trafficking and modern slavery and the damaging effects that it had on you', which for her is 'a statement toward empowerment'. More importantly, she discovered that freedom is not immediate. She said that it is popular for people to say that 'you achieve freedom the moment you are freed from your trafficker', which she says, 'is just not true'. Rather, the idea that freedom is a process of adjustment means that it may take some time for an individual to feel truly free.

This largely inductive process structured around different phrases relating to freedom, and revealed across three groups of respondents in two different countries, represents an innovative way to understand what freedom means to people. Juliana hopes that her work finds resonance in the minds of policy makers, who she argues 'do not really think about freedom' when drafting different measures to support survivors of modern slavery. She wants policy makers to think more carefully about what 'survivors are being given freedom to' and she sees her work as 'holding up a mirror' to reveal 'exactly what we are thinking' about freedom. For service providers, she is keen that processes and support measures become 'more efficient' in addressing the needs of survivors by knowing more about freedom in their work. The idea that freedom is a *process* and *not a status* carries much weight within the community of survivors for whom each day is a struggle to live a free life.

Law and Institutions

Human rights law in general and anti-slavery law in particular are a 'bulwark against the permanent threat of human evil'[31] and provide a framework of protection for freedom in the ways we discovered in our conversations with David, John and Juliana. The evolution and proliferation of anti-slavery legislation come with state duties to give effect to the different instruments to which they are a party and to implement their own legislation within their

---

31 S. Mendus, "Human Rights in Political Theory," *Political Studies* 43 (1995): 10–24.

own legal jurisdictions. While the promulgation of anti-slavery law and legislation is laudable, the actual implementation of these laws, as we saw above,
remains a key challenge in the struggle against modern slavery. In order to
understand the complex legal terrain of anti-slavery legislation, we spoke
to Katarina Schwarz from the Rights Lab and Laura Dean from Millikin
University in Illinois, who joined us from her field mission to Latvia.[32]
Katarina specialises in international and domestic human rights law, carried
out her doctoral research on reparations for historical slavery[33] and with Jean
Allain from Monash University created the world's first comprehensive database of anti-slavery legislation for all 193 UN Member States.[34] Laura Dean
specialises in anti-trafficking and anti-slavery policies primarily in Eastern
Europe and Central Asia, regions that have experienced high levels of prevalence of modern slavery, particularly after the end of the Cold War and the
collapse of the former Soviet Union.[35] Beyond law, we were also interested in
anti-slavery governance through institutions, and spoke to James Cockayne[36]
on the ways in which the international system seeks to bring about an end to
modern slavery. James is Professor of Global Politics and Anti-Slavery at the
University of Nottingham and formerly senior fellow at the United Nations
University in New York. He is the author of numerous publications on organised crime, governance and modern slavery.[37]

We started by asking Katarina whether anti-slavery law has been progressive over time and whether it dates back to before the 1926 Slavery
Convention. She told us that 'it is a bit of both', where anti-slavery sentiment

---

32   K. Schwarz and L. Dean, "Strengthening Laws and Ending Modern Slavery: What Connects
SDGs 16 and 8.7?" The Rights Track, May 6, 2020. http://rightstrack.org/strengthening-laws
-and-ending-modern-slavery-what-connects-sdgs-16-and-87.

33   See K. Schwarz, *Reparations for Slavery in International Law* (Oxford: Oxford University Press,
2022).

34   J. Allain and K. Schwarz, *Antislavery in Domestic Legislation*, online database. https://anti-
slaverylaw.ac.uk/. See also K. Schwarz, J. Allain, and A. Nicholson, "Slavery Is Not a Crime in
Almost Half the Countries of the World – New Research," *The Conversation*, February 13, 2020.
https://theconversation.com/slavery-is-not-a-crime-in-almost-half-the-countries-of-the-world
-new-research-115596.

35   L. Dean, *Diffusing Human Trafficking Policy in Eurasia* (Policy Press, an imprint of Bristol: Bristol
University Press, 2020).

36   J. Cockayne, "How Is the UN Working to End Modern Slavery?" The Rights Track, July 3,
2019. http://rightstrack.org/how-is-the-un-working-to-end-modern-slavery.

37   J. Cockayne, *Hidden Power: The Strategic Logic of Organised Crime* (New York: Oxford University
Press USA, 2016); Centre for Policy Research, *Developing Freedom: The Sustainable Development Case
for Ending Modern Slavery, Forced Labour and Human Trafficking* (New York: United Nations University,
2021). https://www.developingfreedom.org/report/.

is represented historically through the issue of 'decrees' and 'declarations' that have seen moments of rollback, but that since the late 1800s, there has been a 'truly international effort to engage all states' in the anti-slavery agenda through law. The evolution of this body of law includes a move from an exclusive treatment of slavery, to expand to include forced labour and other forms of exploitation; however, with this evolution has come 'fragmentation and confusion', as well as differences across 'laws, practices, and agents'. These different laws are not yet coherently woven together, but there is significant 'overlap'. To understand this panoply of laws, Katarina built a 'legibase' of all anti-slavery legislation in the world. Contrary to the popular view that slavery is 'illegal everywhere', her work on the database shows that in nearly half of all states, slavery is not a prohibited crime, and that 'we still have a lot of work to do in the first legislative step'. Subsequent to our conversation with Katarina, she shared a figure that captures the variation across regions in domestic legislation provisions for different categories of slavery and different types of legal instruments (see Figure 8.2).

Beyond this first legislative step, we asked Katarina what needs to be done. She is quick to observe that 'legislation is not implementation', and that globally, 'there are surprising places with good legislation'. For example, she argues that Nauru, a small island state in the Pacific to which 'people do not naturally look', has model domestic legislation that has 'criminal provisions that translate international law into domestic law'. Beyond Nauru, she finds that Latin American countries are more likely to enact constitutional anti-slavery provisions than European countries. We were keen to understand from Katarina how to address the 'implementation gap' between de jure protection and de facto realisation.[38] For her, this is a 'complicated question' that involves 'multiple different pieces of the governance puzzle fitting together'. For example, there are separate provisions for criminal justice prosecution, mechanisms for the socio-economic drivers of slavery, clauses to combat bribery and corruption, and variable provisions for access to justice. She stresses that 'the access to justice question is really fundamental', for those who have a 'need to pursue redress'. Overall, the challenge of 'multi-level governance' involving inter-governmental organisations, TANs and domestic actors in the public and private sector requires a real 'grappling with complexity'. There is the need to 'marry each level of governance across different spheres',

---

38 There is a long-held and recurring challenge of legal implementation of human rights in general, and in anti-slavery in particular. See T. Landman, and K. Schwarz, "Rights Indicators and Implementation," in *Research Handbook on the Implementation of Human Rights in Practice*, ed. Rachel Murray and Deborah Long (Cheltenham: Edward Elgar, 2022).

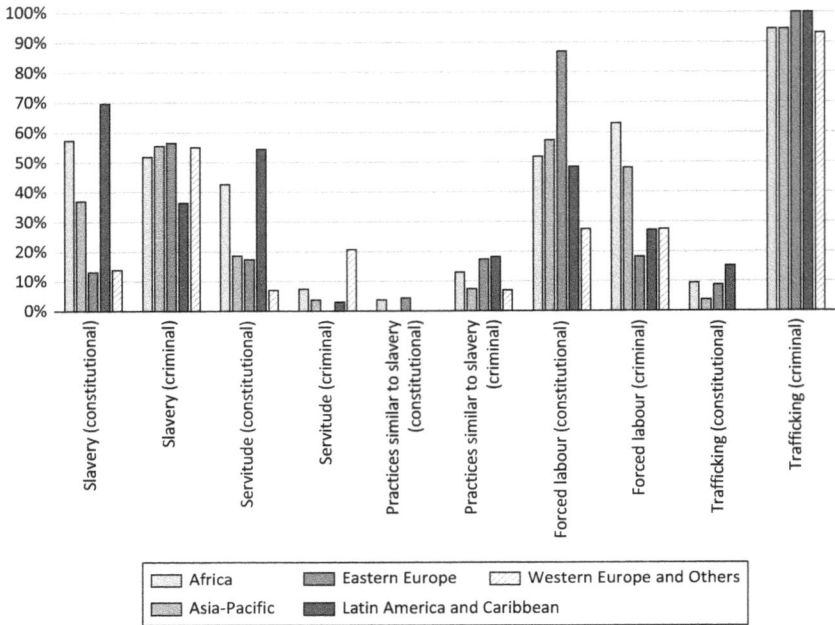

Figure 8.2 Proportion of States with domestic legislative provisions by region. *Source:* Anti-Slavery in Domestic Legislation, available at: https://antislaverylaw.ac.uk/. This figure also appears in Landman and Schwarz (2022) 'Human Rights Indicators and Implementation', in Rachel Murray and Debbie Long (eds.) (2022) *Research Handbook on the Implementation of Human Rights in Practice*, Edward Elgar. Reproduced with permission from Edward Elgar © 2022 Todd Landman and Katarina Schwarz all rights reserved.

including 'labour, immigration, victim protection, and human rights', with a fair degree of 'picking and choosing'.

These themes resonated with Laura, who argues that with respect to the region of the world where she has worked, the 1990s saw the end of the Cold War and the breakup of the Soviet Union, which created more states, different regime types and different orientations about national governmental systems reflecting ideas from the West and the East. The Baltic states of Latvia, Lithuania, Estonia, as well as Central European states such as Poland, the Czech Republic, Poland and initially Ukraine, looked West to the European Union, while countries such as post-Maidan Revolution[39] Ukraine (and the

---

39 Variously known as the Revolution of Dignity, the Euromaidan Revolution or the 2014 Ukrainian Revolution, the Maidan Revolution led to the ousting of President Viktor Yanukovych and the overthrow of the Ukrainian government. Landman was in Kiev a year

Russian invasion of Crimea), Moldova and others looked more towards the 'sphere of influence' of the Russian Federation. In either case, attention in the 1990s and early 2000s primarily focused on the stereotypical 'Natasha' problem. These were Slavic and Eastern European looking women who worked in the sex trade in Western European capitals. Countries in the region developed legislation on sexual exploitation of women with little attention given to the larger issues of forced migration, forced labour and human trafficking, particularly among young men. This lack of attention is partly explained by the fact that 'migration takes time' and 'wasn't automatic with the breakup of the Soviet Union'. She argues further that corruption and organised crime residing in larger society typical in countries outside the region had become part of the state apparatus. Like Katarina, Laura sought to measure legislation through a 'human trafficking policy index' and finds surprisingly that Estonia has the worst developed set of policies, while countries such as Georgia and Moldova have the best. She finds further that democracies in the region 'are better at implementation', but 'score lower on the scope of their policies'.

Laura tells us that legislation needs to move beyond the issue of sexual exploitation, and that through her field research on the ground, efforts to understand implementation tend to focus more on 'outcomes' and 'victim rehabilitation' than on 'arrests' and 'referrals' of victims to services. She sees 'street-level bureaucrats' as essential to the policy process, and that there continues to be a bias towards women and rehabilitation, but more needs to be done for male victims, who are stuck in the 'continuation of the trafficking cycle', where the top destination countries include Germany, Russia and Ukraine. Both Katarina and Laura agree that the legal developments and implementation require 'stronger institutions' and 'enhanced state capacity'. Across all regime types, democratic and authoritarian alike, Laura argues that 'if we really care about victims, we need to strengthen institutions'.

It is precisely to the role of institutions that our conversations with James Cockayne focused, with particular emphasis on the role of the United Nations. James agrees with the observation that the United Nations is huge, complex and full of multiple agencies, interests and incentives that shape its work around the world. He starts by saying that the United Nations is a 'forum for member states', is comprised of a series of 'technical agencies' and

---

before the revolution working with civil society groups and academics as part of a project led by the Westminster Foundation for Democracy to develop frameworks to measure the quality of democracy in Ukraine, where he worked with groups whose focus was on the EU and NATO at the time.

a variety of very different 'organisations that can respond to problems on the ground'. Taken together, this multitude of functions and structures does give the United Nations a 'holistic perspective' with which to address global problems. James states that the United Nations does take a broad human rights-based approach to modern slavery, but that it treats the problem differently through its different parts. Through its human rights machinery based on the Universal Declaration of Human Rights and subsequent legal instruments, it formally labels the problem as 'contemporary forms of slavery'. The organs with responsibility for labour label it as a 'labour rights' issue. Other organs, such as the UN Office on Drugs and Crime, see it as a 'criminal justice' problem. The differences in anti-slavery 'lenses' for James mean that the different parts of the United Nations are 'holding a different part of the elephant', and in echoing Katarina and Laura, 'grappling with the different manifestations of the problem'.

James reminds us that the UN Global Compact[40] on business and human rights with its focus on 'respect, protect, and remedy' is also an important part of the United Nations' work and 'increasingly part of the story' with respect to modern slavery. The anti-slavery movement, however, 'has been a little slow in addressing this' and in recognising that both states *and* large companies have a responsibility to tackle the problem. In addition to business and human rights, James is keen to stress that modern slavery is also a problem for sustainable development, and hence has featured as part of the United Nations' SDGs. Totalling 17 goals and 169 separate targets, the SDGs represent a tremendous achievement in bringing together all member states to agree on how the United Nations will help address a wide range of inter-related development problems, of which modern slavery is one. Announced in 2015 with a target of achievement for 2030, James says that UN agencies are 'digesting this framework' and the whole UN development programme has been reorganised to fit within the framework.

For the issue of modern slavery, James argues that science and measurement play a crucial part in addressing the problem (see Chapter 4), but he recognises that even though significant progress has been made, much more work is needed, with 'some distance to go'. He notes that the recent estimate from the ILO and Walk Free Foundation of 40.3 million enslaved people means that a net difference of 9,000 people a day must be freed, a number that takes

---

40 The UN Global Compact is a voluntary programme for multinational corporations and businesses to recognise their role in realising and advancing human rights. The Compact currently comprises over 12,000 companies located in over 160 countries around the world. See https://www.unglobalcompact.org/.

into account the existing number of enslaved people and any new people who fall into slavery. To give some perspective on the scale of this problem, he cites the case of Brazil, which over the past twenty years has freed 55,000 people, a rate that does not even come close to what is needed given the estimated prevalence in the world. As we set out in Chapter 4 in this book, James argues that it is 'much easier for people, [and] policy actors' who want to know 'what is the evidence', 'what can I reliably know about this problem, particularly in my country'. To this end, James tells us that the United Nations established Alliance 8.7 and he was the main architect in setting up Delta 8.7, which is a knowledge platform for sharing country-level information on 'slavery and related issues' that is easy to navigate. He also hosted the Code 8.7[41] meeting at the United Nations, which brought together the artificial intelligence world and the anti-slavery world to explore how the latest advances in data science, machine learning and AI can be harnessed to provide greater insight and evidence into the problem of modern slavery. On the back of this meeting, James is optimistic that new forms of data and collaboration will provide the United Nations with 'every source of data that we can'.

James agrees with Katarina and Laura that modern slavery is an 'umbrella term' for a wide range of practices and many different 'legal nuances'. The 'articulation of Target 8.7' has accelerated action on the problem and in many ways means that the United Nations now 'talks with one voice' on this issue. This voice, however, for James, also needs to include the voices of survivors, who 'need to be at the heart of this'. He points out that when we speak of a 'case' of modern slavery, we are using a 'theme that has come from someone' and if we do not observe ethics and responsibility in working with survivors, there is the potential for a 'horrible resonance between the act of non-consensual taking and the form of exploitation that they have been through'. This idea of 'voice', as we learned from David and John through history, is essential for the struggle against modern slavery, and sits at the heart of the UN system, which is founded on the opening line 'we the peoples'. James sees a natural tension between this commitment to people and the governance of the United Nations through a system of states. He worries that this distance and dissonance between inter-governmental politics and 'the people' could be a 'recipe for alienation of the people we are supposed to be benefiting'. In short, 'we are their representatives' and 'we need to learn from them'.

---

41 Code 8.7 was a meeting at the United Nations in February 2019 that featured an anti-slavery consortium comprising the Rights Lab, the Computing Consortium, the Turing Institute, Arizona State University and Tech Against Trafficking. Landman was part of two plenary sessions and a working group as part of this conference.

The Freedom Blueprint

It is clear from our conversations on history, freedom, law and institutions relevant to the fight against modern slavery that there is a burgeoning community and emerging consensus on the urgency of the problem and the provision of a set of tools and actions that can be deployed to address it. Our conversation with Zoe Trodd, director of the Rights Lab, brought these issues together under what she calls 'the freedom blueprint', which is an overarching rubric and framework to realise the aspirations of SDG Target 8.7 to end modern slavery by 2030.[42] Zoe is an historian with a scholarly background in American protest literature, co-author of *Picturing Frederick Douglass* and a series of books and articles on historical and modern slavery,[43] an anti-slavery policy expert and is now Professor of Modern Slavery and Human Trafficking in the School of Politics and International Relations at the University of Nottingham. As director of the Rights Lab, she leads its work across five main research areas[44] and engages with a large network of anti-slavery stakeholders around the world.

We spoke to Zoe shortly after 'Anti-Slavery Day',[45] to understand more about the current work of the Rights Lab and its plans for the future in conducting research to end modern slavery by 2030. Zoe starts with the latest estimate of 40.3 million enslaved people produced by the ILO, the Walk Free Foundation and the IOM. She argues that in absolute terms, the problem affects the largest number of people in the history of the world, but as a proportion of global population, it is both tractable and relatively small. She is quick to point out that the phenomenon is not isolated to developing countries and that while it varies in prevalence, there is not one country in the world without cases of modern slavery. For many years, it was commonly claimed that 'the only slavery-free country is Iceland', but Zoe assures as that this is simply not true. In the UK, she argues, the original estimate in 2014 of

---

42 Z. Trodd, "Blueprint for Freedom: Ending Modern Slavery by 2030," The Rights Track, November 9, 2017. http://rightstrack.org/blueprint-for-freedom-ending-modern-slavery-by -2030.

43 J. Stauffer, Z. Trodd, and C.M. Bernier, *Picturing Frederick Douglass: An Illustrated Biography of the Nineteenth Century's Most Photographed American* (New York: W.W. Norton and Company, 2015).

44 The five research programmes are (1) data and measurement, (2) communities and society, (3) ecosystems and the environment, (4) law and policy and (5) business and economies.

45 Anti-Slavery Day takes place annually on 18 October and was established through the Anti-Slavery Day Act 2010, a private members bill passed in the UK to raise awareness of the problem of modern slavery. https://www.legislation.gov.uk/ukpga/2010/14/pdfs/ukpga_20100014_en .pdf.

between 10,000 and 13,000 slaves is very likely a conservative one given what we now know about the problem.

For her, the past 20 years of mobilisation against slavery represent 'the fourth great wave of abolition'[46] and that having an explicit SDG dedicated to the problem is a real sign of success of the movement to get this issue on the global agenda. As one of the key architects of the Bellagio-Harvard Guidelines on the Legal Parameters of Slavery, Zoe adopts a conservative definition of slavery that draws on the legal content of the 1926 Slavery Convention, which emphasises the 'condition with powers attaching to ownership'. As an historian, she recognises that this idea of ownership in the strictest sense no longer exists, but she is keen to point out that modern slaves are still defined with the notion of 'the rights of possession', where people are treated 'as if' they are property. This means that today there remain a large number of people in the world who are bought, sold and traded. These people are 'paid nothing, cannot walk away, who have lost freedom of movement, free choice [...] whose labour power is being stolen'. While her work focuses on these extreme forms of exploitation, she argues that 'abusive labour' of any kind represents a significant 'pathway into slavery'.

The work of the Rights Lab thus operates within this bounded definition of modern slavery and comprises over 100 academic researchers whose work is engaged in 'harnessing, borrowing, and fusing together' many of the theories, methods and tools that come from a broad range of different academic disciplines. These different approaches range from 'slavery from space', which engages in the systematic analysis of satellite images of sites of slavery (see Chapter 4 in this book) to local-based research on building 'slavery-free communities'. This broad arc of work from the local to the transglobal includes topics such as 'armed conflict, mental health, migration, survivor narratives, economic struggles, the value of the economic dividend to ending slavery, supply chains, and monitoring and evaluation'. Through all of this work, her teams are committed to 'rigorous measurement' and 'research-led interventions' to help address the problem. She sees this approach as moving beyond short-term measures, such as 'rescue and prosecution' to create an 'integrated programme' of research that focuses on the root causes and the variety of interventions that 'work' to combat the problem. This integrated programme for Zoe is the 'Freedom Blueprint', which she hopes will be an endorsed and internationally recognised document that 'sets out the results' of the Rights Lab work with a strong degree of 'transferability' since the terrain of modern

---

46 The four waves include (1) eighteenth-century England, (2) nineteenth-century United States, (3) twentieth-century Congo and (4) twenty-first century for the whole world.

slavery varies considerably around the world. The Freedom Blueprint, needs to be 'global' in its approach, is a basic 'set of techniques and tools' that 'have room to be modified' to fit particular country contexts. Founded in June 2017, the Rights Lab has become the 'go to' place for research on modern slavery and its nearing its goal to produce the Freedom Blueprint.

Giving Voice and Bearing Witness

Across the many guests featured in this chapter, we have seen a set of common themes running through our conversations. David and John both see a strong degree of continuity between the slavery of the past and the slavery of the present. The denial of agency and denial of voice are mainstay features of slavery that continue to this day, where the current 'fourth wave' of abolitionism, like abolitionism of the past, strives to give voice to victims and survivors with a view to regaining agency for all. Agency and free will sit at the heart of conceptions of freedom as revealed through Juliana's work with survivors, service providers and law enforcement officials. The legal developments and efforts of a multitude of international institutions provide significant frameworks and multiple levels of governance through which to address the problem and realise freedom; however, Katarina, Laura and James all agree that given the complexity, partial development and coordination problems, much work remains to be done. Zoe's approach is to focus on building a research platform that uses the latest tools and methods from a variety of disciplines to understand the nature and extent of the problem, the drivers of modern slavery, the reasons for its persistence and the ways in which the evidence she and her team collect helps inform effective interventions. In this way, leading this research platform is a form of what John calls 'bearing witness', and as an historian working on a contemporary problem, she values the human element in all of her work, especially the voices of victims and survivors. In thinking about the Freedom Blueprint, she says, 'my hope is that we never build and enact an intervention without working with survivors first'. This focus on survivors echoes the lessons from Frederick Douglass, himself a survivor, who said that abolitionists had developed '[t]he tools to those who can use them' and '[l]et every man work for the abolition of slavery in his own way. I would help all and hinder none'.[47]

---

47   F. Douglass, *Life and Times of Frederick Douglass* (Boston: De Wolfe, Fiske and Co, 1892), 381.

Chapter 9

PERPETRATORS AND SURVIVORS

Abstract

This chapter delves into the lives of slavery perpetrators and slavery survivors. It starts with a 'socially embedded slavery model' we developed to illustrate the complex set of factors that affect the fundamental relationship between perpetrators and victim-survivors, and helps situate the conversations we had with our guests. We discussed slaveholders in India with Austin Choi-Fitzpatrick (Rights Lab and San Diego University); Andrea Nicholson (Rights Lab), who has developed qualitative methods for interviewing survivors of slavery; and Minh Dang (Rights Lab and Survivor Alliance), a survivor-scholar who works to empower survivors and to rebuild their lives. These conversations further deepen our understanding of freedom, voice, loss, trauma and recovery.

'How does it feel to be in that moment when you realise that the thing you are doing is no longer acceptable?'

– Austin Choi-Fitzpatrick, Rights Lab and San Diego University

'Just listen to the people who have been through this.'

– Andrea Nicholson, Rights Lab, University of Nottingham

'Freedom isn't just the absence of slavery.'

– Minh Dang, Survivor Alliance and Rights Lab, University of Nottingham

Lives Lived Hard

Aanan is a *Brahmin*[1] in India who runs a quarry that extracts large boulders, the gravel from which are then crushed to make silica for the sole supply

---

1 A Brahmin is a member of the highest caste in India.

of raw materials to the multinational firm Tata. The mines for these supplies are open and involve long days of manual labour, where the workers are provided subsistence food and clothing, but are kept in small groups, and controlled so as not to involve themselves in unionisation efforts or engage in revolt or insurrection against Aanan and his firm. Avoiding disruption to the production process is paramount, while the overall operation illustrates the many contradictions between 'culture and capital', 'relationship and extraction' and 'care and exploitation'.[2] Tung is a young man from Vietnam who, at the age of 15, was brought to the UK through Russia and then a migrant camp in France. He was drawn to the promise of reuniting with his father who, unknown to Tung, was heavily indebted. Once in the UK, Tung worked 19-hour days in a Chinese takeaway without breaks, pay or a proper form of accommodation. In the subsequent six years, he was trafficked within the UK and found himself forced to work in a cannabis farm,[3] followed by being forced into sexual slavery and ultimately suffering genital mutilation before being liberated and receiving support.[4]

These accounts are exemplars of perpetrators and survivors of modern slavery in the world today, and they illustrate the many complexities associated with the individuals caught up in this set of practices. Our previous chapter showed that slavery has persisted as a practice for millennia with many different continuities and discontinuities over time and an evolution in attempts to prohibit it formally through domestic and international law, as well as through different institutions at the domestic and international level. Our conversations with slavery scholars and activists about slavery past and present focused on key questions surrounding conceptions of freedom, voice and bearing witness. Absent from our conversations, however, was a deeper

---

2   Aanan is one of the 40 perpetrators that Austin interviewed as part of his field research. See A. Choi-Fitzpatrick, *What Slaveholders Think: How Contemporary Slaveholders Rationalize What They Do* (New York: Columbia University Press, 2017), 1–2.

3   In the UK, cannabis farms are typically established in rented properties, where the rooms are converted into hydroponic growing cells and involve 'minders' who are forced to harvest the cannabis and package it for onward distribution. In the tiny hamlet of East End in East Bergholt, Suffolk, Landman lived across the street from one such farm established in an idyllic five-bedroom house typical of the English countryside. New tenants arrived late at night with a truck, proceeded to lower the blinds in the windows and for a period of months produced cannabis. Police infrared cameras found an unusually large heat signal from the property, and subsequently raided it early on an August morning in 2011. The perpetrators higher up the operations supply chain were not found, while the inhabitants of the house were arrested.

4   Tung was interviewed in 2017 in the UK. See A. Nicholson, M. Dang, and Z. Trodd, "A Full Freedom: Contemporary Survivors' Definition of Slavery," *Human Rights Law Review* 18 (2018): 701.

understanding of how the practice of slavery is located in contemporary society, the relationship between perpetrators of slavery (slaveholders) and victims of slavery of the kind captured by the brief individual accounts above. Also absent has been a more thorough consideration of how the voices of survivors of modern slavery play a crucial role in combatting it and help create programmes of support for life after slavery. In order to understand more deeply the complex world of perpetrators and survivors, this chapter first presents our own 'embedded slavery model' to illustrate the array of factors in which the relationships between perpetrators and survivors are located at different levels. This model draws on extant modern slavery and other social science research, and sets the scene for our conversations with several Rights Track guests who have carried out research on perpetrators and worked with survivors.

Our conversation with Austin Choi-Fitzpatrick from the Rights Lab, the Carr Centre at Harvard University and the Joan B. Kroc School of Peace Studies at San Diego University features his work on perpetrators, which has included field research and in-depth interviews with slaveholders in India.[5] His work challenges popular and simplistic understandings of slavery as a simple crime and explores the complex social and cultural contexts in which slavery is a de facto and accepted form of practice. We explore these insights from India further through our conversation with Andrea Nicholson and Minh Dang from the Rights Lab. Andrea is a lawyer and political scientist who uses 'cognitive interviewing' with survivors of slavery to produce rich analysis of modern slavery narratives.[6] Minh is a survivor-scholar who completed her doctoral work on survivor well-being through 'constructivist grounded theory' and in-depth interviews with survivors in the UK. She is also founder of the NGO Survivor Alliance, which since 2018 has developed its strategic priorities, grown its membership and supported survivors around the world through a variety of events and resources.

---

5   A. Choi-Fitzpatrick, *What Slaveholders Think: How Contemporary Perpetrators Rationalize What They Do* (New York: Columbia University Press, 2017).
6   Z. Trodd and A. Nicholson, "Integrated and Indivisible: The Sustainable Development Agenda of Modern Slavery Survivor Narratives," in *Fighting Modern Slavery and Human Trafficking: History and Contemporary Policy*, ed. G. LeBaron, J. Pilley, and D. Blight (Cambridge University Press, 2021); K. Schwarz and A. Nicholson, "Collapsing the Boundaries between De Jure and De Facto Slavery: The Foundations of Slavery beyond the Transatlantic Frame," *Human Rights Review* 21 (2020): 391–414; A. Nicholson, M. Dang, and Z. Trodd, "A Full Freedom: Contemporary Survivors' Definitions of Slavery," *Human Rights Law Review* 18, no. 4 (2018): 689–704.

Socially Embedded Slavery

In order to situate our conversations about perpetrators and survivors, we developed a 'socially embedded slavery'[7] model, which conceives the practice of slavery operating in layers of complex factors at five different levels: (1) individual, (2) household and family, (3) community, (4) national and structural and (5) international (see Figure 9.1). At the individual level in the centre of the figure, slavery is fundamentally a 'dyadic' relationship between a *perpetrator* (actor *A*) and a *victim-survivor* (actor *B*).[8] The relationship between *A* and *B* is *unequal* and laden with *power*. In this simple formal representation of power, actor *A* gets actor *B* to do something that actor *B* would not normally do without the presence of actor *A*.[9] Our daily lives are full of examples of these kinds of power relations, where we are only ever able to exercise our *relative freedom* vis-à-vis other actors with whom we have relationships. In contrast to much theorising about individuals, choice and volition popular in economic and political analysis, however, slavery involves the *intentional denial of agency*, where the source of power as John Stauffer reminds us is fear, violence and coercion, and where normal power relations reach a 'threshold of slavery' owing to their extreme nature of exploitation.[10] As we have seen in the previous chapter, victims of slavery are not free to choose their conditions of labour, work or other forms of exploitation, nor are they free to leave these

---

7 This idea of 'socially embedded' originates from political scientist Mark Lichbach, for whom 'the socially embedded unit act' constitutes any individual-level decision making as a function of some autonomy and responsibility, purpose and free will, and reason and actions. These elements of agency relate to their desires (i.e. goals, purposes and ends), beliefs (i.e. information and knowledge) and choices (i.e. act, do and perform) (Ibid., 261). At a collective level, individuals are part of different social orders, where desires produce a larger set of norms, beliefs reflect material conditions and individual choices aggregate into and respond to collective action (Ibid., 262). See M. Lichbach, "Social Theory and Comparative Politics," in *Comparative Politics: Rationality, Culture, and Structure*, ed. M. Lichbach and A. Zuckerman (Cambridge: Cambridge University Press, 1997), 239–276. See also J.S. Coleman, *Foundations of Social Theory* (Cambridge, MA: Belknap Press of Harvard University Press, 1990); C. Sartorio, *Causation and Free Will* (Oxford: Oxford University Press, 2016).
8 While we concede that individuals are 'victims' of slavery and upon their release from their enslavement are considered 'survivors'. We are additionally persuaded by the evidence on survivors that their condition of 'freedom' is not fully achieved at time of release (see the section of Chapter 8 on Juliana Semione's research), and as we learn from Minh Dang, both 'freedom' and 'well-being' are not a status, but rather a process that is highly relational and volatile. Hence, we use the couplet 'victim-survivor' throughout this book.
9 This is a well-established concept of power from political science. See R. Dahl, "The Concept of Power," *Behavioural Science* 2, no. 3 (1957): 201–215.
10 See T. Landman, "Out of the Shadows: Transdisciplinary Research on Modern Slavery," *Peace Human Rights Governance* (2018): 1–15.

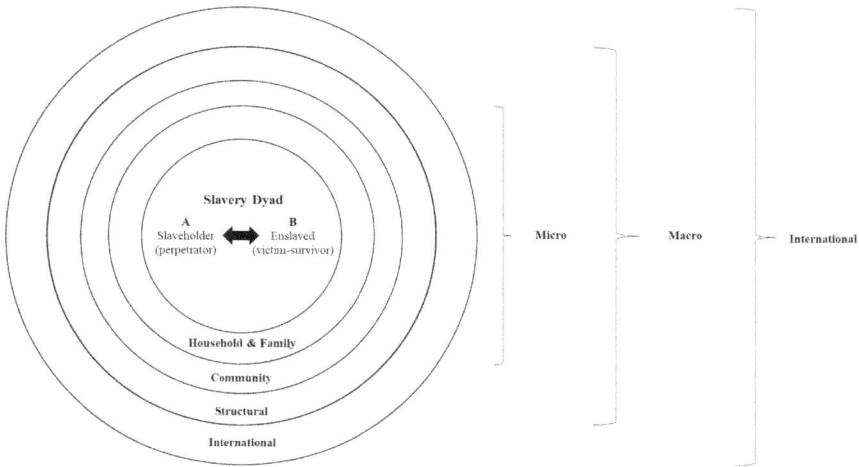

Figure 9.1 Socially embedded slavery: micro, macro and international factors. *Source:* Compiled by the authors and adopted from International Office for Migration (2019) *IOM Handbook on Protection and Assistance to Migrants Vulnerable to Violence, Exploitation and Abuse.* Geneva: International Office for Migration, available at: https://socialprotec-tion.org/discover/publications/iom-handbook-protection-and-assistance-migrants-vulnerable-violence.

conditions without significant or severe repercussions, often involving violence or other sanctions.[11] This absence of choice and control over decisions aligns with what Juliana Semione found among her respondents concerning an individual's 'freedom to' do things and 'freedom from' undue coercion and restraint (see Chapter 7).

These individual-level relationships are often set within the context of the family and household, as well as larger community relationships, about which we learn much more from our conversation with Austin in this chapter. Grounded anti-slavery work from NGOs shows that this level of our model captures the cultural context in which slavery becomes acceptable and self-reinforcing as a practice. In the case of India, there are inter-generational lineages within families and communities for different forms of 'debt-bondage', where loans made at some time in the past bring with them an obligation for work that passes down from one generation to the next. At the national level, there are further structural factors in the economy, society and polity that contribute to the probability that any one individual may become trapped in

---

11 For a formal articulation of this dyadic relationship, see D. Acemoglu and A. Wolitzky, "The Economics of Labour Coercion," *Econometrica* 79 (2011): 555–600.

a condition of slavery with little by way of legal redress or means of escape. These factors can include caste, class, economic inequality, ethnicity, race and other social attributes, as well as political control and power across different institutions. At the international level, as we shall see in our next chapter, there are additional drivers for slavery that involve the economics of trade and development,[12] as well as a complex interdependency between the drivers for migration and increased vulnerability to slavery (see also Chapter 6 of this book).[13]

For us, slavery is thus embedded in these different relationships at the micro, macro and international levels, with an array of different factors that impinge on the ability for individuals to make free choices over their own destiny in life. Anti-slavery work is beginning to bring analysis together across these different levels, where there are scholars and practitioners working directly with individuals, studying household and community drivers for slavery, and seeking to understand the variation in slavery across different national contexts, as a function of both domestic and international variables. The purpose of this chapter is to reveal what can be learned by focusing on the individual lived experiences of perpetrators and survivors through our conversations with Austin, Andrea and Minh.

Situating Perpetrators

Popular commentary on perpetrators, such as Aanan's case above, particularly in the criminal justice frame[14] that characterises much contemporary work on ending modern slavery, sees them as evil criminals engaged in illegal activity that is in need of investigation, prosecution and punishment (see Chapter 11). As a dominant actor in the dyadic relationship, perpetrators exert power, control and coercion over victim-survivors in ways that exploit

---

12 See T. Landman and B.W. Silverman, "Globalization and Modern Slavery," *Politics and Governance* 7, no. 4 (2019): 275–290; G. LeBaron, *Combatting Modern Slavery: Why Labour Governance Is Failing and What We Can Do about It* (Cambridge: Polity; Centre for Policy Research, 2020); *Developing Freedom: The Sustainable Development Case for Ending Modern Slavery, Forced Labour and Human Trafficking* (New York: United Nations University, 2021). https://www.developingfreedom.org/.

13 See International Office for Migration, *IOM Handbook on Protection and Assistance to Migrants Vulnerable to Violence, Exploitation and Abuse* (Geneva: International Office for Migration, 2019). https://socialprotection.org/discover/publications/iom-handbook-protection-and-assistance-migrants-vulnerable-violence.

14 The modern anti-slavery movement can be broadly divided into four main frames or lenses: (1) criminal justice, (2) human rights, (3) forced labour and (4) sustainable development. Each of these frames is based on different claims about the root causes of the problem and what should be done in a practical sense to address them.

them as commodities and objects in a highly unequal and transactional way. Against this framing, our conversations with Austin[15] revealed a much more complex picture, where slavery is often an accepted and culturally determined practice across communities in India. Austin's motivation for this research rests on the idea that so much of anti-slavery work concentrates on policy, legislation and publicity about victims and survivors, but 'we know less than we should about perpetrators', which for him is the 'broken relationship of slavery'. In this sense, he poses a fundamental question: 'what role do perpetrators have in slavery and emancipation?' He was drawn to the case of India, which has an estimated eighteen million people in some form of bonded labour or other forms of exploitation understood as part of modern slavery,[16] where he discovered that perpetrators are in a 'set of relationships' in which perpetrators 'don't often think of themselves as criminals'. They are 'not hiding from the law', and they are 'violating human rights, but not social norms'.

This tension between locally created and accepted norms and violations of human rights makes his work particularly difficult to undertake as an outsider conducting highly sensitive research. Rather than entering this context as an alien researcher, he approached his work as a 'puzzle about how we enter a space in way that is humble and appreciative of individuals and the experiences of their own lives'. He did not walk up to people and ask direct questions about slavery, but rather opened with questions such as 'What's going on around here?' and 'What's new here?' He did not use the language of 'perpetrator' and started from a position that recognises 'all of us do things that we are not proud of'. His approach was to use what he calls 'a leapfrog method', where if his first encounter did not go well, he would move on quickly to others to ask, 'who else in your community experienced what you did?' In evaluating the answers he would receive, he remained conscious to 'try not to catch them in the lie in way that is obvious, but do a lot of triangulation on the fly to determine which bits add up, and which bits do not add up'. In this evaluation, he needed to decide if his respondents were being 'forthright or not' and he needed to exercise his own judgement in trying to decide if they were telling the truth.

---

15 A. Choi-Fitzpatrick, "Face to Face: Researching the Perpetrators of Slavery," The Rights Track, June 19, 2018. http://rightstrack.org/face-to-face-researching-the-perpetrators-of-modern-slavery.

16 International Labour Organisation and Walk Free, *The Global Slavery Index*, 2018. https://www.globalslaveryindex.org/.

In addition to his strategic use of lateral questioning and leapfrogging across the community, at a personal level he grew his beard out to be longer than usual and engaged in storytelling of his own life to build rapport with his respondents. For Austin, his long beard gave him 'additional spiritual status', while his storytelling focused on inter-generational changes and transformations. He recounted that his grandfather was a farmer in rural Pennsylvania, his father went to university and his own educational journey ultimately led to obtaining his PhD. In this way, he was communicating that things change and that things move on in an effort to relate to the inter-generational changes that had taken place in the communities he was studying. His grounding in a rural background had resonance locally and acted as a significant entry point for him to carry out his research.

Austin's strategies did develop rapport with and empathy for the people with whom he spoke, where he collected interview data from 40 perpetrators, which included 20 perpetrator–victim 'dyads'. His interviews revealed that through the many changes that had taken place over time, perpetrators had a profound 'sense of loss, lost relationships, lost community, with workers in their area that had been seen as family who had been treated with dignity and honour'. The perpetrators felt that they were 'no longer paid respect', which had been 'earned out of relationships'. They acknowledged the 'relational embeddedness', were 'opposed to the language of justice', and instead used the 'language of relational loss'. The survivors with whom he spoke could openly identify perpetrators in the community, while changes that had taken place included women's collectives, stories of abuse, stories of struggle and victory, and growth in a number of self-help groups. He witnessed public acknowledgement that 'exploitation took place in the community', where perpetrators are not 'extracted' from this community, but very much part of it. For him, there was a strong recognition that 'prior to, during, and after exploitation', the members of the community 'have lived together and have to find ways of relating and relating anew'. Given the size of the affected population, Austin argues that some form of restorative and community-based justice is a better way to move forward, as it is simply impossible to 'arrest our way out of the problem'.

For their part, Austin tells us that some perpetrators did express remorse for their actions, and that if they 'have the means to persist, they had a choice to either give up' and 'quit', or in other cases, 'they were able to persist without repercussions', owing to having access to 'status' and 'cash'. Some perpetrators had status, police support, but little accumulated capital, while others had 'positional power' and saw their status as a 'hereditary form of livelihood'. He learned that they engaged in a calculus that analyses the trade-off between political cost and economic gain, where their 'range of opportunities is much larger' than those available to victims and survivors. Overall, it 'takes both of the communities to work toward broadly distributed justice'.

We asked Austin if what he discovered from his work in India could 'travel' to other cultural contexts. He feels that in 'the case of India, exploitation as a cultural practice is *sui generis*', and that in many ways, the case illustrates the phenomenon of 'human rights violations' that are 'not quite human rights violations'. Beyond the particularities of the Indian case, he argues that there remains a significant question: 'How does it feel to be in that moment when you realise that the thing you are doing is no longer acceptable?' This question for Austin applies far beyond his particular work on India and raises questions about the degree to which the universal language of human rights lands effectively in local contexts, and whether the cultural system of paternalism at work within the community led to a set of 'self-deceptive' practices, which in the end have been identified as wrong.[17]

Valuing Survivors

On the other side of the perpetrator–victim dyad, we spoke to Andrea and Minh about their work with survivors.[18] Like Austin, they see great complexity in the lived experiences of survivors that challenges preconceived notions of victims, freedom and the strains of living life as a survivor. We began with Andrea by asking more about definitions of slavery and how these align with survivor understandings of their own definitions. As a lawyer, Andrea is keenly aware of the definitions from the 1926 Slavery Convention, but sees these as more applicable to 'people who are going through a legal case, a prosecution, criminal law, or talk about the offence that has occurred'. Andrea concedes that there are 'elements that correlate with 19th Century chattel slavery', but she is more interested in understanding the 'struggles in survival' and 'unravelling the complexity' of life as a survivor. She argues against the simple binary between 'free and not free' with respect to survivors, who are 'people who emerged from slavery who don't see themselves as victims who are trying to form some agency in freedom, and it is an empowering term'.

---

17   This idea of self-deception and cultural practice with respect to human rights violations has been frequently observed in other contexts, such as among police in Brazil who tortured people, and local communities in Bolivia that engaged in public lynching of criminals as a form of community justice. See M. K. Huggins, *Violence Workers: Police Torturers and Murderers Reconstruct Atrocity* (Berkeley: University of California Press, 2002); D. Goldstein, *The Spectacular City: Violence and Performance in Urban Bolivia* (Chapel Hill: Duke University Press, 2004).

18   A. Nicholson and M. Dang, "Voices of Slavery: Listen and Learn," The Rights Track, February 1, 2018. http://rightstrack.org/voices-of-slavery-listen-and-learn.

Against the sole focus on victimhood and the past, she makes the point that survivors are 'scholars, activists, and leaders', and that we 'need to start viewing these people as those things'.

Minh is one such survivor-scholar, who identifies 'as a survivor of slavery in the United States'. She became active in this area of work because she 'saw that what was being done did not represent my own experience', nor 'what supported me and what support I didn't have'. More fundamentally, and in echoing our conversation with Zoe Trodd in our previous chapter, she observed that 'research and practice, and the people leading that didn't include the voices of survivors'. Her work in the UK asks, 'how do we include survivors in research and in the process when designing interventions', which has significance for slavery research and practical solutions for ending it. This inclusion of survivors is born from her involvement in a 'community-based action-research project in the United States' that has a particular focus on trafficking in San Francisco and represents the 'first survivor-led research project'. The project was hosted by the Anti-Trafficking Task Force, but its research questions and research methods have all been survivor informed. Her work in the UK focuses on 'how do we define well-being to inform metrics to design mental health interventions', where she argues that 'practitioners can leave out the population they're serving in designing interventions'.

In similar fashion, Andrea's work examines what are called 'survivor narratives'[19] comprised of contemporary narratives from 'NGOs, testimonies to the US Congress, autobiographies, and cognitive interviews' that encourage 'free telling' of stories, as well as the use of drawings and images in which 'the expressions, the marks, and the emotions come out much more strongly in a drawing'. This work involves 'deep textual analysis', and the application of 'corpus linguistic' methods to uncover new insights into definitions as well as the linkages between the content of the narratives and the 169 UN SDG targets. For definitions, the idea of 'ownership' does not resonate much, while there has been a tendency to miss 'sexual slavery against men and boys' and a 'bias towards forced labour'. For the SDGs, there is considerable overlap between the narrative content and the different targets, but more importantly, there are many concepts and terms in those targets outside SDG 8.7 on slavery that 'relate to their experiences and the things that made them vulnerable to slavery', including 'climate change, armed conflict, [and] gender bias'.

---

19 For examples on how narrative analysis can be applied to human rights, see T. Landman, "Narrative Analysis and Phronesis," in *Real Social Science: Applied Phronesis*, ed. Bent Flyvbjerg, Todd Landman, and Sanford Schram (Cambridge: Cambridge University Press, 2012), 27–47.

In talking to survivors, Minh observes that there is less mention of slavery per se, and a more frequent discussion of 'poverty, domestic violence, or racism', which act as entry points to a fuller discussion of slavery. Survivors, in her experience, 'don't start by identifying [as slaves] until it is introduced', and it these other issues that frame their initial discussions. Minh is an academic and feels a certain sense of privilege in using more formal terms and language, but this is 'not quite what survivors are interested in'. Once these terms are used, however, she feels that it is 'empowering to have a label' while at the same, using the label 'makes it too real, and then it is painful'. As a survivor, she has experienced this pain, which in turn provides the necessary empathy to do the work that she does.

Andrea agrees that labelling is important, as it leads to the formation of an identity and can thus make survivors feel less isolated. A label lets them know 'what's happened to them' and provides them with 'a community' of people with similar and shared experiences. Her analysis of the narratives reveals complex references to survivors' sense of 'trauma, recovery, perceptions of freedom, perceptions around definitions'. At a deeper level, she has discovered that survivors display a 'lack of futurity' or the 'inability to perceive any future beyond their existence as a slave' and an inability to 'divorce' themselves entirely from their time in slavery. In addition, survivors express a 'lack of privacy', a 'lack of self-purpose', the 'inability to choose for oneself' and a 'lack of care for well-being'.

These feelings and observations are often born of struggling for many years as a survivor. In one case, Andrea interviewed someone who has been a survivor for over twenty years, who is 'still suffering the effects of trauma'. For her, trauma is a 'complex state of being, state of existence' that 'can go one for many years and decades', where other trauma survivors (e.g. from the Holocaust[20] or victims of domestic abuse) 'still don't quite compare'. Both Andrea and Minh agree that the trauma experienced by survivors of slavery is not simply equivalent to 'post-traumatic stress disorder', and that there is a real need to 'acknowledge the radical nature of it'. In addition to this acknowledgement of the radical nature of trauma, Minh also stresses that anti-slavery interventions 'have tended to focus on the moment of freedom',

---

20 One of the most famous accounts of this kind of survival can be found in P. Levi (1947) *Survival in Auschwitz*. Also known as *If This Is a Man*, his book provides a daily account of life in the Nazi death camp, and how he used his expertise as a chemist to work in the camp and avoid the gas chamber. It is telling that despite his survival of this set of experiences, he died in 1987 after a fall from a third-storey apartment, an event that has been assessed as either an accident or a suicide. See P. Levi, *The Complete Works of Primo Levi* (New York: Penguin Classics, 2015).

which in her view is only 'the beginning of a hard road', where 'freedom isn't just the absence of slavery'.

While legally, survivors of slavery are free, emotionally and psychologically, it is very likely that they are not quite free. This is a significant observation that for both Andrea and Minh must inform the ways in which social and political institutions need to create more suitable solutions to help survivors. Andrea argues that there is a need for 'public awareness, education for vulnerable communities, monitoring of employment agencies', the development of a 'platform for survivors to speak' that gives them direct representation, 'tougher state monitoring on anti-slavery spend' and 'reports on countries suppressing anti-slavery efforts'. The attention to survivors, their experiences, their feelings and their inclusion in the study of slavery and the design of interventions and programmes of support are thus crucial, where we need, echoing the words of Bill Simmons, to 'just listen to the people who have been through this'.

Finding Freedom and Exercising Human Rights

It is clear from our conversations with Austin, Andrea and Minh that perpetrators and victim-survivors are in a complex dyadic relationship that is deeply embedded in a wider set of factors at many different levels that impinge on this relationship and which shape our thinking about freedom after slavery. Across all three conversations, it is clear that there are not strict binary or dichotomous categories of 'free' and 'unfree', or 'perpetrator' and 'victim-survivor'. Rather, these concepts and understandings are deeply *relational* and *relative*. In this way, a perpetrator does not exist without a victim-survivor, and a victim-survivor does not exist without a perpetrator. The first to conduct a focused study on a specific set of perpetrators in India, Austin has uncovered the complex ways in which slavery is culturally determined and based less on the transactional nature of the relationship and more on the hereditary expectation for bonded labour and other forms of exploitation. The tensions between 'human rights violations' and 'social norms' provide a deep lesson for anyone working to advance human rights. For their work with and for survivors, Andrea and Minh have revealed the instability of victim-survivor identities, the long-term process of post-traumatic healing and recovery and the need for survivor inclusion in all efforts to analyse the problem and provide solutions to it. In this and the previous chapter, we have now seen how voice, bearing witness and freedom must come from those who have been denied them, and only then can we take the necessary steps to provide support and prevent recurrence.

Chapter 10

BUSINESS, ECONOMICS AND MODERN SLAVERY

Abstract

From the clothes we wear to the products we buy, business operations have become more attuned to the degree to which modern slavery may or may not be present in their supply chains. The chapter draws on our conversations with Genevieve LeBaron (University of Sheffield) and John Gathergood (University of Nottingham) on the business and economics of modern slavery. This is followed by our conversations with Baroness Lola Young of Hornsey (House of Lords and University of Nottingham) who has been leading reform to transparency laws, Alexander Trautrims (Rights Lab) on how having a slavery free supply chain is good for business, Siddharth Kara (Rights Lab) on cobalt mining and technology and Hannah Lerigo-Stephens (Rights Lab) on business and modern slavery. We conclude with our conversation with Elaine Mitchel-Hill (Marshalls plc) and Arianne Griffiths (Rights Lab) on how some businesses are 'walking the supply chain' in their efforts to combat slavery.

'Could we have capitalism without slavery?'

> – Genevieve LeBaron, University of Sheffield

'The drive to make cheaper products at a given quality results in an *unbelievable product.*'

> – John Gathergood, University of Nottingham

'To guarantee that a supply chain is perfectly slavery free is actually almost impossible.'

> – Alex Trautrims, Nottingham University Business School and Rights Lab

'Even a rounding error on their balance sheet would be utterly transformative.'

> – Siddharth Kara, Rights Lab

'We would always want to be able go back to source, back to raw materials, back to holes in the ground.'

> – Elaine Mitchel-Hill, Business and Human Rights Lead, Marshalls plc

Supply, Demand and Production

The next time you use your mobile device, pause and think about its components and from where they may have come. The next time you bag a bargain at a clothing retailer, think about who made the item and under what conditions. The next time you get your car washed, think about how many people are engaged in the process and how little you pay for the service. Our daily lives are replete with products and services that have complex processes of production, long supply chains that in many cases reach around the world and micro-business models that bear further scrutiny in how their pricing mechanisms work and under what conditions their services are being delivered. These and other examples are mainstay features of the modern economy and over the last two decades. Human rights and modern slavery scholars and practitioners have been asking significant questions and collecting increasingly robust evidence on these many complexities of the modern global economy and the role that modern slavery plays in it. From geospatial analysis, EO and artificial intelligence approaches to in-depth interviews with survivors of slavery, we are learning more and more about the drivers for slavery, conditions of slavery and the many economic and business factors that need to be addressed in order to end it.

The modern economy is comprised of a multitude of firms that vary in size from micro-enterprises to multinational corporations whose annual turnover is larger than that of many countries in the world. For example, latest estimates show that the annual turnover for multinational corporations is USD 11.48 trillion (13.72 per cent) while the total turnover of countries is USD 72.17 trillion (86.28 per cent). In comparative terms, the top economic performers in the world are the United States, China, Japan, Germany, France, the UK and India, followed by Apple and Saudi Aramco.[1] The subsequent list of top performers includes Amazon (12th), Microsoft (14th), Alphabet (19th), Alibaba (23rd), Facebook (24th) and Tencent (25th), followed by Switzerland, Saudi Arabia, Turkey, Taiwan, Iran, Poland, Sweden, Thailand and Belgium. In a recent report published by the Council of Foreign Relations, human trafficking alone accounts for an estimated USD 150 billion annually for

---

1   The last few decades have seen the rise of 'tech giants' like Apple and Microsoft, whose annual turnover figures have eclipsed those of more traditionally understood multinational corporations, such as Shell, Exxon and Unilever. For country annual turnover statistics, see statistics times.com/economy/projected-world-gdp-ranking.php. For company annual turnover, see https://www.gfmag.com/global-data/economic-data/largest-companies.

perpetrators,[2] while there are many more billions leveraged from activities that have other elements of modern slavery somewhere within the production and service delivery process. The estimated total number of enslaved people in the world is equivalent to the population of California and its overall economic size makes it a big business on its own, but the dispersion of this group of people around the world and its hidden nature mean much of this practice remains obscured within larger economic structures and business processes.

Our conversations in this chapter reveal some of these hidden elements to the modern economy, how they are uncovered and the ways in which they can be prevented from continuing. Before delving into the many sector-specific insights offered by our guests, we locate our conversations in a brief overview of economic development, capitalism and the global economy provided by our guests Genevieve LeBaron and John Gathergood.[3] Genevieve is Professor of Politics at the University of Sheffield and works on forced labour and labour standards in the global economy. John is Professor of Economics at the University of Nottingham and works on consumer behaviour in financial markets. Together, they discuss with us the history of capitalism, its main features and its main contradictions in understanding the role that enslaved people play in the modern global economy today.

John opened our discussion on the business and economics of slavery with a general summary of the historical process of capitalist development and economic growth, which for him is the 'bringing together of production, be that land and resources, and human labour to increase goods and services that are produced in the economy over time'. Whether involving small agricultural and agrarian activity or large corporations, this 'bringing together' of production has varied over time and increasingly involved 'new and more efficient mechanisms to produce goods and services' and 'training workers to have greater and more diverse skills to use technology in more efficient ways', which when combined, has seen 'persistent economic growth'. While aggregate growth has increased persistently, John asks whether such growth is 'equally beneficial to all' and 'who wins, and who loses' from these processes. He argues that throughout these processes, there have been many disenfranchised people, various gaps in skills, 'imbalances and unevenness' and within these, 'abuse of workers and others'.

2 J. Biglio and R.B. Vogelstein, *Ending Human Trafficking in the 21st Century* (New York: Council of Foreign Relations, 2021). https://cdn.cfr.org/sites/default/files/report_pdf/ending-human-trafficking-in-the-twenty-first-century_3.pdf.
3 G. LeBaron and J. Gathergood, "The Business of Modern Slavery: What Connects SDG 8.7 with Its Overarching SDG8?" The Rights Track, August 11, 2020. http://rightstrack.org/the-business-of-modern-slavery-what-connects-sdg-87-with-its-overarching-sdg8.

While these initial reflections focused on domestic processes, the various waves of trade and globalisation have been based on the 'fundamental tenets of capitalism: specialisation and comparative advantage'. One country may specialise in the production of food, and another may specialise in the production of clothes, where trade between two such countries raises overall levels of production and growth for both countries. For John, 'big waves' of globalisation have seen the 'movement of people, goods, and services' and increasingly, 'the movement of capital'. Accompanying trade and globalisation has been a rising complexity of operations, with long supply chains that are 'cross-country' and where firms have become 'complex entities'. While these developments have been 'good for growth', for modern firms, this means that the 'supply chain is very difficult to track'. John emphasises that 'fragmentation of production, and [that there are] elements of a supply chain that might appear to be cheap and quick and accessible, but only because they are using less legitimate or potentially forced forms of labour'.

In taking a slightly different perspective, Genevieve argues that 'mainstream narratives' about the success of capitalism tend to 'overlook that some business models are fundamentally rooted in mass production, retail economy, premised upon fast turnover, cheap disposable goods'. The supply chains that are part of these models are 'hard wired to produce these inequalities and especially to produce labour exploitation [...] in terms of the structural ways they are set up'. She argues further that one of the secrets of capitalism lurking behind its 'narrative around individual liberties, freedom, freedom in the labour market, freedom of exchange, freedom to participate in the economy as one might wish [...] is that it has relied very heavily on slavery and other forms of forced labour since its origins a few hundred years ago'. For her, there is a long and problematic historical relationship between capitalism and slavery, such that 'supply chains since the origin of capitalism have often been about locating and exploiting people who for various reasons don't have full rights in the economy'. Her observations apply to modern and historical forms of capitalism, which she sees as a 'long-standing problem', where benefits accrue to some, but the system is 'hard-wired to produce adverse and unequal outcomes to the most vulnerable people on the planet'.

Her assertions are based on in-depth research across many different parts of the world on retail, tea and cocoa, and the garment industry. Across these different sectors and geographies, she finds that 'forced labour is not surprising' and certainly not the case of a 'few bad apples', but rather she sees 'patterns both in terms of why some businesses have demand for forced labour, [and] why supply chains are set up to facilitate the unfair treatment of workers and exploitation of workers'. The prevalence and persistence of these patterns leads her to ask 'Could we have capitalism without slavery?'

since in 'reality [...] it is very difficult to identify any moment in the history of global capitalism where there hasn't been a reliance on some form of forced labour or slavery'. As in our conversations concerning slavery past and present (Chapter 8), Genevieve agrees that this persistence of forced labour and slavery has involved different types of people and different geographies over time, while she believes solutions to the problem 'can't just be focussed on tinkering around the edges of supply chains'.

John agrees that a 'persistent facet' of capitalism involves the 'anonymity of the transactions that occur' where there is a 'lack of accountability through the production process'. For him, one of the main virtues of capitalism – the fragmented, specialised and competitive market of suppliers – is also one of its main vices. Firms have tremendous choice in how they source their raw materials necessary for production, where the economic and financial incentives drive firms to look for 'good, cheap and efficient' sources for their supplies. While this certainly can lead to economic efficiency, it remains highly problematic, since it 'encourages exploitation further down the supply chain' and allows firms to 'wash their hands' of any problems in the conditions of supply. For John, the 'feature of the current organisation of production [...] strongly encourages firms that work and exist in contexts with strong institutions to source from countries and contexts with weak institutions' where the 'prevalence of *effective* slavery or unfree labour induced by the activities of producers in those nations may be far higher'. He likens this activity to other types of 'negative externalities'[4] of firm activity (such as pollution) and argues that 'individuals should be responsible for the full cost of their production or consumption'. In this way, the use of forced labour is an 'unfair cost' of production for which firms should bear responsibility. In the absence of exercising this responsibility, some form of state intervention in terms of regulation and sanction is needed, but John argues that this 'fundamentally challenges the organisation of production'.

Genevieve's research over the years has been focusing precisely on the kinds of private and public mechanisms for accountability and constraint that are in place and those that should be in place to combat forced labour and modern slavery. Private mechanisms include the general commitment to 'corporate social responsibility' (CSR), 'social auditing' and 'ethical certification', which she argues remain voluntary in nature, where firms 'set

---

4 A negative externality is a cost suffered by a third party as a consequence of an economic transaction. Pollution is a common example, where a firm may process raw materials to make a finished product, but dispose of the unwanted materials that result from that process in a way that pollutes water supplies (e.g. mercury from gold production) or other parts of the environment.

their own standards'. Public mechanisms include regulations on immigration, subcontracting, business compliance and the international architecture comprised of interstate agreements and treaties. She believes that there is still an over-reliance on voluntary codes of conduct, where states are 'unwilling to perform their regulatory' duties and company adherence to their own principles represents 'pretty bad news for the effectiveness of CSR'. For example, her own research on tea and cocoa production found no evidence for a difference in labour rights between those firms with ethical certification schemes and those without.[5] Beyond these specific sectors, Genevieve argues that current deep economic structures in the global economy mean that 'political economic conditions allow for wildly unequal value distribution along supply chains'. She sees high levels of 'wealth and profit at the top of the supply chain' and 'insufficient margins at the bottom', leading her to assert further that 'governments have been the architects of globalisation'.

In order to ground these arguments in concrete cases, our conversation turned to the city of Leicester in the UK, where its garment industry has been heavily criticised for its use of forced labour. In line with the opening questions of this chapter, John says that there are key markers in Leicester that should raise concerns, such as an 'untoward production price' that simply cannot reflect the 'national living wage' for workers with prices that are 'unbelievably cheap'. The £3 top sold in retail outlets that is virtually 'disposable' is evidence that the 'drive to make cheaper products at a given quality results in an *unbelievable product*'. Genevieve agrees with John and says that it is an 'open secret in the garment industry that sourcing takes place very often below the cost of production'. She sees this as a 'sector wide problem' with frequent reports of 'labour exploitation, gender-based violence, lack of severance pay, problems with unionisation' and the exercise of labour rights. She notes that the mainstream media, such as the *Financial Times*, has acknowledged these problems for years and that 'what industry has said what it would to do to fix it have simply not come to fruition'. Against the public commitments to pay the living wage, firms have 'done largely nothing'. For her, the prevailing business model has 'systemic risk', where the 'costs of production are not being covered', but also where no one will disrupt the business model.

---

5 G. LeBaron, *The Global Business of Forced Labour* (Sheffield Political Economy Research Institute (SPERI), University of Sheffield, 2018). http://globalbusinessofforcedlabour.ac.uk/wp-content/uploads/2018/05/Report-of-Findings-Global-Business-of-Forced-Labour.pdf.

Business Models and Modern Slavery

These insights and observations from John and Genevieve align with our conversation with Alex Trautrims,[6] which shows that more needs to be discovered about business models, business operations and the relatively weak frameworks for international and corporate governance with respect to supply chains and the use of labour. Alex is Associate Professor in the Nottingham University Business School and Associate Director of the Business and Economy Programme in the Rights Lab. He works on transparency in supply chains and has been seconded to the OSCE in Vienna to address how to implement due diligence and strengthen governance, particularly in the area of procurement.

For Alex, the issue of supply chains hinges on the processes of sourcing and procurement, where there is great variation and complexity across different kinds of business models across different sectors. He cites steel production as a relatively straightforward process and business model, while the production of an iPhone is hugely complex, involving an 'ecosystem of actors' around the world that influence business practices. Geographically, he says that some countries (e.g. North Korea) are relatively closed and engaged in production processes where supply chains are relatively confined nationally, while in 'an advanced economy, that's very hard to imagine' where it would 'take a lot of effort to avoid global sourcing'. Alex sees that one of the main drivers for the potential for forced labour and modern slavery in supply chains is cost, but even here, there is great variation depending on the product and the availability of supply. In global supply chains, the 'only thing that matters is the price' such that 'if a high proportion of your cost is labour cost, then the only way to win a contract against your competitor is cheaper labour' and that's when 'people start cutting corners'. He cites Brazil as having a particularly strong legal framework on forced labour and modern slavery that makes business responsible in the supply chain, while the UK has a relatively weak regime that has seen an increase in the use of 'outsourcing' to suppliers that 'pay their people worse, treat them worse', particularly in public sector outsourcing. There is thus a matrix of many different business models and varying complexities in their associated supply chains. Some have short and visible supply chains. Others have long and less visible supply chains. The variation across these different models and supply chains affects the degree to which they may have problems with forced labour and modern slavery.

---

6 A. Trautrims, "Unchained Supply: Eradicating Slavery from the Supply Chain," The Rights Track, January 8, 2018. http://rightstrack.org/unchained-supply-eradicating-modern-slavery -from-the-supply-chain.

In addition to the 'race to the bottom' for cheap labour, there is the additional problem that 'labour is a replaceable commodity' particularly in those areas of production that use 'low-skilled manual labour'. This group of workers, for Alex, represents 'the most vulnerable part of the supply chain' since it has 'no bargaining power'. The practice of forced labour and modern slavery is thus common in supply chains, where extreme forms of coercion are clear cut and easy to detect while less extreme forms remain difficult to detect for law enforcement officials. Details about someone who is not allowed to leave their place of work, who have had their freedom taken away and who have their travel documents taken away from them are 'more obvious'. The persistence of the less obvious forms of abuse and the absence of a law enforcement response for Alex manifest itself in the 'unethical normalisation of people being treated badly'.

Alex and his research team focused some of their work on a very localised issue involving 'hand car washes', which are typically located in sectioned off pieces of car parking areas across large supermarket chains, or facilities established through the adaptation of disused gas stations on the periphery of towns and cities, which are quite prevalent in the UK. Alex's first observation concerning these facilities is that there is 'no business model that would allow them to pay these workers a minimum wage'. The fact that six people can wash a car by hand in less than thirty minutes for £6 or £7 means that unfair working conditions are 'clearly observable'. To get around local regulations, the workers at these facilities are often registered as 'self-employed', where Alex says some use of coercion is evident. He and his team observed one facility, used a stopwatch to record the duration of each wash, looked at the price list for services and counted the passing cars to estimate the proportion of cars that used the facility, controlling for weather as this has an impact on the demand for car washing. His work has led to media interest,[7] more formal modelling of the business model with 'agent-based' computer simulations and the development of a car wash app[8] to record signs and markers of untoward practices, but in the end, he feels that while 'citizens are worried, there are no other car washes left', and thus they continue to use them. In other cases, 'most consumers are wilfully ignorant', and there is less of a comparison to the 'free range' food movement, since there are additional health benefits to consuming organic food that are simply not apparent in the car

---

7 See, for example, A. Strangwayes-Booth, "Safe Car Wash App Reveals Hundreds of Potential Slavery Cases," *BBC News*, April 7, 2019. https://www.bbc.co.uk/news/uk-england-47829016.
8 For more on the 'Safe Car Wash App,' see https://theclewerinitiative.org/campaigns/safe-car-wash.

wash sector. In the UK, the Gangmasters and Labour Abuse Authority and
the Independent Anti-Slavery Commissioner (IASC) have used Alex's work
to raise awareness of the problem, while the app that he helped develop with
the Clewer Initiative (see Chapter 5 in this book) has led to 'citizen-science'
reporting of suspicious conditions at car washes that have helped law enforcement agencies.

Beyond this specific example, Alex is encouraged by the 2015 UK Modern
Slavery Act, which requires that all firms with a turnover of over £36 million
registered in the UK must file a Modern Slavery Statement setting out how
they will prevent modern slavery in their supply chains. Alex asks, 'Could
this company have reasonably known that this is going on?' and 'Do they
have the right systems in place?' This relatively new piece of legislation challenges 'supply chain practitioners to learn about their own supply chains' and
'encourages good supply chain practice'. Any attempt to monitor and address
the problem, however, becomes a function of the sector of the business and
the complexity of its supply chain, which for Alex means that 'to guarantee
that a supply chain is perfectly slavery-free, is actually almost impossible'.
Where companies have come together, Alex believes that they have collective
buying power to change things, but often times, because of the fragmented
and distant nature of supply chains, as well as the 'anonymity' that John has
also pointed out, there remains considerable risk around the world. Suppliers
working across many sectors can choose among buyers in ways that avoid
monitoring and scrutiny, and much work in this area remains.

Fast Fashion

Baroness Lola Young[9] is an independent cross-bench peer in the House
of Lords, Honorary Professor in the Rights Lab and Chancellor of the
University of Nottingham. Lola was one of the main architects of the UK
Modern Slavery Act, and as Chair of the All-Party Parliamentary Group on
Ethics and Sustainability in Fashion, she has been working on transparency
in supply chains in the fashion industry and in sports. Her initial interests
were focused on the creative arts, such as theatre, film and the media, but
when she joined the House of Lords, she was asked to focus on one key issue
to pursue, and someone mentioned 'ethical fashion' as a starting point. She
began talking with 'a lot of people in the industry' who wanted her to 'do
something in Parliament' and to make 'politicians sit up and take notice'. It

9 L. Young, "Fast Fashion and Football: A Question of Ethics," The Rights Track, June 29,
2019. http://rightstrack.org/fast-fashion-and-football-the-ethics/.

was not until the 2013 Rana Plaza disaster in Bangladesh that the issue began to make inroads into the minds of the public and in the minds of politicians. The disaster itself was one of a building collapse, but it raised larger questions about the conditions of work in the garment industry.[10] The problems at Rana were not immediately 'labelled as modern slavery', but there were 'features of production' that were related to 'demand for fast throwaway fashion'. She argues that like other ethical consumer issues, fashion involves 'people [...] always making choices regardless of how much money they've got' and the question of 'How do you spend as wisely as possible?'

'Fast fashion' for Lola is driven by an increasing cycle of demand that has moved beyond mere seasonality, to include the rise and fall of a certain look and the somewhat contradictory observation that people 'want to be like everyone else, but don't want to be like everyone else'. Lola is quick to observe that 'we live our identities through what we wear'. This mindset has led to increased demand, quick trends and a system of 'just in time delivery', where it is not uncommon among online retailers for a garment to arrive at a company, a photo to be taken quickly and the item to appear on a website within a very short period of time. Lola says that there are now 'week on week changes' in demand and a real drive for cheap and disposable clothing. She recalls a woman on a bus with large bags of clothes who explained to her that 'she didn't bother about trying on the clothes, since if they did not fit, she would simply throw them away'. The secular decrease in prices, reflecting problematic production processes, makes these clothes both highly afford-able and disposable at the same time, while the continuous demand for these clothes leads firms to subcontract and outsource to a wide range of suppliers to meet this demand quickly. For Lola, 'this is so habitual, people don't know how to get out of this cycle, this loop'. Moreover, she notes that the same fac-tories that make fast fashion also make garments for high-end brands. While the raw materials for these brands (e.g. for an £80 t-shirt) may be superior to those used for a £3 t-shirt, the same production process using the same workers sits at the heart of the supply chain, which raises questions around responsibility and accountability across suppliers, buyers and retailers.

Lola sees herself as having an important role as a member of the House of Lords in advancing concerns around forced labour and modern slavery. For her, the House of Lords has great 'convening power' to assemble delega-tions of companies to come together to provide evidence, to 'build up rap-port with them' and to 'work with them to improve and change'. Her role

---

10 For more on the Rana Plaza disaster in Bangladesh, see https://www.ilo.org/global/topics/geip/WCMS_614394/lang--en/index.htm.

gives her 'access to people with power and influence' and her work on cross-party groups has been 'almost as effective as the select committees'. With the 2015 Modern Slavery Act now in place, she uses her position in the Lords to make progress on this issue in the fashion industry and has turned her attention to the business of sport. As a football fan, she has noted that across many of the business fora she has attended, there is a noticeable absence of Premier League football clubs, even though their annual turnover is huge. She says that their initial modern slavery statements were 'pitiful' but she has seen some improvements more recently. She is also interested in looking at 'trafficking in and through football'. Beyond the players and events, she is also concerned with the production of football-related merchandise, which has its own complex 'hyper-distributed supply chain', as well as the construction of large stadia for global sporting events and the recruitment of international players.

Cobalt, Technology and Business

Siddharth Kara[11] is a British Academy Global Professor in the School of Sociology and Social Policy at the University of Nottingham and Associate Professor in the Rights Lab. He has spent many years conducting field research on human trafficking, sex trafficking and modern slavery in South Asia and Africa, as well as teaching at the Carr Center for Human Rights at Harvard University. His most recent work focuses on cobalt extraction in the Congo, where he has combined his site visits and interviews with geolocation data on cobalt mines.[12] Our conversation[13] focused on this recent work in order to understand the importance of cobalt in global supply chains and the conditions under which companies extract this resource, which is in very high global demand given its use in computers and mobile technology devices. We also spoke with Hannah Lerigo-Stephens, who has worked with leading food retailers like the Co-op and Morrisons to improve labour standards in

---

11   S. Kara, *Modern Slavery: A Global Perspective* (New York: Columbia University Press, 2017); S. Kara, *Bonded Labour: Tackling Systems of Slavery in South Asia* (New York: Columbia University Press, 2012); S. Kara, *Sex Trafficking: Inside the Business of Modern Slavery* (New York: Columbia University Press, 2009).

12   During one of his recent field missions in the Congo, Siddharth brought a hand-held GPS location device with him to tag the location where he carried out his interviews and send the location data to research teams in the Rights Lab for further geospatial analysis.

13   S. Kara and H. Lerigo-Stephens, "The Congo, Cobalt, and Cash: What Connects SDGs 9 and 8.7?" The Rights Track, August 26, 2020. http://rightstrack.org/the-congo-cobalt-and-cash -what-connects-sdgs-9-and-87.

their global supply chains and who has worked in the Rights Lab, where she translated research evidence into resources for businesses and organisations looking to work ethically and sustainably.

For more than twenty years, Siddharth has travelled to over fifty countries to document 'thousands of individuals directly' who are in conditions of 'forced labour, child labour, and modern slavery'. He has seen high degrees of 'hazard, coercion, and subhuman conditions' where 'no country is immune, no sector is immune'. He makes the strong claim that if you 'go down the list of the great industries across the global economy, and at the bottom of their various and variegated supply chains, you will invariably find severe labour exploitation and in the worst cases, slavery and child labour'. His most recent work has focused on the extraction of cobalt in the DRC, where the highly concentrated area in its southeast corner (see Figure 10.1) is the source for 70 per cent of world supply needed for a wide range of products, including mobile phones, laptops and electronic vehicles. Any product that has a rechargeable battery has cobalt as one of its primary ingredients, which means that the issue of cobalt extraction passes through our daily lives.

The cobalt mines and the process of extraction include 'horrific, devastating, and subhuman conditions that involve mass environmental destruction, grievous injury to thousands upon thousands of the most vulnerable people in the Congo, as well as death through tunnel collapses, toxic exposure, and even violence from military forces on the ground'. The physical geography of the mining region means that cobalt is relatively close to the surface of the earth, such that the process of extraction can involve either capital-intensive

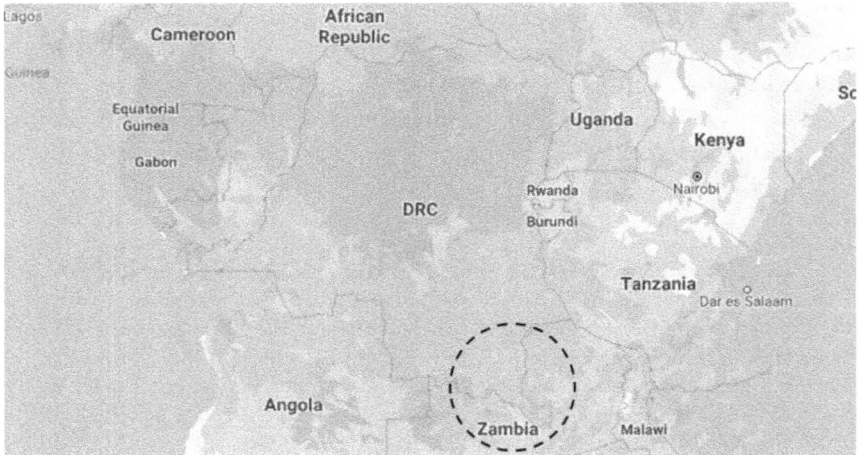

Figure 10.1 Cobalt mining region in the DRC, southeast mining zone marked in the dotted circle. *Source:* Google Maps.

methods or the use of manual labour. Thirty to forty per cent of the industry relies on manual labour, which, for Siddharth, represents the 'most extreme form of modern slavery', where with 'hacks and picks and shovels', workers face 'radioactive uranium', 'toxic' cobalt and use their bare hands 'with no PPE' (personal protective equipment) to 'fill up sacks with stones'. The use of 'artisanal mining', Siddharth argues, takes us 'back centuries', with 'no support in the tunnels' which collapse all the time and where miners become 'buried alive'. The supplies that result from these processes are then traded on an informal market through a 'layer of informality of traders and buying houses' before entering the more formal supply chains for purchase by well-known global brands. From top to bottom, this process of extraction and onward sales represents the 'widest asymmetry in the share of value at the top of the chain [...] and the pennies that are sprinkled down to the bottom of the chain'.

Hannah argues that what Siddharth describes is 'unfortunately typical of what you would see in any global value chain, global production network, [or] global supply chain' where there are 'multiple buyers' and great complexity. Too often than not, people use complexity as an excuse for inaction on this issue, but in reality, she argues that the 'instability of relationships, instability of connections between different stages of the supply chain, and the imbalance of power between the actors' sit at the heart of the problem. There is a lot of concentration of power and 'market imbalance' where companies are either attracted to countries without strict legislation or in the case of cobalt, where supply is highly concentrated in one area. In echoing Genevieve's perspective, Siddharth agrees with Hannah and argues that the 'anaemic share of value' is the 'construct and nature of contemporary global capitalism', where at the bottom of the supply chain, 'value is virtually nil'. Cobalt miners earn one to two dollars a day at the bottom of the chain and the resulting products are 'sold at robust margins at the top', certainly for such high-end products like mobile phones, tablets and laptops. Siddharth argues that there needs to be 'the simple will and desire to be more equitable'. In reality, the sums of money involved are such that 'even a rounding error on their balance sheet would be utterly transformative' for those people working at the bottom of the chain, who are not seen as 'employees' and whose conditions constitute 'the futility of the suffering'.

Both Hannah and Siddharth agree that despite this bleak picture, there are several solutions available. At a normative level, they both argue that there needs to be a greater 'will to be decent' and embrace a stronger principle of 'redistribution'. At a pragmatic level, Hannah cites the emerging legislation on modern slavery as a positive step, but such legislative frameworks need to move beyond mere 'reporting' and 'due diligence' to include real

sanctions and legal punishment. She argues that the 'modern slavery statements' required of firms under the UK Modern Slavery Act should instead
be 'modern slavery strategies' that include measurable and actionable targets
and greater accountability mechanisms.[14] She also adds that it is possible to
make progress through making the business case for addressing these issues.
She knows that companies focus on the 'bottom line', but she also contends
that firms simply need to think more about 'what else needs to be in place,
having a weakness in any part of the supply chain will be a risk for them in
future'. This combination of risk and resilience is important for her, such that
'if people can't understand risk, they severely undervalue resilience, and if
they are not resilient, they won't continue to be successful'.

At a more radical level, Siddharth had 'reached the end of his tether'
through what he discovered in his research and has engaged in a process of
'strategic litigation' by filing a case on behalf of 14 plaintiffs from the Congo in
the US Federal Court in Washington, DC, against 'Apple, Google, Microsoft,
Dell, and Tesla'. He recognises that this legal strategy has a low probability
of success, but 'even if the case is not successful, it is the opportunity for *voices*
to be heard' (see Chapter 8 in this book). He locates his work and its many
challenges as 'the latest chapter in a long history' of the inherent problems of
capitalism, characterised as the 'same process of pillaging resources, exploiting labour, extracting massive amount of value for the Northern half of the
planet'. He does see the potential for further legal cases in other jurisdictions
against different companies and is hopeful that perhaps now a 'reckoning is
happening'.

Walking the Supply Chain

Elaine Mitchel-Hill is the business and human rights lead at Marshalls plc,[15]
a leading hard landscape company serving both the commercial and domestic construction markets with multiple operating sites in the UK and supply
chains across the globe. Arianne Griffiths is a lawyer and led the deploy-
ment of research in the Rights Lab for business application. Her work focuses

---

14   A recent review of modern slavery statements shows that modern slavery statements are
increasing in number, size and sophistication; however, companies are 'not necessarily engaging
with modern slavery risks in a thorough and meaningful way, or acknowledging the contribution
that their price-driven commercial models make towards increasing the risk of modern slavery in
supply chains'. See Modern Slavery and Human Rights Policy and Evidence Centre, *Effectiveness*
of Section 54 of the Modern Slavery Act: Evidence and Comparative Analysis, February 2021. https://mod-
ernslaverypec.org/assets/downloads/TISC-effectiveness-report.pdf.
15   For more on Marshalls, see https://www.marshalls.co.uk/.

on effective law and policy to tackle modern slavery in supply chains and the application of business and human rights frameworks to the anti-slavery agenda. Our conversation with Elaine and Arianne examined the practical steps that companies can take to gain deeper insights into their supply chains and how international and corporate governance can be strengthened to make companies more accountable for their practices.[16]

Marshalls plc's commercial operations focus on hard landscaping and construction. Founded in Yorkshire in 1875, the company has supplied natural stone and other products for large capital projects, including the stone paving for London's iconic Trafalgar Square. Since its founding, the company has grown and now has supply operations in over thirty countries around the world. Elaine says that the company provides 'natural stone from a whole range of geographies, across the globe: Brazil, India, China, and Vietnam' where she is very open that such countries pose the 'highest risk for human rights abuse and modern slavery'. For her, 'in those high-risk geographies, for natural stone, we would always want to be able go back to source, back to raw materials, back to holes in the ground'. She adds further that her company does not 'tend to buy from the open market place', which allows her personally to 'go back to quarry locations to see the conditions'. Her physical visits to sites allow her to 'have the relationships that are required' for knowledge about these conditions and allow human rights concerns to be 'more up front for us than the suppliers'.

For Marshalls 'all of the stone that we take is extracted using some form of machinery', where Elaine has seen 'less and less people involved' over time. In some quarries, however, she still sees 'the splitting of the stone done by hand'. Her awareness of potential human rights abuse took place in 2005, when her own 'walking the supply chain' in India revealed that the biggest issue 'was actually the issue of child labour', particularly for the use in the production of 'cobbles', 'taking water' and 'lifting spoil'. She says that if we 'fast forward to where we are now: [Marshalls has had an] interesting and winding journey with perhaps not as much progress as I would have liked to have seen overall'. She feels that much of what she saw in the past is 'now hidden, moved out of the way, moved out of sight', where child labour is 'inextricably linked with bonded labour and forced labour'.

Arianne argues that the evolution evident to Elaine is mirrored in the 'dramatic increase in the amount of attention' now given to modern slavery and

---

16 E. Michel-Hill and A. Griffith, "Walking the Supply Chain to Uphold Human Rights: What Connects SDGs 12 and 8.7?" The Rights Track, June 5, 2020. http://rightstrack.org/walking -the-supply-chain-what-connects-sdgs-12-and-87.

other human rights abuses. She sees 2011 as a major turning point with the establishment of the UN Guiding Principles on Business and Human Rights, the development of 'other international instruments' and measures specific to different industries. Under the Guiding Principles, there are the 'duty of states to protect human rights, responsibly of companies to respect those rights, and the joint responsibility of both states and business to afford effective remedy'. She is quick to assert that 'corporate responsibility to respect exists independent of whether states are willing or able to do their part of the bargain' and that the 'Guiding Principles reflect and capture human rights obligations that states already have in international human rights law'. This 'increasing normative value' or 'normative weight' means that 'even in the absence of legislation, companies are demonstrating that they understand that they have these responsibilities', but that there is 'still a lot of work to be done'. In her view, we 'need mandatory due diligence legislation' in order 'to move past the first generation of legislation' that focused primarily on transparency of supply chains.

Elaine agrees and says that within the Marshalls DNA as a 'Victorian philanthropic company' there was a 'match' between its own values and the emerging importance of human rights in business operations, such that it was 'not a hard push' to align to the Guiding Principles and where Marshalls was an early member of the UN Global Compact. Both in terms of the customer base and the company itself, Elaine sees a 'strong set of values' that are aligned and the 'the sail is set' for their 'sustainable approach, embracing all the values that come with that' creating a real 'congruence in the business'. She sees her company's efforts as 'commercialising our approach to sustainability' in order to 'stay in business and do the right thing'. She makes the economic case for their approach in saying 'unless as we have a robust business, we don't have a vehicle in terms of a business to support human rights'.

Arianne and Elaine agree that the UK's Modern Slavery Act has put renewed focus on these issues, where Marshalls was an early firm to file required modern slavery statements, and that their work in this regard provides 'a real platform to engage with the spirit of the act' versus 'the letter of the law'. At the time of the act's passage in 2015, Elaine felt that there was an 'un-level playing field in terms of the work we were doing'. The act 'gave it some focus and demanded that others engaged in the conversation' about the 'depth and breadth of what we have done', including 'what kind of training, with whom, how many suppliers, how many on our team, spot and report'. Her work has helped in 'improving due diligence' and allowed the company 'go beyond complying with the act'. Despite these advances in due diligence, Elaine and Arianne both argue that so much more can be done. Elaine feels that we are at the 'cliff face' and need to 'get right back to the raw materials and where they come from', where more effort is required to understand the blurred relationships between the 'formal supply chain' and 'informal supply chain'. Given this complexity of relationships, she does think that there are 'defensible limits to transparency' and that much more 'government to government work' is required to enhance this understanding and make continued progress.

The Time Is Now

Our conversations with these Rights Track guests suggest to us that the time is now for significant recognition of and concrete action on tackling the vulnerability of global supply chains and business operations to modern slavery. While companies like the Body Shop spearheaded attention to the 'fair trade' movement,[17] our conversations in this chapter demonstrate that the scrutiny and regulation of business must also include attention to modern slavery in addition to value chains and fair remuneration to suppliers. The global regulatory environment remains relatively weak and primarily comprises voluntary codes of conduct and reporting requirements that have very few sanctions in place. Much popular commentary places the responsibility to address the issues on companies themselves, but a richer and perhaps more fruitful approach involves a combination of responsibility for nation states and companies working together on this global challenge.[18] Both Genevieve and John recognise the negative externalities to economic activity and the need for much stronger regulatory frameworks and sanctions for non-compliance. Alex argues for the development of a modern slavery risk barometer based on company financial accounts and other data, while across their different sectors of interest, Lola, Siddharth, Elaine and Arianne, all show us not only the problems in current practices, but also practical and pragmatic ways in which companies can do better. As Alex notes, there is an emerging cadre of company roles expressly defined to address these issues that need to be dedicated to legal compliance and real concrete action to bring about

---

17 See A. Roddick, *Business as Unusual: The Journey of Anita Roddick and The Body Shop* (Thorsons, 2000). See also H. Shultz, *Onward: How Starbucks Fought for Its Life without Losing Its Soul* (Rodale Incorporated, 2012).

18 For a strong argument on how such an approach can be developed and implemented, see I. Bantekas, "The Linkages between Business and Human Rights and Their Underlying Root Causes," *Human Rights Quarterly* 43, no. 1 (2021): 117–137.

lasting change.[19] While the United Nations recognises the problem of modern slavery as articulated in the SDGs, the process of economic development involves international actors, the public sector and the private sector working together to achieve Target 8.7. Only through a public and private cooperative approach can the world move towards ending modern slavery.

---

19 Landman and some of his colleagues at the University of Nottingham teach on the Masters in Sustainability Leadership programme at the Judge Business School at Cambridge University, whose students come from a wide range of, and different levels in, world's leading private companies. This growing body of professionals have a much better awareness of sustainability issues, which include human rights, forced labour and modern slavery. See https://www.cisl .cam.ac.uk/.

Chapter 11

FIGHTING SLAVERY ON THE GROUND

Abstract

Grassroots and frontline organisations are working hard to help free people from conditions of modern slavery, and this chapter discusses these efforts with a wide range of academics and practitioners around the world. We discuss bonded labour in India with Pradeep Narayanan and Anusha Chandrasekharan (Praxis); forced labour in Vietnam, Uganda and Albania with Patricia Hynes (University of Bedfordshire) and Patrick Burland (IOM); interventions in 'slavery hotspots' with Dan Vexler (Freedom Fund); the pursuit of perpetrators with David Westlake and Steven Webster (International Justice Mission); collective public health and modern slavery in Brazil with Luis Leão (Federal University of Mato Grosso); forced marriage and women's rights with Karen Sherman (Akilah Institute) and Helen McCabe (Rights Lab); and the idea of how to achieve a network of 'slavery free cities' with Alison Gardner (Rights Lab).

'These are not going to be our demands, these are already our basic rights.'
— Anusha Chandrasekharan, Praxis

'We are dealing with really high levels of trauma here.'
— Patricia Hynes, University of Bedfordshire

'You cannot try and rescue your way out of slavery.'
— Dan Vexler, The Freedom Fund

'It is even harder to prove there is forced marriage when there is no legal record of the marriage.'
— Helen McCabe, The Rights Lab

Women are 'potential agents of change, capable of transforming their lives, and in turn the lives of the families and communities.'
— Karen Sherman, Akilah Institute, Rwanda

'Local areas are bringing in tactics for disruption.'
— Alison Gardner, Rights Lab

On the Ground

The portraits of certain forms of modern slavery revealed though the work of our Rights Track guests Siddharth Kara and Elaine Mitchel-Hill make us focus on the 'holes in the ground' and the 'futility of human suffering', where there is widespread evidence of what can only be described as medieval systems of economic production and extraction. Leading modern slavery scholar Kevin Bales titled one of his recent books *Blood and Earth*, which captures the visceral and organic nature of much of the work being carried out today by many enslaved peoples around the world.[1] Beyond these portraits, we have learned from our many other guests that the phenomenon leaves no country untouched, with patterns of forced labour, human trafficking, forced marriage, sexual exploitation and modern slavery affecting the wealthy countries of the so-called Global North, albeit to a lesser degree than in other regions. As we saw in our last chapter, leading economies of the world have persistent problems with current business models in which there is strong evidence of modern slavery across many different sectors. For example, in her *2020–2021 Annual Report*, Dame Sara Thornton, the UK's IASC, shows that there has been a secular rise in the number of modern slavery referrals to the Home Office from between 1,000 and 1,200 people per quarter in 2017–18 to between 2,800 and 3,000 people per quarter in 2020–21.[2] These trends are for only those cases that have been referred to the Home Office and thus represent a partial picture of the true nature and extent of the problem in the UK. The trends do show, however, that the largest proportion of referrals to the Home Office comes from the UK, followed by Albania, Vietnam, Sudan, Romania, Eritrea, Iran, China, Iraq and Nigeria.[3]

Against this bleak picture of human suffering and coercion, since the 1990s, there has been a proliferation of anti-slavery NGOs at the national and 'transnational' level with dedicated intervention and support programmes. The work of these NGOs with victims and survivors on the ground helps extricate them from their conditions of exploitation and provides them with much needed assistance to help them to become part of

---

1 Kevin Bales, *Blood and Earth: Modern Slavery, Ecocide, and the Secret to Saving the World* (Spiegel and Grau, 2016). His earlier work equally captures the severity of the issue and is entitled *Disposable People*. See Kevin Bales, *Disposable People: New Slavery in the Global Economy* (Berkeley: University of California Press, 1999).

2 Independent Anti-Slavery Commissioner, *Independent Anti-Slavery Commissioner Annual Report 2020–2021*, Presented to Parliament pursuant to Section 42 (10) (b) of the Modern Slavery Act 2015, July 2021. https://www.antislaverycommissioner.co.uk/media/1642/independent-anti-slavery-commissioner-annual-report-2020-2021.pdf.

3 Ibid., p. 65.

the formal economy and leave their particular forms of enslavement. This burgeoning network of NGOs, financially supported by inter-governmental agencies, national aid agencies, trusts and charitable foundations, involves a number of concrete actions and long-term programmes aimed at ending slavery by 2030. These NGOs are also part of the larger human rights movement, which has had a major role in shaping the law and practice of human rights (see Chapter 3 in this book). The conversations that feature in this chapter cover many different geographies and national political contexts, including India, Vietnam, Albania, Brazil, Thailand, Ethiopia, Rwanda and the City of Nottingham, among others. Throughout our conversations, we were interested in understanding how anti-slavery efforts are designed and delivered, and to what degree they 'work' in bringing people out of enslavement in a sustainable way.[4]

Bonded Labour in India

The prevalence of modern slavery is particularly high in India, where one of the most dominant forms is that of bonded labour. Also known as debt bondage or peonage, bonded labour is a form of labour that is traded in exchange for a loan or as function of an inherited debt within households that is passed down through generations. As we saw in Chapter 9 in this book, the prevalence and practice of bonded labour is rooted in local communities and embedded in larger cultural understandings, institutions and social norms. Pradeep Narayanan is Director of Research and Capacity Building and Anusha Chandrasekharan is Senior Programme Manager of Communications for Praxis,[5] an India-based not-for-profit organisation, which works to democratise development processes and institutions in order to ensure that the voices of the poor are heard and that concrete actions for positive change are formulated from these voices. We spoke to Pradeep and Anusha about the problem of bonded labour in India and their organisation's efforts to address it on the ground with a particular focus on the *Dalit* community, the lowest level of people and 'untouchable' group that is technically an illegal part of the Indian caste system even though it comprises 17 per cent of the total population.

---

4 See Katharine Bryant and Todd Landman, "Combatting Human Trafficking Since Palermo: What Do We Know about What Works?" *Journal of Human Trafficking* 6, no. 1 (2020): 1–22.
5 Pradeep Narayanan and Anusha Chandrasekharan, "Bonded Labour: Listening to the Voices of the Poor and Marginalised," The Rights Track, May 30, 2019. http://rightstrack.org /listening-to-the-voices-of-the-poor-and-marginalised-a-participatory-approach-to-ending-slavery-in-india.

Pradeep and Anusha work with the 'most vulnerable and most excluded' people in India, including the Dalits and in particular Dalit women. In addition to being illegal, the Dalits are actually 'outside the caste system'. They are reached through Praxis' work in hamlets and villages in an effort to 'get their voices into various policy platforms', which for Pradeep and Anusha is achieved 'not through us, but they themselves'. Praxis uses what are called 'ground level panels' to collate voices to reach 'high level panels' to effect change. They reach these communities through participant 'action research' processes and the use of 'audio-visual materials' and other communications strategies.

Despite the Bonded Labour System (Abolition) Act of 1976 and the illegal status of the Dalit community, the bonded labour tradition continues as an extension from earlier periods for work in the agricultural sector to the contemporary period, which now includes the manufacturing and other sectors. Anusha explains that these people are 'forced to work and not get paid', a situation that emerges from the fact that the community does not have 'access to easy, safe loans' for 'emergencies, weddings, deaths, or serious illness'. In addition, the 'health infrastructure is not sufficient', and community members seek access to 'private hospitals for which they require more money'. This money typically comes in the form of an 'advance' particularly during 'festival time' where there are 'a lot of expenses' and where 'agents go to the hamlets' and 'identify vulnerable families'. The system means that these people 'get paid money and have to work it off', where they are 'not allowed to leave the place of employment' and suffer abuses, such as physical violence, sexual violence and threats—conditions that mean that their holders 'use them in whatever way they feel justified'.

In the 'brick kiln' industry (see Chapter 4), workers live close to the site of the kiln and experience 'physical violence' and 'threats' to force people to work, and in the event that workers are ill or unable to come to work, the brick kiln operators demand that the workers' families send their children. Pradeep argues that it is very likely that only 1 per cent of workers are coerced in this way, but the 'threat becomes manifested' through the rest of the group to the degree that many 'may not be able to find out that this threat exists' leading to a 'situation where the bonded labourer does not feel bonded'. In this sense, there is an 'invisibilisation of threats'. Anusha recalls a woman worker who, after spending a day carrying out agricultural work, then stayed on to carry out 'household work' for her holder for no pay. When asked why she engaged in this work, the woman said, 'I do it out of love', since she sees him 'as a provider'. This account aligns with the insights we gained from our conversation with Austin Choi-Fitzpatrick (see Chapter 9) about the broader cultural acceptance, local social norms and a sense of obligation that persists in this system of bonded labour.

Pradeep and Anusha work with the Freedom Fund and engage in an 'action research group within the community' to understand the 'drivers for their bonded labour' through lateral discussions of 'health [...] how their being in bondage affects them'. Through 'layers and layers of questions', their work raises awareness and identifies new and previously unknown areas that have bonded labour, such as schools, where 'it's about teachers who are not even getting paid'. They see this work as slow and incremental, where 'even though you can rescue them, you will not be able to help them with an alternative'. Pradeep and Anusha work to find these alternatives and have begun to take on the issue of CSR to challenge the perception that bonded labour is understood only as 'citizen versus the state'. Their Corporate Responsibility Watch documents bonded labour throughout corporate supply chains for the top 100 companies, which tend to 'ignore the lowest levels of the supply chain'. The Indian government now has a National Action Plan on business and human rights. In reflecting on the fact that India is the world's largest democracy, Pradeep admits that 'there are flaws in the democratic way of functioning, but the solution is more democracy' with stronger 'rights-based legislation' in an effort to 'make many of these things entitlements'. Anusha agrees that there remain 'barriers' to achieving these basic entitlements and wants to know 'how they can be addressed'. For her 'all these answers will come from our engagement with these communities'.

Forced Labour in Nigeria, Albania and Vietnam

We discussed the causes, determinants and 'vulnerabilities' to human trafficking with Patricia Hynes from the University of Bedfordshire and Patrick Burland, Senior Project Officer for Human Trafficking and Modern Slavery for the IOM.[6] In addition to the root causes of human trafficking, we also discussed the support needs of people from countries who have experienced trafficking into the UK, including from Nigeria, Albania and Vietnam. Patricia tells us that while some gains have been made, we 'still have things that we need to understand better', where there is a 'disproportionate amount of knowledge generated around sexual exploitation', but 'very little knowledge

---

6 P. Hynes and P. Burland, "Becoming a Slave: Who's Vulnerable to Being Trafficked?" The Rights Track, February 19, 2019. http://rightstrack.org/becoming-a-slave-whos-vulnerable-to -being-trafficked.

around the trafficking of men and boys' from the three countries featuring in her work. She continues with 'we know very little about what recovery means' and that there are significant 'gaps in recording statistics', such that 'whether we have all the knowledge already is a big question'. Patrick agrees with Patricia about the gaps in knowledge. He argues there is 'a significant lack of knowledge about trafficking to the UK as a consequence of having worked with a very small number of survivors of trafficking' and 'very little knowledge of people who have returned from the UK'. Moreover, he observes that 'if they are returning to their countries of origin, they are not returning to comprehensive programmes of support and assistance', where there remain 'questions and concerns about the possibility for them to be re-trafficked in their futures'.

Patricia and Patrick adopt the IOM's 'Determinants of Vulnerability' model to understand the drivers for human trafficking, modern slavery and migration. The model has four different levels: (1) the individual, (2) the household, (3) the community and (4) the structural (see also Chapter 9). Patrick sees these four different levels working separately and interacting in complex ways that create conditions for people becoming embroiled in modern slavery and human trafficking. He highlights individual factors, such as poverty, gender, education and basic skills, alongside household expectations, community practices and understandings, and variation in institutional capacity and government responsiveness. Patricia argues that this set of factors is operating in Albania, with 'a strong honour code that operates in an unspoken way'. In her conversations with survivors, she says that 'nobody really mentioned it' effectively making it an 'omnipresent social norm', which when combined with a lack of 'state capacity to protect against those rights violations', there remains 'a lot of silence around some of the aspects'.

Patrick paints a similar picture from his work in Vietnam and Nigeria, where 'traffickers can often have a strong connection to an individual who ends up exploited' that allows them to 'take advantage and exploit existing relationships' while at the same time drawing on the 'status and role of the family'. Traffickers make promises of riches and paid work, exploit their own status in local hierarchies and lure people into situations of unpaid work and trafficking. He argues that 'we see a lot of intermediaries, a lot of complicated relationships, which might start with the household or direct community, but the intention is unclear' leading to an 'ambiguous sense of family, where everyone is an uncle or an auntie'. Like Albania, there are unspoken and invisible norms and expectations in Vietnam and Nigeria surrounding trafficking practices that present many challenges in finding solutions to helping people on the ground.

Albania, Vietnam and Nigeria are in the top four or five 'sender' countries for trafficked people referred to the Home Office in the UK under the
NRM. The NRM is part of the UK's Modern Slavery Act and, at the time
of our podcast, included 45 days of support for victims and survivors. Both
Patricia and Patrick welcome this support, but argue that it is inadequate
to address the needs of these people. Patricia observes that 'we are dealing
with really high levels of trauma here' and upon arrival and referral to the
NRM, people 'experience a system that does not really support them'.[7] For
those victims and survivors who return from the UK, there are also limited
resources for supporting them. Indeed, Patrick is surprised that in the case of
Nigerian returnees between 2013 and 2017, only *six people* were supported by
the Nigerian government. He observes that 'we can assume that the number
might be greater than six given it's a top five country' for referred cases to the
NRM in the UK. There is thus a 'disconnect between the process of leaving
the UK and having access to support' upon return. Patricia and Patrick's
work in Albania, Vietnam and Nigeria has involved in-depth interviews with
over 170 people, sixty-eight of whom are survivors of trafficking and from
whom they have expanded our understanding of the drivers for trafficking,
the levels of support available in the UK and levels of support available upon
their return. The results of their research and engagement with these communities have been submitted in a report to the UK Parliament.[8]

Slavery 'Hotspots'

Freedom Fund is one of the leading anti-slavery organisations in the world and
featured widely in the popular press in June 2021 after receiving significant

---

7 Lord McColl's Modern Slavery (Victim Support Bill) seeks to extend the period of support,
and a judicial review case found against the Home Office, leading to the period of support being
extended. See https://bills.parliament.uk/bills/2543. A cost–benefit analysis carried out by the
Rights Lab showed that extending the period of support would bring net positive benefits to
government in terms of direct and indirect expenditure, the reduction in re-trafficking and programmes of support. See A. Nicholson, K. Schwarz, T. Landman, and A. Griffith, *The Modern
Slavery (Victim Support Bill): A Cost-Benefit Analysis* (University of Nottingham: Rights Lab, 2019).
https://www.nottingham.ac.uk/research/beacons-of-excellence/rights-lab/resources/reports
-and-briefings/2019/august/the-modern-slavery-victim-support-bill.pdf.
8 See P. Hynes, P. Burland, A. Thurnham, J. Dew, L. Gani-Yusuf, V. Lenja, and H.T. Tran,
with A. Olatunde and A. Gaxha, "'Between Two Fires': Understanding Vulnerabilities and the
Support Needs of People from Albania, Viet Nam and Nigeria Who Have Experienced Human
Trafficking into the UK," University of Bedfordshire, International Organisation for Migration,
Institute of Applied Social Research, 2019. https://www.beds.ac.uk/media/266832/between
-two-fires-finalreport-29062019.pdf.

funding from MacKenzie Scott and Dan Jewett to help support its work.[9] International Justice Mission works in 14 countries to combat trafficking and slavery, violence against women and children, and police abuse of power.[10] We spoke to Dan Vexler, Director of Programmes at the Freedom Fund, about its approach to addressing 'slavery hotspots' around the world and to David Westlake and Steven Webster from the International Justice Mission about its criminal justice approach to modern slavery.[11] Our conversation revealed a difference in seeing modern slavery as a 'criminal justice' problem on the one hand and a much broader problem on the other that needs additional and focused attention on its 'root causes'. While both organisations are dedicated to addressing modern slavery, this difference in approach raises a number of significant questions around the strategies for ending it.

After 20 years of working to combat modern slavery, David and Steven explain that the International Justice Mission fundamentally sees the problem as a crime. Working in partnership with local authorities, law enforcement and other public sector organisations, they work on 'building a case that demonstrates that slavery is taking place in a particular location, gather evidence around perpetrators, victims and how that breaches the legal requirements'. They 'share [their] work with police', who then 'lead a raid' to 'rescue' victims, and then provide immediate 'after care' to survivors. They argue that in addition to the trauma of enslavement, there is 'trauma that goes along with being released to freedom'. Their approach means that they view slavery as 'a crime scene' and that it needs to be addressed as such. They do not think slavery should be 'demoted to a humanitarian crisis', but rather see that their role is to 'help and equip and support the justice system in any particular place to deal effectively and to deliver consistently and constantly justice for the most vulnerable, for the most poor'. In contrast to many of the perspectives shared in this section of the book, they 'do not think it is the job of companies or NGOs to end slavery', but 'it is the job of governments and law enforcement to enforce laws that protect the poor and the vulnerable'.

---

9   MacKenzie Scott is an American billionaire businesswoman who has pledged to give half of her wealth to charity. Among her many gifts, Freedom Fund was selected to receive support for its work on ending modern slavery. See https://freedomfund.org/press-release/our-thanks-to -mackenzie-scott-and-dan-jewett/.

10   Landman is part of a project to develop a framework to estimate the prevalence of child sexual exploitation in the Philippines in partnership with the International Justice Mission using complex and unstructured data across a variety of practices and international transactions.

11   D. Vexler, D. Westlake, and S. Webster, "Fighting Slavery on the Ground: What Does It Look Like?" The Rights Track, December 17, 2018. http://rightstrack.org/fighting-slavery-on -the-ground-what-does-it-look-like.

They thus challenge formal authorities wherever they work to 'rise up and deliver justice'.

Dan agrees that 'prosecutions are critical' and that 'modern slavery is a crime', but he argues further that 'the law enforcement side of fighting modern slavery is only part of the solution'. His organisation 'takes a step back' to look at why certain groups of people, certain classes of people around the world are in modern slavery' and to focus on power dynamics and people who are treated as 'second-class citizens'. Such groups include, for example, the 'lower caste in South Asia, workers in some of the Gulf States', such as 'Qatar, Saudi Arabia, the UAE [United Arab Emirates]' or 'forced labour in the seafood industry' in Thailand. In the Thai case, Dan sees 'xenophobia' at play, making forced labour practices 'permissible' often with the complicity of the police. In some popular accounts, migrants from Myanmar and Cambodia who become forced labourers in the seafood industry are referred to as 'ATMs', as 'cash machines' in ways that allow people to 'extort them' and through which there is 'wider social acceptance' of this practice.

The Freedom Fund works with over one hundred and twenty frontline organisations in Thailand, Nepal, India and Ethiopia combatting modern slavery across different sectors, providing information; raising awareness about risks, deception and tricks; the available legal protections; and how to organise through unions, informal worker cooperatives and local community groups. In the Gulf States, they focus their work on migrant workers in the construction industry and migrant domestic workers, where there are patterns of 'coercion and deception all the way along'. For example, it is quite typical for a woman in Ethiopia to decide that she would like to work abroad. Her decision is then mediated through a 'broker' and she may well arrive in a different country, or confront radically different conditions than expected upon arrival, where she is treated in a 'degrading way' that is 'not much more than a dog'.[12] Often, women such as these will have their passports confiscated, rendering them unable to leave their place of employ or unable to seek help from the authorities, which for Dan constitutes the practice of slavery. For Dan, 'migration is an entry point for where bad things can happen' and 'it happens in every country in the world'.

---

12   This portrait of an Ethiopian woman engaging in migrant domestic work is similarly recounted by Mende Nazer, a Nuba tribe member from war-torn Sudan, who, after eight years of sexual slavery and forced domestic servitude, organised her own route to freedom from the home of a Sudanese embassy official in London in 2000. See M. Nazer, *Slave: The True Story of a Girl's Lost Childhood and Her Fight for Survival* (London: Virago, 2004).

Freedom Fund has adopted a 'hotspot' model for its work that is predicated on the basic principle that 'let's not spread ourselves too thinly'. They have two hotspots in India, two in Nepal, one in Ethiopia and one in Thailand. Dan explains that these hotspots are chosen on several criteria: (1) slavery prevalence is high, (2) there are civil society organisations with whom Freedom Fund can work, (3) there is a possibility that their intervention will make a difference, (4) the government is 'open' enough to the issue area and (5) there are available resources and funding to carry out their work. Once in a hotspot, they work to 'support a cluster of civil society organisations' and 'community-based organisations', which are 'sometimes led by survivors'. This approach allows them to 'get as close to the coalface of the issue as we can' and to 'build them into a coalition to press for systemic change'. In the case of Thailand, their work has led the government to focus on how 'to protect migrant workers and regulate the seafood industry', while in Ethiopia, they have been 'changing the government policy' on migrant workers with a view to 'making migration safer'. Dan admits that their work is a 'long-term game' that seeks to build resilience instead of focusing on the shorter-term act of rescue. Dan is clear that 'we can't rescue our way out of slavery'. The contrasting approaches of the International Justice Mission and the Freedom Fund are best seen as complementary efforts to address the reasons for slavery as well as to help those people currently enslaved and recently rescued.

Public Health and Slavery in Brazil

Brazil has a large number of enslaved people, but also stands out as a country with strong legal frameworks in place and a positive record in making progress against the problem, primarily through its use of 'labour inspectors'.[13] A vast and highly variegated country with over two hundred million people, Brazil has a long history of colonial forms of transatlantic slavery and commodity production that ended with its formal abolition in 1888, and since then has seen patterns of differentiated economic development, populism, authoritarian rule and democracy. Rich in natural resources and agricultural production, the country has seen long-standing conflicts over land, access to health, education and social protection, and has stark and persistent

---

13   Centre for Policy Research, *Developing Freedom: The Sustainable Development Case for Ending Modern Slavery, Forced Labour and Human Trafficking* (New York: United Nations University, 2021). https://www.developingfreedom.org/wp-content/uploads/2021/01/DevelopingFreedom_MainReport_WebFinal.pdf. On the case of Brazil, see pp. 92–111.

inequalities in terms of land and income distribution.[14] Our conversation with Luís da Costa Leão focused on a 'collective public health' approach to combatting modern slavery.[15] Luis is a Professor of Social Psychology in the Department of Collective Health at the Federal University of Mato Grosso in Brazil and was a visiting research fellow in the Rights Lab.[16]

We began our conversation by discussing the concept of 'collective health', which for Luis is a 'Latin American' concept developed in the middle of the nineteenth century and is a holistic view of health that includes 'epidemiology, public policy, and management in general'. This broader concept stands in sharp contrast to the idea of 'medical health' typically represented by a focus on doctors 'wearing white' and people 'with diseases' to include the 'whole of population' who 'take health in their own hands in terms of power to under-stand the determinants of health'. Luis connects this more holistic concept of health to that of work, where 'work is a very deep and powerful determi-nant of health'. Brazil made a formal and legal commitment to the right to health in its 1988 Constitution, but 'collective health' was a 'social movement' that developed throughout the 1970s during the military dictatorship.[17] The 1988 Constitution establishes health as a 'universal right', which Luis argues needs people to 'defend the right to health for everyone', and where the 'sur-veillance of conditions of work' needs to be carried out 'to reach poorer areas' and to 'fight the current government and plans to privatise health'.

In addition to its main connections to conditions of work, 'collective health' for Luis also 'has a close dialogue with environmental systems and studies' with linkages that cut across 'work, environment, and health'. And it is across these linkages that Luis sees a connection to the fight against modern slavery in Brazil. He has engaged in 'strategies to carry out surveillance of the entire

14 See T. Landman and M. Larizza, "Inequality and Human Rights: Who Controls What, When, and How," *International Studies Quarterly* 53, no. 3 (2009): 715–736.
15 L. da Costa Leão, "Health and Slavery: What Connects SDG 3 and SDG 8.7?" The Rights Track, February 19, 2020. http://rightstrack.org/health-and-slavery-what-connects-sdg-3-and -sdg-87.
16 As Luis is a non-native speaker of English, we translated and transcribed his conversation with us to represent his thoughts in a more readable fashion. For example, his use of 'America Latin' has been transcribed to read 'Latin America'. This process in no way compromises the meaning of his words used in the podcast episode.
17 Brazil experienced a military coup in 1964, which ushered in a prolonged period of authori-tarian rule until 1985, followed by elections in 1989. The period of authoritarianism featured various military rulers, some ability for opposition parties to compete in congressional elections and waves of social protest from a variety of different social movement organisations, culminat-ing in a managed transition to democracy. See J. Foweraker and T. Landman, *Citizenship Rights and Social Movements: A Comparative and Statistical Analysis* (Oxford: Oxford University Press, 1997).

commodity chain' across production processes of many different commodities, including, for example, 'sugar cane, meat, timber, corn, and soya beans'. He argues that such surveillance needs to move beyond attention to the 'quality of good or products' and 'expand this view' to include 'the entire process' of production. Tracking products in this way, Luis explains 'reveals the presence of slavery' where the quality and 'intensity' of workplace environments affect levels of health and intersect with the problem of modern slavery.

From a governance perspective, Luis is cautiously optimistic. He tells us that Brazil has a 'multi-level' approach that involves 'municipal governments, state governments, and the federal government'. He says that the complexity of the modern slavery problem requires 'complex solutions' involving these different levels of government, each of which has 'obligations to take care of each stage of production'. The Brazilian Penal Code formally cites 'conditions analogous to slavery', which include 'degrading conditions of work', 'exhausting work hours', 'servitude' and 'forced labour'. Degrading working conditions include 'exposure to risk, inadequate lodgings, disease, and lack of medical care'. Exhausting work hours involve 'not only working time' but also the 'intensity of work'. Servitude is manifested though the 'over charging for being able to work' including for the 'tools for working' and 'commuting', where workers accrue 'debts' and effectively experience the kind of 'debt bondage' we have seen in the case of India. Forced labour for Luis means that people 'work against their free will'.

As the current system operates, however, Luis notes that there is very little recognition for 'public health'. While there are 'a lot of actions against slavery practices', Luis is concerned that 'you can't find participation of health institutions, health professionals, or the health system'. In his interviews with 'freed' and 'rescued' slaves, Luis has learned that 'health is related to life', and that 'good working conditions' include the provision of 'water, food, and shelter'. In the testimonies that he has collected, he notes that there are patterns in the 'denial of each of these elements', such that 'slavery is not the opposite of freedom' but also 'the opposite of health'. For Luis, 'slavery causes severe consequences to health', including 'mental health, disease, physical health, [and] psychological, and psycho-social dimensions'.

Beyond the concerns over recognition of these links between freedom and health, Luis shared with us that since 1995, there have been a large number of labour inspections, which over fifteen years led to between 4,000 and 5,000 people being rescued from slavery, with more than 90 per cent of the cases coming from agriculture. Over 90 per cent of those rescued were young men, and Luis continues to be concerned that it is rare for any attention to be given to women, which is partly explained by the fact that the current system does not recognise sexual exploitation as a form of modern slavery. In addition to the absence of this form of modern slavery, Luis explains that Brazil's efforts to combat slavery are constrained by the persistence of corruption. Beyond the notorious and contested corruption cases against former presidents Dilma Rousseff and Luiz Inácio Lula da Silva, Luis says that corruption is a 'huge problem for us' and that 'all of the Brazilian story is full of corruption', where the 'Brazilian government always makes deals with private companies to become rich'. He explains that 'Brazil is a rich country, but corruption blocks our real development' across its 'political, social, and cultural development'.

Forced Marriage and Women's Rights

Our conversation with Luis identified that in the case of Brazil, women have been under-represented in the struggle against modern slavery. Yet, in its 2018 GSI, the ILO and the Walk Free Foundation report that 71 per cent of the estimated 40.3 million enslaved people are women and that an estimated 15.4 million women are in forced marriage.[18] A forced marriage is one in which one or both people in the marriage have not or could not give(n) consent to the marriage, and where pressure and abuse are used to force them into marriage.[19] 'Force' in this case can include physical, psychological, sexual, financial and emotional pressure, where choice and the freedom to make choices are absent.[20] Forced marriage is also the focus of UN SDG Target 5.3, which seeks to 'eliminate all harmful practices, such as child, early and forced marriage and female genital mutilation'. To understand the disproportionate impact of modern slavery on women and the issue of forced marriage in particular, we spoke to Helen McCabe and Karen Sherman.[21] Helen is Associate Professor in the School of Politics and International Relations and a member of the Rights Lab at the University of Nottingham working on a multi-year project on forced marriage. Karen is a renowned author[22] and speaker on global women's issues. She was formerly a senior executive at Women for Women International and is currently the president of the Akilah

18 International Labour Organisation and Walk Free, *The Global Slavery Index*, 2018. https://www.globalslaveryindex.org/.

19 See https://www.gov.uk/government/publications/what-is-a-forced-marriage.

20 See, for example, https://rightsofwomen.org.uk/get-information/family-law/forced-marriage-law/.

21 H. McCabe and K. Sherman, "Forced Marriage and Women's Rights: What Connects SDGs 5 and 8.7?" The Rights Track, March 8, 2020. http://rightstrack.org/forced-marriage-and-womens-rights-what-connects-sdgs-5-and-87.

22 See K. Sherman, *Brick by Brick: Building Hope and Opportunity for Women Survivors Everywhere* (Lanham, MD: Rowman & Littlefield, 2020).

Institute, Rwanda's only women's college, leading its strategy, growth and partnerships.[23]

We published our episode with Helen and Karen on International Women's Day and began our conversation with them about marriage, the legalisation of marriage and the problem of forced marriage. After 30 years working in Rwanda, the Former Soviet Union and Central Asia, Karen argues that legalised marriage provides women with the 'rights to child custody, inheritance, property ownership', rights that do not 'convey to women that did not have a legally sanctioned marriage'. For Karen, 'marriage ensures women's rights and rights of children', but even where such 'rights are on the book', women 'are unable to access them, can't or don't know about them'. In addition, across many of the countries where she has worked, 'men are resistant' to the idea of legalised marriage and see such legal guarantees as 'reduced freedom' for men, which precludes the practice of having 'multiple partners' and 'multiple wives'. Against this increased 'accountability' through the law, 'men are baulking at the idea of a legal marriage'.

Helen agrees with Karen that women who 'don't have a legal marriage, don't have rights'. In the case of forced marriage, including the forced marriage of children, it is 'even harder to prove there is forced marriage when there is no legal record of the marriage' and calls for 'better record keeping'. Helen is a political philosopher, where her work on the nineteenth century reveals that various critiques of marriage raise very similar concerns that are in operation today concerning legalisation, rights and obligations.[24] For Helen and Karen, there is a 'strange dichotomy' between the 'need' for 'legal marriage to codify women's rights' and the reality of '40 million women across Africa being forced into marriage before their 15th birthday'. For Karen, the question comes down to 'what do women want?' and 'what are they defining in their best interests?' In the case of Rwanda, the 1994 genocide created 'an opportunity for women to redefine their rights' since they were 'leading the process and the rebuilding that followed'. Women's collective action in Rwanda was born out of necessity and circumstance, and the country has in many ways become a model in women's leadership, representation and positive change.

Karen argues further that women need 'education' and 'the ability to earn an income', which provide the 'skills, knowledge, [and] expertise to link up to the workplace'. Education 'gives women choice' over (1) 'sending and keeping

---

23 See https://www.akilahinstitute.org/.
24 See H. McCabe, *John Stuart Mill, Socialist* (Montreal and Kingston, London and Chicago: McGill-Queen's University Press, 2021).

kids, particularly daughters, in school'; (2) 'choices when a woman is suffering violence and abuse in the home' and (3) 'choices about how money is saved and spent'. Helen agrees that there is a cycle at work: 'girls who stay in school, get married later', and that 'girls who stay in school have more options about to whom and when they get married'. Against this, however, girls who stay in school will often find in some cultures that they are 'unmarriageable' given the very young age that girls are forced into marriage and/or considered 'suitable' for marriage. Helen's work has shown that 'forced marriage happens to women across the world', and some contexts, such as in the UK, there is still the 'racist perception that it only happens to people from South Asia', but the practice is far more extensive and pervasive. Helen and Karen are both hopeful that the raised awareness that forced marriage is one form of modern slavery can help reduce the practice. For Helen, the linking together of 'servile marriage, forced marriage, and slavery is a way to get the global community on board to take forced marriage seriously' where the 'action on gender can be leveraged'. She sees a complicated and sequential relationship between forced marriage and other forms of modern slavery. Women 'escape forced marriage' but are 'susceptible to trafficking'. Women who 'escape trafficking' are 'vulnerable to forced marriage'. Karen agrees that widening the struggle against forced marriage and slavery along lines of gender has been helpful, and through her own work is committed to converting women from victims to survivors to active citizens, making them 'potential agents of change, capable of transforming their lives, and in turn the lives of the families and communities'. In conceiving of women in this way, Karen believes they can 'rebuild their lives a brick at a time'.

Slavery Free Cities

Cities around the world are vulnerable to modern slavery, owing to their overall patterns in population density, the blend of their formal and informal economies and their lure to those individuals seeking a better life and enhanced economic opportunities.[25] Cities vary in size and complexity from small provincial cities like Nottingham to megacities such as Mexico City, São Paulo and Tokyo, as well as their variable ability to address the prob-

---

25 The dominant economic explanation for rural–urban migration focuses on the *expected* wage differential between rural and urban labour markets. In reality, the 'pull' from cities owing to this expected difference creates burgeoning city populations with chronic unemployment and the growth of the informal sector. This model of migration was first articulated in J.R. Harris and M.P. Todaro, "Migration, Unemployment and Development: A Two-Sector Analysis," *American Economic Review* 60, no. 1 (1970): 126–142.

lem of modern slavery. We spoke to Alison Gardner about her 'resilience framework'[26] and her advocacy for the establishment of 'slavery free cities'.[27] Alison is a Nottingham Research Fellow in the School of Sociology and Social Policy and Associate Director of the Communities and Society Programme in the Rights Lab, while she has prior experience over many years working in local government in Nottingham.[28]

Alison begins by telling us that approaches to combatting modern slavery in the UK have been at the 'national level'. The 2015 Modern Slavery Act, increased funding and 'raised awareness' in the media – all good developments in her view; however, she has not seen 'attention to how policy is implemented at a local level', which is 'a real problem' since 'slavery is primarily first encountered at the local level' and is 'prevented at the local level'. At the local level are found 'prevention', 'discovery' and 'recovery', which are 'managed by local level services and local voluntary sector services'. She says that as we move 'beyond recovery [...] you want to create communities that are resilient to this', where we need to work out 'how we fill that gap, respond to modern slavery, using the services we have on the ground'. For Alison, this response must focus on 'how can we serve people better to ensure that slavery cannot flourish in the places in which we live'. She says we need a 'systemic view' that 'runs from prevention through discovery and recovery, and what you do beyond recovery so it doesn't come back'.

There is great fear and a lack of systematic information pertaining to the return to slavery. There is 'no systematic tracking' of individuals who have been identified as victims and survivors of slavery, referred into the NRM, and then re-enslaved. Under the NRM, individuals receive housing and benefits, but then after the mandated time of support comes to an end, they face what Alison calls a 'cliff edge', are 'left destitute' and are therefore vulnerable to re-enslavement, with 'no systematic attention to how that problem is fixed on the ground'. Alison observes that 'a significant group' of those in the NRM are UK nationals who face 'conditions of vulnerability' that include 'substance abuse, homelessness, indebtedness, and poverty', as well as 'psychological trauma', while 'benefits sanctions mean that people are left in extreme poverty'.

---

26 A. Gardner, P. Northall, and B. Brewster, "Building Slavery Free Communities: A Resilience Framework," *Journal of Human Trafficking*. doi: .

27 A. Gardner, "Slavery-Free Cities: Why Community Is Key," The Rights Track, December 1, 2017. http://rightstrack.org/slavery-free-cities-why-community-is-key.

28 A. Gardner, "How the Home of Robin Hood Is Trying to Free Itself of Modern Slavery," *The Independent*, October 21, 2017. https://www.independent.co.uk/news/uk/home-news/how -the-home-of-robin-hood-is-trying-to-free-itself-of-modern-slavery-a8011481.html.

At the local level, there is a variety of stakeholders who seek to address the problem of modern slavery, but there remains a lack of inter-agency coordination and a truly coherent multi-stakeholder approach. Alison tells us that the 'police have certainly had some direction' but she says that they are 'not necessarily the best agency to be in the lead' on this issue. She sees the need for enhanced involvement from the health and local government services, and that the 'local voluntary and community sector' needs much more of a role. Under the NRM, the Salvation Army holds the main contract for supporting victims and survivors and subcontracts to other NGOs, but these organisations tend to operate at the regional and national level and not the local level. Local groups have a 'very limited' role to play at present, which for Alison is a real problem she has sought to address through her work. Beyond formal organisations, Alison says that she has not seen much 'work with the state to produce the kinds of services and changes on the ground'.

In the City of Nottingham, Alison has been involved in community organising across different faith-based groups, civil society organisations, local government agencies and law enforcement, which led to a formal declaration to make Nottingham a 'slavery free city'.[29] With its long history of radicalism and resistance, its long-standing myth of Robin Hood and its many disparities and inequalities, Nottingham appeared to be an ideal provincial city to launch such a commitment. For Alison, the basic tenants of her call for a slavery free city are 'public awareness raising, training of front-line staff, strong victim support services, and engagement with law enforcement'. She sees a strong role for uncommon stakeholders in her vision who do not have a formal remit to tackle modern slavery, such as energy supplier E.ON, whose meter readers are out in the local community. The company can raise awareness of its employees, who 'see these people all the time' and can 'spot the signs of slavery'. Beyond this company, she sees 'businesses and business practices that would strengthen the community against slavery', who need to 'look beyond supply chains' to 'what their role is as employers within a community, as corporate citizens of that community'. She also sees a role for banks, who can use their information on 'suspicious transactions', such as multiple cash deposits and cash withdrawals from the same people, an indicator of benefits fraud and benefits hoarding that typically takes place among perpetrators. Data on these kinds of suspicious transactions can be combined with data on 'houses in multiple occupation' and 'antisocial behaviour', such as the accumulation of uncollected refuse and the frequent movement of people at odd hours of the

---

29 On 18 November 2016, more than 800 representatives from Nottingham-based organisations pledged to make the city 'slavery free'.

day. Rather than focusing on detection and prosecution for slavery directly, Alison believes that multi-agency approaches can 'disrupt practices' related to slavery, where visits from 'pollution control, environmental health, trading standards' and others can 'get them on something'. Ultimately, Alison is optimistic about this kind of approach at the local level: 'I believe it is possible to shift people's mind set' in ways that will address the problem.

From the Ground Up

From Nottingham to Nigeria, we have seen from our conversations with representatives from leading frontline organisations and modern slavery scholars that there is currently much work focused on combatting modern slavery with much work that remains. We have seen different approaches to the problem, including criminal justice, public health, 'hotspots' and resilience frameworks. It is clear from our conversations that there are high quality and dedicated efforts taking place, but there remains the absence of a coordinated approach that addresses the root causes and drivers of slavery alongside efforts to liberate and support victims and survivors. It is also clear that the drivers for slavery vary across sectors with many different vulnerability factors operating at the individual, household, community and structural levels. Victims and survivors are often tipped into different forms of modern slavery owing to their perceived status in social hierarchies and being treated as second-class citizens, a status that is coupled with deeper cultural understandings and norms of social acceptance that are either visible or invisible. There are inadequate support mechanisms in place to prevent re-enslavement or to foster full economic and social reintegration of victims and survivors. The concerted efforts of anti-slavery groups, even in the absence of coordination, however, are gaining ground against the problem, where short, medium and long-term approaches are beginning to bring about positive change. Brick by brick, city by city, it is now more possible than ever to bring about a slavery free world for all.

Part IV

THE FUTURE OF HUMAN RIGHTS

Part IV of *The Rights Track* brings us full circle to consider what we have learned about human rights and modern slavery through the medium of podcasting. It argues that the two dominant scholar and practitioner communities engaged in the advance of human rights and the fight to end modern slavery have limited accessibility for their work through extant forms of dissemination and communication. We make the case for why podcasting gave us new insights into their work and how this form of communication can be effective in reaching larger audiences. It also demonstrates how podcasting has put the *human* back into human rights. It does so through pulling out the main themes that have emerged from our conversations across six series of the Rights Track and then looks to the future by addressing the key challenges facing the international community in what promises to be a very difficult century.

Chapter 12

COMMUNICATING HUMAN RIGHTS

Abstract

This final chapter considers the future of human rights and modern slavery through the lens of strategies of communication. It argues for a plurality of communications approaches, including the special contribution that we feel we have made using a podcast. It sets out the two dominant scholar and practitioner communities engaged in the advance of human rights and their extant forms of dissemination and communication, and makes the case for the use of podcasts. It does so through pulling out the main themes that have emerged from our conversations across six series of the Rights Track and then looks to the future by addressing the key challenges facing the international community in what promises to be a very difficult century.

'Fantastic coverage of cutting-edge research in human rights. Professor Todd Landman's interviews have helped me to develop my understanding of complex human rights research further – that is engaging and easy to digest. These podcasts are a great way to discover ground-breaking approaches to analysing human rights from across the world – on the go.'

– Rebecca Cordell, University of Texas at Dallas

'This podcast gives an insight into the work of practitioners in a very apprehensible manner. If you are a human rights law student (or want to become one), it might be a good one to share with a friend or parents who are wondering what is that you want to do as an international lawyer. It vigorously engages with different topics and makes it easy not only to solidify existing knowledge but also to be introduced to something new.'

– Apple Podcast Review

'As a college student, I used multiple episodes of his podcast in a research project I had to do, and they were extremely helpful. Cannot recommend this podcast highly enough.'

– Apple Podcast Review

'The 2018 Annual UK Top100 Corporate Modern Slavery Influencers' Index has played a significant role in raising awareness of modern slavery and labour exploitation amongst the business community whose supply chains are at risk, often unwittingly, of exposure to abuse.'

– Dr Shamir Ghumra, BREEAM Director at
Building Research Establishment (BRE) recognising
Todd Landman as a top 10 corporate influencer

– Top 20 Best Human Rights Podcasts 2021, *Welp Magazine*

Talking about Human Rights and Modern Slavery

As the world continues to grapple with the impacts and consequences of the COVID-19 pandemic, there has never been a more important time to consider, discuss and advocate for human rights. The Rights Track podcast has provided a unique and special platform to engage in important conversations and generate new insights into the lives of people around the globe and to highlight evidence-based approaches that could help the most vulnerable. Talking about human rights and modern slavery during the pandemic and since the 2015 inception of the Rights Track has given us so many new avenues to understand the people, places and problems affecting us all at many different levels. The people we have spoken to and the people who listen to our podcasts have a deep passion for human dignity and the human condition during times of extraordinary change and challenge in the world. Our encounters and conversations have revealed tremendous hope in recognising how many people are working hard every day on so many important and difficult issues. We have been listening to so many voices from around the world about everyday forms of violence, abuse, vulnerability, inequality and intersectionality, and our listeners have ingested, digested and used our audio content for a variety of different purposes ranging from education to advocacy. Our guests have inspired us and our listeners have encouraged and supported us. Across our many episodes, we know that the challenges of human rights and modern slavery leave no corner of the world untouched, and it has been a fascinating journey through the voices of so many who are working so hard to understand, explain and change for the better the ways in which human life is organised, protected and improved. In this final chapter, we provide our view on what we have learned, why podcasting gave us a new window on the world and what we can say about the future of human rights and modern slavery.

Scholars and Practitioners

Human rights have come about through the recognition that after two world wars in the twentieth century, the international community needed to articulate and ultimately codify a set of claims and protections for human dignity and human agency. As we have shown in this book, this commitment to basic human values has expanded in ways that the original drafters of the Universal Declaration of Human Rights could never have imagined. As Chapter 3 has made clear, the genesis of human rights has a very long philosophical and practical history, and the formal expression of human rights has been achieved through consensus across many different fora involving a very large number of stakeholders from around the world. The history of the advocacy for the Universal Declaration of Human Rights in 1948 includes important precedents, such as the establishment of the League of Nations in 1920, the promulgation of the 1926 Slavery Convention and the founding of the United Nations in 1945. Each of these developments sought to bring the family of nations together through the promise of inter-governmentalism in order to address common problems facing all of humanity. The growing body of international human rights law is also reflected in national constitutions and finds expression in the significant development of regional instruments in Europe, Latin America and Africa with hopes to expand the legal remit to other regions. There is now a comprehensive international, regional and national institutional 'machinery' for the promotion and protection of human rights. This machinery, however, would not function without people, who embody these rights, make them real and move them from the page to practice.

These people comprise the loosely defined 'human rights movement', which has included scholars, practitioners and activists who have increasingly used the language of human rights to provide a moral compass on how state and non-state actors ought to conduct themselves. In the academic world, human rights have been embraced and largely propelled forward by scholars in the discipline of law; however, attention to human rights goes beyond law to include history, philosophy, education, geography, political science, economics, business, culture and media studies, and after its initial rejection, anthropology.[1] Across these disciplines, scholars have problematised human rights; expanded the set of human rights protected through international, regional and domestic laws; studied the variation and interdependence of human rights; and sought to understand popular attitudes towards and experiences of human rights, among many other issues. Their work has also involved human rights education at all levels of provision, with dedicated undergraduate programmes, master's programmes, PhD programmes and

---

1   See American Anthropological Association, "Statement on Human Rights," *American Anthropologist*, 49, no. 4 (1957): 539–543. See also M. Freeman, *Human Rights: An Inter-disciplinary Approach*, 2nd ed. (London: Wiley, 2011).

postdoctoral programmes, which have seen growth in interest from many generations of students who have gone on to be scholars and practitioners themselves. Since the 1990s, this community of scholars has forged a new research and practical agenda to end modern slavery: a calling that has now been formally embraced by the United Nations.

Outside the academy, practitioners, primarily but not exclusively working for international and national non-governmental organisations, have been driving a progressive and cumulative human rights agenda. They have focused on individual cases and support for political prisoners, victims and survivors of human rights violations, including survivors of modern slavery. They have raised awareness of human rights problems around the world and advocated for change and sought justice. They have carried out their own research and issued reports and calls for action to bring positive change to the promotion and protection of human rights. The network of these organisations has grown in depth and breadth over many decades, while the history of many of these groups predates the 1948 Universal Declaration of Human Rights, such as ASI[2] and the International Federation for Human Rights.[3] Working at the domestic level and putting pressure on states and international organisations, they represent a 'TAN' that seeks to advance human rights across the world. Most recently, work from this network, according to Zoe Trodd from the Rights Lab, now includes the 'fourth great wave' of abolitionism.

For us, these are two important and in many cases, overlapping communities of people who write, analyse and advocate for human rights, and to date the primary form of dissemination and work has been the written word. Research monographs, textbooks, peer-reviewed journal articles, policy briefs, reports and other written content on human rights have proliferated significantly since the Universal Declaration of Human Rights covering a broad range of topics within the theory and practice of human rights. Their work has developed a specialised vocabulary and form of communication that remains difficult to access, while many of the findings, claims and recommendations remain complicated and difficult to communicate in ways that are legible for a wider public. This has meant that their work, as advanced and high quality as it is, still reaches a relatively small audience. Moreover, the 'revolving door' between and among the academy, human rights organisations and

---

2 Anti-Slavery International was founded originally as the British and Foreign Anti-Slavery Society in 1839, see https://www.antislavery.org/.
3 The International Federation for Human Rights was founded in 1922, see https://www.fidh.org/en/.

formal institutions runs the risk of creating a human rights 'echo chamber' that advances human rights discourse, law and practice, and yet continues to remain difficult to access for the non-specialist.

The Value of Podcasts

The relatively limited accessibility of this specialised and hermetically sealed 'epistemic community' of human rights experts motivated us to turn to the medium of podcasts to enhance dissemination and *humanise* human rights in ways that have not been done before. As set out in Chapter 2, our 'fireside chats' with scholars, practitioners and activists around the world have given space for free expression, reflection and a platform for an ongoing global conversation that provides a new way to capture the 'human part of knowledge creation'.[4] This conversational and dialogic approach to getting the hard facts about human rights challenges has been responsive to real-time human rights issues and questions and has allowed us to engage with people differently. We timed the release of each series with International Human Rights Day (10 December) and dedicated a whole series to the impact of COVID-19 on human rights (Chapter 7), which was unforeseen when we initially created the Rights Track. Our conversations allowed our guests to leave the 'ivory tower' of academia, the halls of power in major international and national institutions and the day-to-day struggle to improve human rights in order to paint a personal and human portrait of their work and how it is making a difference. We learned how they dedicated their entire lives to the pursuit of justice, the advance of law, understanding how to count and compare human rights violations, how to understand the gap between the de jure protection and de facto realisation of human rights, and most importantly, what can be done to address this gap. Rather than reading their work, we asked them to talk about it, challenged their answers, pushed them to share and invited them to join others in our curated conversation. This enabled them to speak to us, with us and with others in ways that can only be done through the power of the podcast.

Our conversations showed us that the path to knowledge creation and impact is often long and lonely, requiring resilience, curiosity and dedication, as well as a mindset that asks difficult questions in search of meaningful answers. From survivors to a baroness, statisticians to business leaders, young scholars to world leading experts, our guests have amazed us and our listeners

---

4   Some of the content in this section draws on T. Landman, "Podcasting is Perfect for People with Big Ideas. Here's How to Do It," *The Guardian*, January 13, 2016. https://www.theguardian .com/higher-education-network/2016/jan/13/podcasting-is-perfect-for-big-ideas.

with their stories and insights. Examples from our many guests capture this idea of personal and raw human endeavour. Dixon Osburn led a 17-year battle to repeal the 'Don't Ask, Don't Tell' policy in the US armed forces and then went on to fight deep injustices and widespread human rights abuses. Shareen Hertel travelled in Mexico and South Asia to understand the plight of workers. Genevieve LeBaron spent years visiting tea plantations to understand production processes and value chains, while Elaine Mitchel-Hill walked the supply chains for her company's product lines and Siddharth Kara visited the cobalt mines of the Congo and saw first-hand how children were exploited to provide the developed world with mobile devices. Patrick Ball worked in South Africa, Peru, Guatemala, Sierra Leone and East Timor to provide the best statistical evidence possible for use across many Truth Commissions. Mahi Ramakrishnan spent decades travelling between Myanmar and Malaysia to help refugees and migrant workers. Across these and our many other guests, we witnessed their unrelenting commitment to bring about positive change to the world, and we shared our conversations with a growing audience who listened to the Rights Track in so many different contexts and environments. From our monthly recordings to writing this book, we have been in awe of their dedication and their hard work across so many difficult and agonising topics.

Themes and Lessons

It is clear to us given the rich content shared through this book, that human rights are a complex area of research, policy, advocacy and action. In addition to its long history, the topic of human rights has expanded considerably throughout the twentieth and twenty-first centuries. The complexity comes from the fact that there are now over sixty human rights codified in international, regional and domestic laws. This set of rights is further differentiated across the state obligations to respect, protect and fulfil human rights. The resulting matrix of human rights categories and obligations has many additional temporal, spatial and disciplinary differences. This complexity means that in the face of limited resources, states face many challenges in prioritising their activities in order to uphold these different rights. It means that there is a continued and pressing need to build a strong and sound evidence base to provide important pathways for the greater protection of human rights. Most importantly for this book, it means that communicating human rights remains a significant challenge. It has been a difficult story to tell and across our many guests, we have sought to use the medium of podcasts to really understand the many different dimensions of this complexity in ways that are more accessible and conversational than traditional forms of communication.

We have learned that it is difficult to establish a sound evidence base for understanding the current state of and future prospects for human rights and modern slavery. The hidden population of human rights victims and survivors, the hidden nature of their circumstances in terms of actions and events and the deeper structures and inequalities that underpin them present research and practical limits for understanding the true nature and extent of human rights issues. Each of our guests approaches these problems with their own life experiences, educational and professional backgrounds and their own assumptions about how the world works and on what we should focus to improve and advance human rights. Despite these many differences, however, we have seen a remarkable agreement across a wide range of common themes that run through our different chapters, podcasts and topics of discussion, a golden thread that brings coherence and optimism in equal measure. Given the 'unobservable' nature of much of this area of work, we have seen dedicated approaches leveraged to build a knowledge base on human rights around the world. We are of the view that the evidence we now have has grown in scope and sophistication, which allows us to make some stylised observations in this final chapter. We recognise, however, that communicating and translating these observations can be all the more difficult in an age of social media and misinformation, which have fed suspicion and scepticism about the utility of human rights. We have also learned of the doubt and scepticism that some voice about the nature of modern slavery.

Stylised Findings

We learned from many of our guests that human rights are advancing in ways that are much more than popular perception, attitudes and the media may suggest. At a global aggregate level, Chris Fariss (Chapter 4) has produced truly seminal work that has shown that even though we have a higher standard of expectation about state behaviour, the long-term trends in human rights have been ones of improvement. These trends uncovered by Chris are complemented by the work of James Ron (Chapter 4), who tells us popular attitudes about human rights, particularly among mass publics outside the 'Global North', are strong and positive. These more optimistic findings about trends and attitudes about human rights are complemented by the case work that has been done by people such as Dixon Osburn (Chapter 3). Bill Simmons reminds us how we need to be mindful of the joyful dimensions of the lives of victims and survivors, and at the same time of the ever-present tendency for different communities to 'marginalise the other' through their discourses, actions and policies. Certainly, our whole series on the impact of COVID-19 (Chapter 7) has shown that this tendency has been evident across many different groups, effectively enhancing and exacerbating pre-existing inequalities.

Across the book, we have learned that 'intersectionality' and 'interdependence' are much more than a simple claim or an official declaration, but the lived experience of many people around the world. Whether discussing torture and other forms of inhuman and degrading treatment, varieties of practices that fall under the rubric of modern slavery or the disproportionate impact of COVID-19, we have seen that gender, class, race, poverty and ethnicity intersect in compound and complex ways. Refugees, migrant workers, forced and child labourers, IDPs, women, people of African descent, and poor and marginalised people have all in one way or another experienced more difficult life conditions and suffered human rights abuse in one form or another disproportionately. From torture to trade, from voting to eating, from moving to working, there is a recurrent pattern across much of the world that reveals this disproportionate experience. These patterns provide evidence that human rights in many countries might make people 'legally equal', but in reality, they remain 'socially unequal'. In other countries, we learned that certain groups remain legally unequal, such as the hundreds of thousands of Rohingya. These trends in experience suggest to us strongly that 'identity', 'difference' and the 'politics of the other' really matter for the relative enjoyment and exercise of human rights.

Part III of the book makes it clear to us that slavery has not disappeared from the world. Over three series of the Rights Track, our 35 guests told us that the problem of slavery is very much a modern and highly complex one. The historical assertion of overt 'property rights' over enslaved people has given way to the treatment of people 'as if' they are property, which continues to affect tens of millions of people in all countries of the world in many different ways across different sectors. We learned that there are certain continuities and discontinuities between the slavery of the past and slavery of the present, while so many of the experiences resonate with those experienced by such notable former slaves and abolitionists as Frederick Douglass. The use of the term 'modern slavery' today is not universally accepted, but with the advent of the UK Modern Slavery Act, the Australian Modern Slavery Act, and in policy and legislative debates in the European Parliament, the term is gaining traction. Whether in the brick kilns of Bangladesh, the cobalt mines of the Congo, the garment factories of Leicester or the nail bars of Nottingham, modern slavery in all its forms is alive, ever-present and often 'hidden in plain sight'.

We also learned that the phenomenon of slavery, the world's truly first human rights issue, in its current incarnation, raises significant questions around 'structure' and 'agency', 'slavery' and 'freedom', 'victims' and 'survivors', and 'economic growth' and 'sustainable development'. The issue of slavery today cannot be reduced to a simple dichotomy between individual volition and agency as against larger economic structures. We learned that the people who have been enslaved do not necessarily become 'free' at their moment of liberation, while the term 'freedom' itself remains fluid and relative. We learned that in certain contexts there are strong cultural and community practices that have made slavery socially acceptable. We learned that many different business models underpin long periods of economic growth, but that the very structure and operation of these models often rely on the use of forced labour, bonded labour and other forms of extreme exploitation that lie at the heart of global supply chains. The United Nations articulation of this problem as one of *sustainable development* asks us to move our gaze away from raw economic growth to one of growth with equity and freedom from modern slavery as a bare minimum while emphasising a larger goal for 'decent work' for all.

Finally, we have learned from all our guests that human rights advance only through people 'giving voice' and 'bearing witness' to their lived experiences. Only through open dialogue; the telling of stories and narratives; and the free exchange of ideas, challenges and inconvenient truths can we begin to right past wrongs, raise awareness about current wrongs and find solutions to prevent future wrongs. It is a voice that we have captured and shared through our work on the Rights Track. The voices we heard shared a wide range of experiences in the struggle for human rights, whether these voices were from scholars, practitioners, victims or survivors. Many of our guests have also borne witness either for themselves or on behalf of others, making the case that difference matters, inequalities are real and deeply felt, and that solutions for a better world must include those who have been most affected by their own experiences. Having space and time for these voices to be shared and the sound evidence that we have uncovered in the ways that we have done in our podcast and in these pages have been hugely enlightening, inspiring and joyful.

The Future of Human Rights

The global human rights community has established a foundation and a framework for the promotion and protection of human rights and has issued a call to end slavery forever. The latter half of the twentieth century gave shape and purpose to this framework, and more nations than ever before were at least formally committing themselves to the ideas and values that underpin this framework. At the turn of the twenty-first century, however, we now know that the world experienced a turning point, where the terrorist

attacks of 9/11 made many nations look inward with great fear and trepida-
tion, while at the same time joining forces to engage in a new round of conflicts, nation building and imposition. The rise of populism, nationalism and
increasing isolationism has raised serious questions about 'globalism', 'multi-
culturalism', 'cosmopolitanism' and 'global citizenship' at a time when communications technologies, the diffusion of values and hyper-mobility have
made the achievement of such ideas even easier. As David Owen (Chapter 7)
reminds us, however, the COVID-19 pandemic has shown us how connected
and interdependent we all are, as its rapid spread and progress across the
world took us all by surprise and changed our lives forever.

The fragmentation of Iraq, the rise and fall of ISIS, the turn towards
authoritarianism and the withdrawal of forces from Afghanistan illustrate the
many limits to foreign interventionism, as well as the many challenges that
remain with us in shaping a better world for all. These setbacks and reversals,
however, do not undermine the fundamental appeal of human rights. The
simple claim that human rights are articulated on the basis of our shared and
common humanity run far and deep. Guest after guest shared with us the
appeal of these ideas and the importance of recognising our shared humanity. After talking to so many people engaged in understanding the many complexities of lived experiences tell us that we do *need to hold tight to human rights*.
Holding tight to human rights is both a normative commitment and a practical embrace of tools that put the human back into human rights. As the world
emerges from the pandemic it faces significant challenges with respect to climate change; inter-generational justice; endemic inequalities; and the continued threat of violence, conflict, terrorism and the abuse of human rights.
In the face of these challenges, individuals, groups and nation states need
to accept their own humanity, use the human rights framework effectively
in ways that recognise and celebrate diversity, while remaining inclusive in
formulating solutions for the future. The pandemic forces us to hold a mirror up to ourselves and asks us to think again about how we should organise
ourselves in more equitable ways. We need enlightened leaders that speak 'an
octave higher than the rest of us understand' for us to realise what needs to be
done to protect the most vulnerable and to avoid the worst forms of our own
behaviour. For us, listening to this higher octave has begun with the Rights
Track and needs to continue in earnest for all our sake.

APPENDIX 1: COMPLETE LIST OF *RIGHTS TRACK* PODCASTS BY SERIES, EPISODES, GUEST (S), TITLE, AND DURATION, 2015-2021

	Ep.	Guest (s) (N=71)	Title	Duration
Series 1	1	Chris Fariss	Are we better at human rights than we used to be?	00:22:15
	2	Amanda Murdie	Do NGOs matter?	00:21:35
	3	Will Moore	How do we count victims of torture?	00:26:16
	4	Kevin Bales	Modern day slavery: counting and accounting	00:38:22
	5	Sakiko Fakuda-Parr	Beyond GDP: a measure of economic and social rights	00:30:54
	6	James Ron	A matter of opinion: what do we really think about human rights?	00:23:53
	7	Patrick Ball	How can statistics advance human rights?	00:30:46
	8	Rhoda Howard-Hassmann	Digesting food crime: is there an appetite for prosecution?	00:22:14
	9	Meg Satterthwaite	Does a picture speak a thousand words when advocating human rights?	00:22:11
	10	Shareen Hertel	Making human rights our business	00:25:42
	11	William Paul Simmons	Human rights: reasons to be joyful	00:27:24
	12	Christopher Phelps and Karen Salt	Does American need a Truth Commission?	00:44:19

(Continued)

	Ep.	Guest (s) (N=71)	Title	Duration
Series 2	13	Richard Beaven	Gay rights – how far have we come?	00:24:33
	14	Elisebth Witchell	Freedom of the press: how do we protect the rights of journalists?	00:20:07
	15	Monica Casper	Women and Trump: a question of rights?	00:29:02
	16	Dixon Osburn	Pursuing justice: what role for research evidence?	00:21:38
	17	Akbar Ahmed	Islam and the West: questions of human rights	00:26:47
	18	Meghna Abraham	Advancing human rights the Amnesty way	00:24:29
	19	Iain Levine	Evidence for change: the work of Human Rights Watch	00:20:58
	20	Claire Thomas	In the minority: the right to identity, culture and heritage	00:24:45
	21	Evelyn Astor	Worker rights: a question of basic income?	00:17:40
	22	Gonzola Vargas Llosa	Refugees: why hard times need hard facts	00:19:48
	23	Garth Lenz	Picture this: using photography to make a case for environmental rights	00:19:27
	24	Heidi Beirich	Hating the haters: tackling radical right groups in the United States	00:23:37
Series 3	25	Zoe Trodd	Blueprint for Freedom: ending modern slavery by 2030	00:22:25
	26	Alison Gardner	Slavery-free cities: why community is key	00:24:05
	27	Alexander Trautrims	Unchained supply: eradicating slavery from the supply chain	00:23:31
	28	Andrea Nicholson and Minh Dang	Voices of slavery: listen and learn	00:23:25
	29	Doreen Boyd	Eye in the sky: rooting out slavery from space	00:21:33
	30	Sir Bernard Silverman	Crunching numbers: modern slavery and statistics	00:20:43
	31	Austin Choi-Fitzpatrick	Face to face: researching the perpetrators of modern slavery	00:24:53
	32	Zoe Trodd and Todd Landman	Modern slavery: a human rights approach	00:33:46

(Continued)

	Ep.	Guest (s) (N=71)	Title	Duration
Series 4	33	David Blight and John Stauffer	The useable past: what lessons do we learn from history in the fight to end slavery?	00:23:35
	34	Dan Vexler, David Westlake, Steven Webster	Fighting slavery on the ground: what does it look like?	00:20:58
	35	Patricia Hynes and Patrick Burland	Becoming a slave: who is vulnerable to being trafficked?	00:23:32
	36	Rt. Rev. Alastair Redfern	How is the church leading the fight to end modern slavery?	00:19:27
	37	Pradeep Narayanan and Anusha Chandrasekharan	Bonded labour: listening to the voices of the poor and marginalised	00:22:34
	38	James Cockayne	How is the UN working to end modern slavery?	00:23:15
	39	Baroness Lola Young	Fast fashion and football: a question of ethics	00:21:41
	40	Juliana Semione	Life after slavery: what does freedom really look like?	00:24:51
Series 5	41	Luís Da Costa Leão	Health and slavery: what connects SDG 3 and SDG 8.7?	00:24:11
	42	Helen McCabe and Karen Sherman	Forced marriage and women's rights: what connects SDGs 5 and 8.7?	00:28:19
	43	Katarina Schwarz and Laura Dean	Strengthening laws and ending modern slavery: what connects SDGs 16 and 8.7?	00:31:03
	44	Elaine Mitchell-Hill and Arianne Griffith	Walking the supply chain to uphold human rights: what connects SDGs 12 and 8.7?	00:29:13
	45	Ravi Prakesh and Phil Northall	Creating stronger places for child rights: what connects SDGs 8.7 and 11?	00:29:20
	46	Jasmine O'Connor and Emily Wyman	Global partnerships to end modern slavery: what connects SDGs 8.7 and 17?	00:31:35
	47	John Gathergood and Genevieve LeBaron	The business of modern slavery: what connects SDG 8.7 with SDG 8?	00:40:15
	48	Siddharth Kara and Hannah Lerigo-Stephens	The Congo, cobalt and cash: what connects SDGs 9 and 8.7?	00:32:18
		Subtotal[1]		**20:29:10**

(Continued)

	Ep.	Guest (s) (N=71)	Title	Duration
Review	49	Todd Landman Omnibus 1	Advancing human rights	00:54:29
	50	Todd Landman Omnibus 2	Ending modern slavery	01:00:00
Series 6	51	Nina Ansary	COVID-19 and women's rights: what impact is the pandemic having?	00:25:58
	52	Dominique Day	Covid, race and inequality: why it is time to hold tight to human rights	00:30:12
	53	David Fathi	Covid and incarceration: how is the pandemic affecting prisons and prisoners?	00:27:08
	54	Alison Brysk	Do human rights provide a pathway out of the pandemic?	00:28:27
	55	Mahi Ramakrishnan	Covid and refugees: protecting the rights of the other	00:26:46
	56	Aoife Nolan	Promoting and preserving children's rights after Covid-19: what needs to happen?	00:27:52
	57	Tom Parker	Tackling Covid-19 and terrorism – the need for a human rights approach	00:29:13
	58	Arlene Tickner and David Owen	Sowing division: COVID-19, democracy, and migration	00:31:40
		Subtotal[2]		**05:41:45**
		Total[3]		**26:10:55**

Source: Compiled by the authors from www.rightstrack.org, 2015–21.

[1]Total duration of Series 1–5 (hours, minutes, seconds).

[2]Total duration of Series 6 (hours, minutes, seconds).

[3]Total duration of Series 1–6, excluding review episodes (hours, minutes, seconds).

INDEX

Note: Bold page numbers refer to figures and tables.

abolitionism 160, 166, 178, 232
Abraham, M. 43, 47, 52, 54, 59
ACA: *see* Affordable Care Act
academic perspective: Business and
   Human Rights Resource Centre 62;
   economic incentives for companies
   63; empirical generalisations 61; petty
   rivalries 62; Ruggie Principles 62;
   struggle for human rights 60; UN
   Global Compact 62–63; United States
   Fish and Wildlife Service 60
Achievement Possibility Frontier 83
ACLU: *see* American Civil Liberties
   Union
Affordable Care Act (ACA) 121
agent-based computer simulations 198
Ahmed, A. 44, 87, 93, 99, 106
Allain, J. 170
Alliance 8.7 175
All-Party Parliamentary Group
   on Ethics and Sustainability in
   Fashion 199
Al-Qaeda 12
American Civil Liberties Union (ACLU)
   45, 99, 140; National Prison Project
   138
Amnesty International 47, 77; additional
   set of rights 52–53; field missions
   to Indonesia 55; forced labour and
   unsafe conditions 54–55; letter-writing
   campaigns of prisoners 52; 'name
   and shame' approach 55; role for
   accountability 54; state obligation
   approach 54
antebellum slavery 21
anti-LGBT groups 97
anti-lockdown and anti-mask protests
   150

anti-Semitism 101
anti-slavery efforts 185, 190, 211
Anti-Slavery International (ASI) 51, 232
anti-slavery legislation 154, 168–71
anti-slavery NGOs, proliferation of 210
anti-slavery sentiment 170–71
anti-terror legislation 11, 146
anti-trafficking 104, 168, 170, 188
Arab Spring 12
Armed conflict between 2000 and
   2020 13
armed militia groups 97
articulation of Target 8.7 175
artificial intelligence 71, 84, 175, 192
asylum seekers 13, 108, 110, 141, 151
Australian Modern Slavery Act 236
*Avoiding the Terrorist Trap: Why Respect
   for Human Rights Is the Key to Defeating
   Terrorism* (Parker) 146

Bachelet, M. 134
Bales, K. 38, 44, 65, 75, 81, 84, 210
Bali attack of 2002 12
Ball, P. 44, 65, 69, 72, 73, 234
ban on travel from Muslim-majority
   countries 110
Barrientos, P.P. 52, 58, 59
Bashar-Al-Assad regime in Syria, case
   against 58, 59
Beaven, R. 44, 107, 123
*Behave: The Biology of Humans at Our Best
   and Worst* (Sapolsky) 126
Beijing Declaration and Platform for
   Action, 1995 135
Beirich, H. 44, 87, 91, 97, 101, 106, 110,
   111, 119
Bellagio-Harvard Guidelines on the Legal
   Parameters of Slavery 160, 177

Black Americans: disproportionality of treatment 117; Kerner Commission, 1967 118; troubling 120; Truth and Reconciliation Commission report 119; two-nation society 118; Universal Declaration of Human Rights 119
black and racial justice mobilisation: antebellum slavery 21; Black Lives Matter 21–22; Civil Rights Movement 21; International Convention on the Elimination of all Forms of Racial Discrimination, 1966 22; Reconstruction 21; 'Unite the Right' white supremacist rally 21
Black Lives Matter movement 21–22, 98, 108, 111, 116, 150
Blair, T. 11
Blight, D. 154, 157, 162
Blood and Earth (Bales) 210
Bolsonaro, J. 13, 14, 58
bombings, 2004 Madrid and 2005 London 100
bonded labour 84, 185, 190, 205, 237
bonded labour, in India 154; Bonded Labour System (Abolition) Act of 1976 212; Corporate Responsibility Watch 213; Dalit community, 'untouchable' group 211–12; debt bondage or peonage 211; ground level panels 212; invisibilisation of threats 212; National Action Plan 213; participant action research process 212; physical violence and threats 212; rights-based legislation 213
'Boxing Day' tsunami of 2004 17
Boyd, D. 44, 65, 84
Brazilian Penal Code 220
'Brick Belt' 84
Brysk, A. 45, 129, 132
Burland, P. 154, 209, 213
Bush, G.W. 27, 74, 122, 130, 131
Business and Human Rights Resource Centre 62
business models and modern slavery: agent-based computer simulations 198; cheap labour 198; complexity in sourcing and procurement 197; use of coercion 198

Calhoun, J. C. 165
capitalism 193; success of 194; without slavery 194–95
Carr Centre for Human Rights (Harvard) 201

Casper, M. 44, 107, 121
cauterisation, strategy of 110, 127
Centre for Justice and Accountability (CJA) 43, 52, 57–59, 63, 67
Chandrasekharan, A. 154, 209
Charter of the International Military Tribunal, 1945 160
cheap labour 62, 198
child labour 17, 105, 159–60, 202, 205, 236
children and COVID-19: impact of digital divide 144; mass de-regulation, of social care 144; rights protections 144
children's rights 56, 143–46
Choi-Fitzpatrick, A. 154, 179, 181, 213
Christian Identity movement 97
Church and modern slavery: anti-trafficking legislation 104; community-based and faith-based networks 106; contribution of church 104; equal value of humans 105; House of Lords, role of 105; labour or other forms of exploitation 104; phone app 105; Redfern, conversation with 103–5; sexual exploitation 104; UK Modern Slavery Act, 2015 104
Cingranelli and Richards (CIRI) Human Rights Data Project 77
citizen journalism 95
citizenship gap 132
Civil Rights Movement 21, 97, 116, 123, 165
civil society organisations 218, 225
civil war in El Salvador 74
CJA: *see* Centre for Justice and Accountability
Clinton, H. 124
cobalt, technology and business: extraction of cobalt in DRC 202; extraction process and research 201–2; extraction, research 201–2; informal market 203; mining region in DRC **202**; modern slavery strategies 204; power and market imbalance 203; redistribution principle 203–4; strategic litigation process 204
Cockayne, J. 39, 154, 157, 170, 173
Code 8.7 175
COE: *see* Council of Europe
coercion, use of 198
collective health 219
Colvin, M. 59
Committed to Rights (Comstock) 15

Committee to Protect Journalists (CPJ) 44; work of 94
Communism 9, 93
community-based action-research project 188
community-based and faith-based networks 106
community-based organisations 218
contemporary terrain 51–52
Convention on the Rights of the Child, 1989 143–44, 160
Corporate Responsibility Watch 213
corporate social responsibility (CSR) 195–96, 213
corruption 94, 95, 142, 171, 173, 221
Council of Europe (COE) 9, 48, 143
COVID-19 pandemic 5, 19, 115; abuse in groceries and pharmacies 133; citizenship gap 132; democracy and migration 149–50; early warning; 130–32; emergence of global pandemic 130; and groups (*see* groups and COVID-19); impact of 235–36; impacts of 45, 132; interdependence 132–33; stringency index 147, **147**; terrorism (*see* terrorism)
cross-border dissemination of information 96
CSR: *see* corporate social responsibility
Cusack, J. 27

Dalit community, untouchable group 211–12
Dang, M. 154, 179, 181
dark figure of slavery crimes 73, 76
Dean, L. 154, 157, 170
debt bondage or peonage 183, 211, 220
Delta 8.7 175
democracy: and Islam 101–2; and migration (*see* migration and democracy)
Democratic Republic of the Congo (DRC) 82, 84, 202
democratic transitions and achievements 13
digital divide, impact of 144
discrimination against women in STEM 135
discriminatory policies and laws 135
domestic human rights documentation 51
domestic legislation 74–75, 171
Dominique Day 45, 136
'Don't Ask, Don't Tell' policy, 1994 57, 58, 234

Domesday Book 70
Douglass, F. 154, 157, 162–64, 166, 167, 176, 178, 236
DRC: *see* Democratic Republic of the Congo
drones, use of 102

earth observation (EO) data 82, 84, 130, 192
Ebola 130
economic incentives for companies 63
economic migrants 108, 110
EDI: *see* equality, diversity and inclusion
elite white feminism, UK 124
Emancipation Proclamation, 1863 97
End of Human Rights (Douzinas) 14
Endtimes of Human Rights (Hopgood) 14, 57
enhanced interrogation techniques 11
enslavement, trauma of 216
equal value of humans 105
equality, diversity and inclusion (EDI) 117; agenda 125
equality and inclusion 124, 151
ethical certification 195–96
ethical fashion 199
European Convention on Human Rights, 1951 9
European Union 2, 9, 13–14, 58, 172
events-based data and multiple systems estimation: abuse during government's conflict with Maoist 72–73; CIRI Human Rights Data Project 77; civil war in El Salvador 74; dark figure of slavery crimes 73, 76; description 72; domestic legislation 74; Ill-Treatment and Torture (ITT) data set 77; International Covenant on Civil and Political Rights, 1966 74; multiple systems estimation (MSE) 73; Pinochet regime in Chile 74; primary sources 74; statistics 74–75; Truth Commission in Peru 75; UK Modern Slavery Act, 2015 76; Universal Declaration of Human Rights, 1948 74
evidence and inference: authenticity and specificity 71; hard-to-find populations 71; human rights evidence, inference and error **70**
Evidence for Hope (Sikkink) 14
evolution in human rights 48
extraction of cobalt in DRC 202
'extraordinary rendition' of terror suspects 11

fair trade movement 207
faith-based groups 225
Fariss, C.J. 37, 44, 65, 78, 235
Fascism 9
fast fashion: drive for cheap and
disposable clothing 200; ethical
fashion 199; hyper-distributed supply
chain 201; Rana Plaza disaster, 2013
200
Fathi, D. 45, 129, 138, 163
Femia, R. 137
fighting slavery on the ground: anti-
slavery efforts 211; modern slavery
referrals 210; proliferation of anti-
slavery NGOs 210
Floyd, G. 21, 108, 116, 136
force, description 221
forced labour 158; intermediaries 214;
IOM's 'Determinants of Vulnerability'
model 214–15; in Nigeria, Albania and
Vietnam 213–15; in seafood industry
217; trafficking 213, 214; and unsafe
conditions 54–55
Forced Labour Convention, 1930 160
Forced Labour Protocol, 2014 160
forced marriage 6, 153, 155, 158, 210;
education 222–23; force, description
221; legalisation of marriage 222;
practice of multiple partners 222;
susceptibility to trafficking 223;
women's collective action in Rwanda
222; and women's rights (see women)
forced migration 108, 173
Foreign Sovereign Immunities Act, 1976
59
formal and informal supply chain 207
formal institutions 232–33
Foster, J. 27
Fourth World Conference on Women
135
free speech champion 88, 91
freedom and modern slavery: anti-
trafficking and anti-slavery legislation
168; freedom, statements 168–69;
National Referral Mechanism (NRM)
167; Q Methodology 167–68; Q-Sort
process 168; UK Modern Slavery Act,
2015 167
freedom blueprint 176–78; Anti-Slavery
Day 176; SDG target 8.7 176; slavery-
free communities 177
Freedom Fund 215; hotspot model,
criteria 218; work of 217

freedom of religion, belief and thought:
International human rights law and
freedom **92**; LGBTQ community 93;
liberation theology 93–94; political and
social revolutions 92; post-9/11 'war on
terror' 93; religiosity 92
Fugitive Slave Law 164
Fukuda-Parr, S. 44, 65, 83

Gangmasters and Labour Abuse
Authority 199
Gardner, A. 155, 209, 224
Garrington, C. 1, 29, 33
Garrison, W.L. 165
Gastil, Raymond D. 77, 78
Gates, B. 130, 131
Gathergood, J. 154, 191, 194
gay rights 57; EDI agenda 125; elite
white feminism, UK 124; equality
and inclusion 124; homophobia 125;
LGBTQ+ awareness 125; Marriage
(Same Sex Couples) Act 2013 124, 125;
rights of transsexuals 123; same-sex
relationships 123
gender-based violence 120, 196
genocide 9, 52, 75, 110, 222
Gervais, R. 27
Ghandi, M. 93
Gibney, M. 77
global economy 154, 192–93, 196, 202
global gag rule 56
global inequalities 149
Global Slavery Index (GSI) 17, 76, 81, 162
Griffiths, A. 154, 191, 204
ground level panels 212
groups and COVID-19: backlash and
xenophobia 142; children 143–45;
COVID-19 hotspots 140; deep-seated
patriarchy 142; discrimination against
women in STEM 135; discriminatory
policies and laws 135; extant hospital
protocols 137; ICE detention cases
140; immigration detention centres
140; impact of digital divide 144;
lack of racial unity 141–42; legalised
discrimination 135; mass de-regulation,
of social care 144; massive racial
disparities 136; medical bias 136;
mixed economy of public and private
prisons 138; Movement Control
Orders 141; people of African descent
135–38; poor ventilation and sanitation
140; pre-trial detention centres 140;

prisoners 138–40; push and pull factors
141; rampant corruption 142; refugees
141–43; rights protections 144; vaccine
hesitancy, issue of 138; women 134–35
Groves, P. 33
Guantanamo Bay 57

Hadji Murat (Tolstoy) 102
Hammersley, B. 26, 27
'Hard Case' of United States: Black
    Lives Matter 98; Christian Identity
    movement 97; civil rights movement 97;
    Emancipation Proclamation, 1863 97;
    First Amendment to the Constitution
    96; 'Klan Watch' intelligence project
    97; Ku Klux Klan 98; multi-racial and
    multi-ethnic democracy 99; Nation
    of Islam 97; National Association for
    the Advancement of Coloured People
    (NAACP) 98; racism 97; Southern
    Poverty Law Centre's work 97–98;
    tragic August 2017 events, Virginia 98;
    women's suffrage 97
HDI: *see* Human Development Index
healthcare 120–21, 133, 136, 141–42
hereditary form of livelihood 186
Hertel, S. 43, 47, 52, 60–63, 234
Heschel, A. 163
Hobbes, T. 101
homophobia 124–25
Hopgood, S. 14, 57
Hopkins, J. 20
HRDAG: *see* Human Rights Data
    Analysis Group
Hughes, L. 120
Human Development Index (HDI) 82;
    Sen, Amartya 83; SERF index 83
human rights 147; abuse, patterns in
    67; effects 17; fatigue 58; future of
    237–38; impacts of pandemic 45, 132;
    instruments 7; interdependence of
    132–33; movement 231; organisations
    232–33; struggle for 60; themes 43–45;
    violations 187
Human Rights Act, UK 9
human rights and the marginalised
    other: ban on travel from Muslim-
    majority countries 110; Black Lives
    Matter movement 111; dismissal of
    voices 111; Immigration and Customs
    Enforcement (ICE) 110; immigration
    debates 111; inter-sectional forms of
    discrimination 112; Rwanda genocide

in 1984 110; strategy of cauterisation
    110; transatlantic slave trade 110; work
    of MRG 113
Human Rights Data Analysis Group
    (HRDAG) 12, 44, 72–73
human rights evidence: authenticity
    and specificity 71; evidence and
    inference 69–71; evidence-inference
    methodological core 69; fundamental
    problem of unobservability 68; hard-
    to-find populations 71; human rights
    evidence, inference and error **70**;
    human rights wrongs 66; inference
    and error **70**; informal death squads
    67; known and unknown violations
    68; making the case 66–67; measuring
    human rights 71–86; nature of abuse
    68–69; secret detention centres 67
human rights in twenty-first century:
    antebellum slavery 21; black and racial
    justice mobilisation 21–23; Black Lives
    Matter 21–22; Civil Rights Movement
    21; COVID-19 19; effects on human
    rights 20–21; global pandemic 19–21;
    International Convention on the
    Elimination of all Forms of Racial
    Discrimination, 1966 22; modern
    slavery 15–17; natural and human
    disasters 17–19; Omicron variant 20;
    power of voice 5–7; reconstruction 21;
    Spanish flu, 1918 19; 'Unite the Right'
    white supremacist rally 21; wildfires
    18–19
Human Rights Measurement Initiative
    (HRMI) 78
Human Rights Watch 47; children's
    rights 56; issues 56; LGBT rights 56;
    organisation's model of change 56;
    refugees 56; reports on abuses 55–56;
    robust evidence base 56; social media
    support 56; women's rights 56
human trafficking 16–17, 132, 158, 173,
    176, 192, 201, 210, 213–14
humanitarian crisis 150, 216
hurricane Katrina, effects 18
Hynes, P. 154, 209, 213
hyper-distributed supply chain 201

IASC: *see* Independent Anti-Slavery
    Commissioner
ICC: *see* International Criminal Court
ICE: *see* Immigration and Customs
    Enforcement

ICTR: *see* International Criminal Tribunal for Rwanda
ICTY: *see* International Criminal Tribunal for the Former Yugoslavia
identity: and difference 126–27; formation of 189
IDPs: *see* internally displaced people
Ill-Treatment and Torture (ITT) data set 77
ILO: *see* International Labour Organisation
immigration 56, 108, 111, 122, 172, 196; detention centres 140–42
Immigration and Customs Enforcement (ICE) 110; detention cases 140
Impunity Campaign 94
Independent Anti-Slavery Commissioner (IASC) 199, 210
informal market 203
Insincere Commitments (Smith-Cannoy) 15
Institute for Social and Economic Research (ISER) 29, 31, 33
intentional denial of agency 182
interdependence of human rights 132–33, 231
internally displaced people (IDPs) 108, 114, 151, 236
International Bill of Rights 7
international condemnation 51
International Covenant on Civil and Political Rights, 1966 7, 74, 89, 147, 160
International Covenant on Economic, Social and Cultural Rights, 1966 7
International Convention on the Elimination of all Forms of Racial Discrimination, 1966 22, 116
International Criminal Court (ICC) 9, 50, 160
International Criminal Tribunal for the Former Yugoslavia (ICTY) 67
International Criminal Tribunal for Rwanda (ICTR) 9, 67
International Criminal Tribunal for the Former Yugoslavia (1993-2017) 9, 160
International Federation for Human Rights 232
International Human Rights Day (10 December) 36–38, 41, 233
international human rights law 143; and freedom of expression **90**; and freedom of religion, belief and thought **92**; growth of 231
international human rights organisations **53**, 81

International Justice Mission 155, 216, 218
International Labour Organisation (ILO) 17, 80–81, 142, 143, 160, 162, 176, 221; and Walk Free Foundation 174–75
International Military Tribunal, Nuremberg 67, 160
International Organisation for Migration (IOM) 154; community 214; 'Determinants of Vulnerability' model 214; Home Office in UK 215; household 214; individual 214; invisible norms and expectation 214; structural 214
internationalism 58
inter-sectional forms of discrimination 112
IOM: *see* International Organisation for Migration
Iraq: fragmentation of 238; Minority Rights Group International (MRG) 113; Second Gulf War 10
ISIS 12, 238
Islam and the West: anti-Semitism 101; commitments in Islam 100; democracy and Islam 101–2; incompatibility of Islam and democracy 101–2; Islamophobia 101; mistaken identity 101; myth busting, conversation 100; radical Islamic terrorism 103; transcendent knowledge 100; Tree of Life Jewish congregation, attack on 101; use of drones 102
Islamophobia 101
isolationism 10, 238

Jackson, A. 59
Jara, V. 58, 59
Jewett, D. 216
Jinnah, Muhammad Ali 101, 102
Jobs, S. 23, 25
Johnson, B. 14, 20
Johnson v. Texas case 91
justice and accountability: case against the Bashar-Al-Assad regime in Syria 58, 59; 'Don't Ask, Don't Tell' policy, 1994 57, 58; Foreign Sovereign Immunities Act, 1976 59; gay rights 57; Guantanamo Bay 57; human rights fatigue 58; internationalism 58; legal incrementalism 59; post human rights era 58; Servicemembers Legal Defense Network 57; targeted drone killings 57; torture 57; Torture Victim Protection Act, 1992 58
Justice Cascade (Sikkink) 14

Kara, S. 154, 191, 201, 210, 234
Kerner Commission, 1967 118
Khaldun, I. 93, 99
'Klan Watch' intelligence project 97
Kroc, Joan B. 181
Ku Klux Klan 97, 98

labour inspections 220–21
labour or other forms of exploitation 104
'lack of racial unity' 141–42
Landman, T. 1, 14, 32, 33
law and institutions: Alliance 8.7 175;
    anti-slavery legislation 169–70;
    anti-slavery sentiment 170–71; anti-
    trafficking and anti-slavery policies
    170; articulation of Target 8.7 175;
    Code 8.7 175; Delta 8.7 175; ILO
    and Walk Free Foundation 174–75;
    implementation gap 171; 'Natasha'
    problem 173; post-Maidan Revolution
    172; proportion of states with domestic
    legislative provisions by region **172**;
    role of United Nations 173–74; UN
    Global Compact 174; Universal
    Declaration of Human Rights 174;
    victim rehabilitation 173
League of Nations 51, 231
Leão, L. 155, 209
'a leapfrog method' 185
LeBaron, G. 154, 191, 193, 234
legal emancipation of African American
    slaves 167
legal incrementalism 59
legalisation of marriage 222
legalised discrimination 135
Lenz, G. 44, 129, 131
Lepore, J. 28
Lerigo-Stephens, H. 154, 191, 201, 203
letter-writing campaigns of prisoners 52
Leviathan (Hobbes) 101
Levine, I. 43, 47, 52, 56, 59
Lewis, J. 163
LGBTQ+ 108; awareness 125; community
    93; rights 44, 56
liberation theology 93–94
London attacks of 2005 12
Lydon, C. 27, 28, 36
lynching, problem of 163–64

Madrid train bombing, 2004 12
Mandela, N. 163
market imbalance 203
Maron, M. 27

Marriage (Same Sex Couples) Act 2013
    124, 125
mass de-regulation, of social care 144
mass publics and freedom of information
    148–49
massive racial disparities 136
McCabe, H. 155, 209, 221
measuring human rights: events-based
    data and multiple systems estimation
    72–77; new forms of data (*see* new forms
    of data, measuring human rights);
    standards-based data 77–79; survey-
    based data 79–81; *see also individual
    entries*
medical bias 136
MENA: *see* Middle East and North Africa
Merkel, A. 108, 115
MERS 131
Middle East and North Africa (MENA)
    12, 56, 113, 115
migration and democracy: anti-lockdown
    and anti-mask protests 150; Black Lives
    Matter protests 150; global inequalities
    149; issues within states 149; mass
    publics and freedom of information
    148; political crisis and humanitarian
    crisis 150; vaccination 149–50; violence
    against women protests 150
minority rights: inter-sectional forms of
    discrimination 112; shared language
    and belief system 112; xenophobia,
    anti-migrant, and anti-refugee
    sentiments 113
Minority Rights Group International
    (MRG) 44, 112; work of 113–14
mistaken identity 101
Mitchel-Hill, E. 154, 191, 204, 210, 234
mobile phone call records 82
mobilisations for civil rights 50
mobilising for human rights: academic
    perspective 60–63; Amnesty
    International 52–55; Anti-Slavery
    International (ASI) 51; Business and
    Human Rights Resource Centre 62;
    case against the Bashar-Al-Assad
    regime in Syria 58, 59; contemporary
    terrain 51–52; domestic human rights
    documentation 51; 'Don't Ask, Don't
    Tell' policy, 1994 57, 58; economic
    incentives for companies 63; empirical
    generalisations 61; evolution in
    human rights 48; Foreign Sovereign
    Immunities Act, 1976 59; gay rights

57; Guantanamo Bay 57; human rights fatigue 58; Human Rights Watch 52, 55–57; international condemnation 51; internationalism 58; issue-based work of human rights organisations 63; justice and accountability 57–59; legal incrementalism 59; list of major international human rights organisations **53**; mobilisations for civil rights 50; people and practice 52; petty rivalries 62; philosophical writings 48; populism 51; 'post human rights' era 58; Ruggie Principles 62; Servicemembers Legal Defense Network 57; Slavery Convention, 1926 48; social construction 49; social mobilisation 51; struggle for human rights 60; TANs 49; targeted drone killings 57; torture 57; Torture Victim Protection Act, 1992 58; transnational partners alliances 49–50; UN Global Compact 62–63; UN Special Rapporteur on Torture 64; United States Fish and Wildlife Service 60; Universal Declaration of Human Rights, 1948 48, 50; universal jurisdiction 51
Mobilizing for Human Rights (Simmons) 14
modern slavery 15–17, 201; description 158–59; referrals 210; SDG target 158–59; strategies 204
modern slavery statement 199, 201, 204, 206
Moore, W. 37, 43, 65, 68, 77
MRG: *see* Minority Rights Group International
MSE: *see* multiple systems estimation
multiple partners, practice of 222
multiple systems estimation (MSE) 73
multi-racial and multi-ethnic democracy 99
multi-stakeholder approach 225
Mumbai attack of 2008 12
Murdie, A. 37, 43, 47, 52, 60, 63
My Bondage and My Freedom (David) 164
myth busting, conversation 100

NAACP: *see* National Association for the Advancement of Coloured People
'name and shame' approach 55
Narayanan, P. 154, 209, 211
Nation of Islam 97
National Action Plan 213

National Association for the Advancement of Coloured People (NAACP) 98, 119
National Crime Agency and the Border Force 105
national living wage for workers 196
National Referral Mechanism (NRM) 167, 215, 225; housing and benefits 224
nationalism 10, 122, 151; rise of 13, 238
natural and human disasters 17–19
Nazer, M. 158
negative externalities of firm activity 195, 207
neo-Nazis 97
neo-slavery 164, 167
new forms of data, measuring human rights: Achievement Possibility Frontier 83; 'Brick Belt' 84; earth observation (EO) data 82; Meg Satterthwaite 84; mobile phone call records 82; open source information 81; satellite images 82; visual storytelling 85
Nicholson, A. 154, 179, 181
9/11 attacks 10–11, 79, 93, 100, 102, 145–46, 238
Nolan, A. 45, 143
non-governmental organisations 8, 43, 232
Nottingham as 'slavery free city' 225
NRM: *see* National Referral Mechanism
Nuffield Foundation 33
number of journalists confirmed killed **95**

Obama, B. 27, 103, 118, 130, 131, 139
Office of the High Commissioner for Human Rights 8
Omicron variant 19–20, 130
open source information 81
Orbán, V. 14
Organisation for Security and Cooperation in Europe (OSCE) 9, 197
Osburn, D. 43, 47, 52, 57, 66, 234, 235
OSCE: *see* Organisation for Security and Cooperation in Europe
'other, the': identity and difference 126; social Darwinism 126–27; Us/Them dichotomies 126
Owen, D. 129, 149, 238
ownership, ideas of 188; and property 15–16, 160

Parker, T. 45, 129, 145
participant 'action research' process 212
Patriot Act 11
Peace Accords, 2016 150

people of African descent and COVID-19: extant hospital protocols 137; massive racial disparities 136; medical bias 136; vaccine hesitancy, issue of 138

perpetrators: 'a leapfrog method' 185; anti-slavery efforts 190; anti-slavery work 185; community-based action-research project 188; complex factors 182; control over victim-survivors 184–85; debt-bondage 183; exploitation 187; formation of identity 189; hereditary form of livelihood 186; human rights violations 187; idea of ownership 188; individual-level relationships 183; intentional denial of agency 182; lateral questioning and leapfrogging 186; legal redress or means of escape 184; micro, macro and international factors **183**, 183–84; NGO Survivor Alliance 181; perpetrator-victim dyads 186; post-traumatic stress disorder 189; relationship between 180–81; relationship between perpetrator and victim-survivor 182; in research 188; self-deceptive practices 187; self-help groups 186; slaveholders in India 181; Slavery Convention, 1926 187; socially embedded slavery 182–84; solutions to help survivors 190; survivor narratives 188; threshold of slavery 182; trauma survivors 189; valuing survivors 187–90; and victim-survivor, relationship between 182

perpetrator-victim dyads 187

petty rivalries 62

Phelps, C. 44, 107

phone app 105

physical violence and threats 212

Picturing Frederick Douglass (Trodd) 176

Pinochet, A. 9, 51, 52, 58, 74; case against 9, 51; regime in Chile 74

podcast, rise of: amateur radio 26; Apple's iPod 26; audioblogging 26; definition 26; Edison Research 26, 28; *Infinite Dial 2021* survey 28; i2GO 26; Last Archive, The 28; Lydon's podcasts 27; Mac's built-in audio editing software GarageBand 25; online radio 26; *Renegades: Born in the USA* 27; *Serial* podcast 28; terrestrial radio show 27; UK with Ofcom 28; UK with Ofcom12 28; US podcast listeners **29**; WTF podcast 27

podcasting: *Conversation UK, The* 31–32; free-flowing conversations 36; about human rights 32–33; human rights in pandemic 40–41; impacts of COVID-19 40–41; interviews over Internet 35; interviews over Skype 34; ISER's web editor 31; modern slavery 38–40; Private Facebook group 34; radio-style interviews 30; about research 29–32; Rights Lab 38; Rights Track Podcast 34; Rights Track visual identity **35**; rise of (*see* podcast, rise of); Series 1 35; Series 5 39; Series 7 41; series 1-International Human Rights Day 36–38; slave-free supply chains 39–40; special episodes 40; technical changes 39; 2012 Russell Group 30; UK Household Longitudinal Study 31; UK Modern Slavery Act, 2015 39; value of 233–34; web expertise 33

Political and social revolutions 92

political crisis 150, 164

Political Terror Scale 77–78

populism 10, 151, 218; rise of 3, 13–14, 51, 238

'post human rights' era 58

post-9/11 'war on terror' 93

post-traumatic stress disorder 189

post-World War II alliances and partnerships 14

Power of Human Rights (Sikkink) 15

pre-emptive attack on electoral integrity 14

press, freedom of: citizen journalism 95; CPJ, work of 94; cross-border dissemination of information 96; number of journalists confirmed killed **95**

Press Freedom Index 89

pre-trial detention centres 140

primary sources 74

prisoners and COVID-19: COVID-19 hotspots 140; ICE detention cases 140; immigration detention centres 140; mixed economy of public and private prisons 138; poor ventilation and poor sanitation 140; pre-trial detention centres 140

private mechanisms for accountability and constraint 195

Prophet Muhammad 87–88, 102

Protecting Human Rights (Landman) 14

public health and slavery in Brazil: Brazilian Penal Code 220; collective health 219; corruption 221; inequalities in income distribution 219; labour inspections 220–21; multi-level approach 220; right to health in 1988 Constitution 219; servitude 220; transatlantic slavery 218; workplace environments 220
public mechanisms for accountability and constraint 196

Q Methodology 167–68
Q-Sort process 168

racial miscegenation 109
racism 22, 97, 116, 118, 122, 124, 136–39, 189
radical Islamic terrorism 103
Rafto Foundation for Human Rights Award 73
Ramakrishnan, M. 45, 129, 141, 234
Rana Plaza disaster, 2013 200
Reconstruction 21, 164
Redfern, A. 44, 87, 94, 103, 106
redistribution, principle of 203–4
re-enslavement 224, 226
refugees: root causes of movements 115; secondary movement 114
refugees and COVID-19: backlash and xenophobia 142; deep-seated patriarchy 142; lack of racial unity 141–42; Movement Control Orders 141; push and pull factors 141; rampant corruption 142
religiosity 80, 92
resilience framework 224, 226
right to free speech: Danish and French cases 91; International Covenant on Civil and Political Rights 89; International human rights law and freedom of expression **90**; Press Freedom Index 89; *Texas v. Johnson* case 91; Universal Declaration 90
right to health in its 1988 Constitution 219
rights of transsexuals 123
Rights Track podcast 34, 52, 108, 230, 239; list of 239–42
rights-based legislation 213
Rodley, N. 64
Rome Statute of the ICC, 1998 160
Ron, J. 44, 65, 80, 235
Ruggie Principles 62
Rwanda genocide in 1984 110

Saied, K. 12
Salt, K. 44, 107, 117
same-sex relationships 123
Sapolsky, R. 126
SARS 131
satellite images 54, 59, 82, 177
Satterthwaite, M. 44, 65, 84–85
scholars and practitioners 230–33
Schwarz, K. 154, 157, 170
Scott, D. 164
Scott, M. 216
SDG: *see* Sustainable Development Goal
Second Gulf War 10
secondary movement of refugees 114
second-class citizens treatment 217, 226
self-deceptive practices 187
self-help groups 186
Semione, J. 154, 157, 167, 183
Sen, A. 83
SERF: *see* Social and Economic Rights Fulfilment Index
Serrano, A. 91
Service members Legal Defense Network 57
sex trafficking 201
sexual exploitation 104, 120, 158, 173, 210, 214, 220
shared language and belief system 112
Sherman, K. 155, 209, 221
Silverman, B. 44, 65, 69, 70, 75
Simmons, B. 14, 44, 107, 109, 112, 118, 190, 235
slaveholders in India 181
slavery: Bellagio-Harvard Guidelines on the Legal Parameters of Slavery 160; business and economics of 193; Charter of the International Military Tribunal, 1945 160; Convention on the Rights of the Child, 1989 160; definition 159–60; encounters and conversations 230; Forced Labour Convention, 1930 160; Forced Labour Protocol, 2014 160; and human rights 230; inception of Rights Track, 2015 230; International Covenant on Civil and Political Rights, 1966 160; during pandemic 230; provisions 160; Rome Statute of ICC, 1998 160; states party participation in core international instruments on slavery **161**; Statute of the International Criminal Tribunal for the Former Yugoslavia

160; transatlantic and imperial
periods 159; Walk Free Foundation
162; Worst Forms of Child Labour
Convention, 1999 160
Slavery Convention, 1926 15, 48, 159,
160, 170, 176, 177, 187, 231
slavery free cities: civil society
organisations 225; enhanced
economic opportunities 223;
faith-based groups 225; housing
and benefits under NRM 224;
multi-stakeholder approach 225;
Nottingham as 'slavery free city'
225; re-enslavement 226; resilience
framework 224; suspicious transaction
information 225, 226; systematic
tracking 224
slavery hotspots: civil society
organisations 218; community-based
organisations 218; forced labourers in
seafood industry 217; Freedom Fund,
work of 217; hotspot model, criteria
218; International Justice Mission 216;
second-class citizens treatment 217;
trauma of enslavement 216
Social and Economic Rights Fulfilment
(SERF) Index 83
social auditing 195
social construction 16, 49, 159; of modern
slavery 16
social Darwinism 126–27
social mobilisation 51, 62–63
social religiosity 80
socially embedded slavery: complex
factors 182; debt-bondage 183;
individual-level relationships 183;
intentional denial of agency 182;
legal redress or means of escape 184;
micro, macro and international factors
183, 183–84; relationship between
perpetrator and victim-survivor 182;
threshold of slavery 182
solutions to help survivors 190
Southern Poverty Law Centre 44, 87, 91,
97–99
Spanish flu, 1918 19
Special Rapporteurs 8, 64, 159
Spotify 27–28, 37
Springsteen, B. 27
standards-based data: *Freedom in the
World* reports 78; Human Rights
Measurement Initiative 78;
methodological steps 78; Political

Terror Scale 77–78; SAT or GRE in
United States 79
state obligation approach 54
state ratification of core human rights
instruments, 2000, 2021 **8**
Statute of the International Criminal
Tribunal for the Former Yugoslavia
160
Stauffer, J. 154, 157, 162, 165, 182
strategic litigation, process of 204
stringency index 147, **147**
structural racism 139
suffragette mobilisations 120
Sundarbans in Bangladesh 84
supply, demand and production: business
and economics of slavery 193;
capitalism without slavery 194–95;
corporate social responsibility (CSR)
195–96; ethical certification 195;
Modern Slavery Statement 199;
multinational corporations turnover
192; national living wage for workers
196; negative externalities of firm
activity 195; number of enslaved
people 193; private mechanisms 195;
public mechanisms 196; social auditing
195; success of capitalism 194; systemic
risk 196
supply chain: increasing normative
value 206; issue of child labour 205;
policy to tackle modern slavery 205;
relationships, formal and informal
supply chain 207; UK's Modern
Slavery act 206
survey-based data: estimation of
prevalence of modern slavery 81;
perceptions and experiences of human
rights 79; Walk Free Foundation 80;
World Values Survey 79
survivors: anti-slavery efforts 190;
community-based action-research
project 188; formation of identity 189;
idea of ownership 188; narratives 177,
188; post-traumatic stress disorder
189; in research 188; solutions to help
survivors 190; survivor narratives 188;
trauma survivors 189
sustainable development 237
Sustainable Development Goals (SDG) 17,
39, 159, 174, 177, 188, 208, 237
Suu Kyi, Aung San 13
swine flu, outbreaks 130
systematic tracking 224

Taking Root: Human Rights and Public Opinion in the Global South (Ron) 80
TANs: *see* transnational advocacy networks
targeted drone killings 57
Tar Sands oil fields in Canada 131
Tennyson, A. 100
terrorism 238; Bali attack of 2002 12; human rights approach 147; London attacks of 2005 12, 79; Mumbai attack of 2008 12; 9/11 attacks 10–11, 79, 93, 100, 102, 145–46, 238; policies 145; socio-economic conditions 148; Tree of Life Jewish congregation, attack on 101; war on terror 145
Thistle and the Drone, The (Akbar) 102
Thomas, C. 44, 107, 112
threshold of slavery 182
Tickner, A. 45, 129, 149
Tohoku earthquake, 2011 17
Torture Victim Protection Act, 1992 58
traffickers 169, 214
trafficking 213, 223; forced labour 213; forced marriage and women's rights 223; human 16–17, 132, 158, 173, 176, 192, 210, 213–14; sex 201
tragic August 2017 events, Virginia 98
transatlantic and imperial forms 15
transatlantic slavery 93, 104–5, 110, 115, 117, 136, 218
transcendent knowledge 100
transnational advocacy networks (TANs) 14, 15, 43, 49, 52, 171, 232
transnational partners alliances 49–50
trauma survivors 189
Trautrims, A. 154, 191, 197
Tree of Life Jewish congregation, attack on 101
Trodd, Z. 38, 154, 157, 176, 188, 232
Trump, D. 1, 10, 13, 14, 20, 56–58, 90, 98, 103, 108, 110, 111, 121, 122, 125, 144, 150
Truth and Reconciliation Commission: in Peru 72; report 119
Truth Commissions 9; in Peru 75; post-Apartheid South Africa 117
tsunami in Japan 17
Tufte, E. R. 85
two-nation society 118

UK Modern Slavery Act, 2015 76, 104, 167, 199, 201, 206, 224, 236
UKIP: *see* United Kingdom Independence Party

UN Convention on the Rights of the Child, 1989 143–44
UN Global Compact 8, 62–63, 174, 206
UN Guiding Principles on Business and Human Rights 8, 206
UN High Commissioner for Human Rights 134
UN Refugee Convention 141, 142
UN Special Rapporteur on Torture 64
UN Women Global Champion for Innovation 134
UN Working Group of Experts on People of African Descent 22, 45, 117, 129, 136
UNDP: *see* United Nations Development Programme
UNHCR: *see* United Nations High Commissioner for Refugees
'Unite the Right' white supremacist rally 21, 88
United Kingdom Independence Party (UKIP) 108, 110
United Nations Development Programme (UNDP) 61, 83
United Nations High Commissioner for Refugees (UNHCR) 38, 44, 114, 142, 143
United Nations Human Rights Council 56
United States Fish and Wildlife Service 60
Universal Declaration of Human Rights 7, 48, 50, 74, 90, 119, 174, 231, 232
universal jurisdiction 9, 51
useable past, concept of: abolitionist movement 166; emancipation 163; Fugitive Slave Law 164; historical abolitionism 166; legal emancipation of African American slaves 167; neo-slavery 167; problem of lynching 163–64; relevance today 164–65; voice in anti-slavery struggle 165–66; work on Frederick Douglass 162–63
'Us/Them' dichotomies 126

vaccination 137, 149–50; hesitancy, issue of 138
Vargas Llosa, G. 44, 107, 114, 141
Vexler, D. 154, 209, 216
victim rehabilitation 173
violence, threat of 238
Visual Explanations (Tufte) 85
visual storytelling 85

voice, power of 5–7; conversational
  network 6; human rights awareness 5;
  Rights Track 6; voices of the people 6
Voting Rights Act, 1965 97

Walk Free Foundation 80–81, 162, 174,
  176, 221
war on terror 10, 93, 102, 145
Webster, S. 155, 209, 216
Westlake, D. 155, 209, 216
WHO: *see* World Health Organisation
Wilberforce, S. 104
Wilberforce, W. 104, 105
wildfires 18–19
Williamson, G. 88
Witchell, E. 44, 87, 89, 94
women 134–35; call to 'defund Planned
  Parenthood' 121; collective action in
  Rwanda 222; and COVID-19 134–35;
  discrimination against women in
  STEM 135; discriminatory policies and
  laws 135; force, description 221; forced
  marriage and women's rights 222–23;
  Fourth World Conference on Women
  135; gender-based violence 120;

healthcare 121; legalisation of marriage
  222; legalised discrimination 135;
  marches 122–23; marches, dimension
  of 122–23; practice of multiple partners
  222; reproductive rights and access
  to abortions 133; rights 56, 120–23;
  suffrage 97; suffragette mobilisations
  120; susceptibility to trafficking 223;
  trafficking 223; UN Women Global
  Champion for Innovation 134; violence
  against women protests 150; women's
  collective action in Rwanda 222
workplace environments 220
World Health Organisation (WHO) 19,
  85, 134, 143
Worst Forms of Child Labour
  Convention, 1999 160

xenophobia 113, 141–42, 217
Xi Jinping 13

Young, L. 154, 191, 199

Zika virus outbreaks 130
zoonotic pandemics 131

www.ingramcontent.com/pod-product-compliance
Lightning Source LLC
Chambersburg PA
CBHW022352280326
41935CB00007B/161